TOP 100

Simplified®

TIPS & TRICKS

Photoshop® CC

by Stan Sholik

Visual™
A Wiley Brand

Photoshop® CC: Top 100 Simplified® Tips & Tricks

Published by
John Wiley & Sons, Inc.
10475 Crosspoint Boulevard
Indianapolis, IN 46256
www.wiley.com

Published simultaneously in Canada

Copyright © 2013 by John Wiley & Sons, Inc., Indianapolis, Indiana

Library of Congress Control Number: 2013936426

ISBN: 978-1-118-64376-1

Manufactured in the United States of America

10 9 8 7 6 5 4 3 2 1

Wiley publishes in a variety of print and electronic formats and by print-on-demand. Some material included with standard print versions of this book may not be included in e-books or in print-on-demand. If this book refers to media such as a CD or DVD that is not included in the version you purchased, you may download this material at http://booksupport.wiley.com. For more information about Wiley products, visit www.wiley.com.

Trademark Acknowledgments

Contact Us

For general information on our other products and services contact our Customer Care Department within the U.S. at 877-762-2974, outside the U.S. at 317-572-3993 or fax 317-572-4002.

For technical support please visit www.wiley.com/techsupport.

U.S. Sales

Contact Wiley at (877) 762-2974 or fax (317) 572-4002.

CREDITS

Sr. Acquisitions Editor
Stephanie McComb

Sr. Project Editor
Sarah Hellert

Technical Editor
Dennis Cohen

Copy Editor
Kim Heusel

Editorial Director
Robyn Siesky

Business Manager
Amy Knies

Sr. Marketing Manager
Sandy Smith

**Vice President and
Executive Group Publisher**
Richard Swadley

**Vice President and
Executive Publisher**
Barry Pruett

Project Coordinator
Sheree Montgomery

Graphics and Production Specialists
Jennifer Goldsmith
Andrea Hornberger
Jennifer Mayberry

Quality Control Technician
Lindsay Amones

Proofreader
Indianapolis Composition Services

Indexer
Potomac Indexing, LLC

**Vertical Websites
Associate Producer**
Rich Graves

ABOUT THE AUTHOR

Stan Sholik has spent over three decades as a commercial, advertising, and illustrative photographer in Orange County, California. During that time he has developed a national reputation in a wide range of technology-oriented specialties for his clients in the computer, electronics, medical device, and food industries. Early in his career he began specializing in close-up/macro photography, motion-simulation, and in-camera photocomposition to enhance the images created with his large-format cameras. He is now working extensively with both 4 × 5 film and high-resolution digital capture. He has also gained a reputation as a writer on both conventional and digital imaging topics with articles in *View Camera*, *Shutterbug*, *Professional Photographer*, *Rangefinder*, and other magazines. He has written books about photographic filters, digital SLRs, and macro photography. This is Stan's third book for Wiley. He has previously written *HDR Efex Pro After the Shoot* and *Photoshop Lightroom 4 FAQs*. Self-taught as a photographer, Stan holds a BS degree in physics and an MA in English from Carnegie Institute of Technology in Pittsburgh, Pennsylvania.

ACKNOWLEDGMENTS

I would like to thank Sarah Hellert, my project editor at Wiley, for her attention to detail and successful efforts to keep my style consistent and readable. I would especially like to thank Stephanie McComb, acquisitions editor at Wiley, for giving me the opportunity to write this book, and for doing her best to keep me on schedule with humor and good will. And finally, thanks to my wife Linda and daughter Amelia and her family for their patience and understanding as I buried myself in this project. Sincere thanks to son-in-law/sound designer/composer/videographer Garrett Montgomery for providing video footage and a royalty-free music track.

HOW TO USE THIS BOOK

Who This Book Is For

This book is for readers who know the basics and want to expand their knowledge of this particular technology or software application.

The Conventions in This Book

① Steps

This book uses a step-by-step format to guide you easily through each task. Numbered steps are actions you must do; bulleted steps clarify a point, step, or optional feature; and indented steps give you the result.

② Notes

Notes give additional information — special conditions that may occur during an operation, a situation that you want to avoid, or a cross reference to a related area of the book.

③ Icons and Buttons

Icons and buttons show you exactly what you need to click to perform a step.

④ Tips

Tips offer additional information, including warnings and shortcuts.

⑤ Bold

Bold type shows text or numbers you must type.

⑥ Italics

Italic type introduces and defines a new term.

⑦ Difficulty Levels

For quick reference, these symbols mark the difficulty level of each task.

Demonstrates a new spin on a common task

Introduces a new skill or a new task

Combines multiple skills requiring in-depth knowledge

Requires extensive skill and may involve other technologies

DECREASE DEPTH OF FIELD with Iris Blur

You can decrease depth of field as well as increase it. By decreasing the depth of field you draw attention to the subject by throwing other parts of the image out of focus. Photoshop has several options for applying blur. Iris Blur is one of the most interesting.

Iris Blur is found in the Filter menu. It is a destructive filter, but there are several ways to apply it so as not to destroy image information. One is to convert the original image to

a Smart Object before you use the filter. Applied as a Smart Filter, the effect is nondestructive and you can return to the image and change the blur effect later.

The subject should be on its own plane in the image and separate from the background to be most effective. You can apply more than one Iris Blur to an image. It is often more effective to apply the softening to several small areas than to try and control one blur to meet your needs.

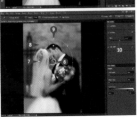

①
- With an image open, right-click the Background layer.
- Click Convert to Smart Object.
  - The thumbnail changes to a Smart Object thumbnail.
- Click Filter.
- Click Blur.
- Click Iris Blur.

The Blur Tools panel opens.
The Iris Blur filter opens with an oval in the center of the image.
- Click and drag the center pin of the oval over the area that you want sharp.
- Click and drag the large white dots to the edge of the area that you want sharp.
- Click and drag the solid oval-shaped line to the edge of the area where you want full blur.
- **②** *Note: The area between the white dots and the solid oval gradually transitions from sharp to blur.*
- Position your cursor over the small white circles on the oval. When it changes to a curved arrow, click and drag to rotate the oval and change the shape.
- Click and drag the Blur slider to set the blur for this pin.

Note: Alternatively, click and drag inside the gray part of the ring around the pin. As you drag, the gray part turns white and the blur increases. The amount of blur is shown in a box above the ring.

#78
DIFFICULTY LEVEL
⑦

- Click another area of the image.
  - Another oval and pin appear.
- Repeat steps 6 to 10 to set the blur for this pin.
- Repeat steps 11 and 12 as needed for other areas.
- Toggle Preview to view the image before and after blur.
- Click OK.
  - The Blur Tools panel closes.
- Save the image as a PSD file.

④ TIPS

Did You Know?
You can use keyboard shortcuts to hide and show different views for Iris Blur. Press and hold H to hide the pins and overlays. Press P to toggle the before and after preview. Press and hold M to view the mask that Photoshop makes for the blur. These same keyboard shortcuts work for many of the blur and other filters.

Did You Know?
You cannot use the Opacity slider or a blend mode from the Layers panel on a Smart Object layer if the effect looks too strong when you close the Blur Tools panel. However, if you immediately click Edit ➪ Fade Blur Gallery, you can both adjust the opacity and change the blend mode.

More Options!
You can have control over opacity of the Iris Blur filter in the future. Instead of applying Iris Blur to a Smart Object, apply it to a copy of the Background layer. You lose the flexibility of returning to the filter to adjust it in the future, but you gain the ability to adjust opacity or the blend mode.

Table of Contents

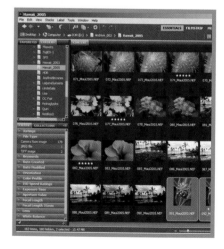

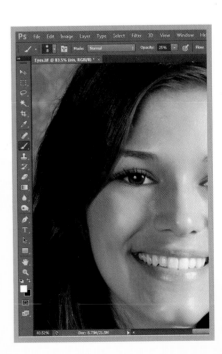

Table of Contents

⑦ Create Stunning Black-and-White Photos

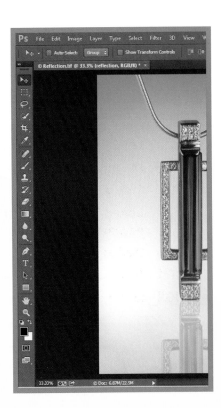

⑧ Create Unique Images with Filters and Special Effects

Table of Contents

11 Use Plug-ins to Extend Photoshop

Take Control of Photoshop

Photoshop is an essential tool for every discipline in the graphics field. Photographers, graphic designers, web designers, videographers, fine artists, and others use Photoshop in their work. Each new version of the program adds tools and capabilities that some users find essential and others never use. With the newest version of Photoshop, Adobe has rebranded the program as Photoshop Creative Cloud (CC). It is no longer available as boxed software, but only by subscription to the Adobe Creative Cloud.

Coming to terms with the large array of tools, panels, and options is essential for working efficiently and productively. And with Photoshop customized to your liking, it becomes a pleasure to use.

For long sessions with the program you may prefer a lighter interface over a darker one, or vice versa. You may prefer to have certain tools quickly available and others hidden that you rarely use.

Saving these options so that they are immediately available each time you open Photoshop minimizes the complexity of the program and makes it easy to begin working even if you have not opened the program in days.

Taking control of Photoshop is easy. The abilities to customize the interface, rearrange panels, quickly change your workspace view, and reset color palettes are all provided within the program.

When you are in control of Photoshop you can command it to perform tasks automatically and even have Photoshop remember the editing steps you make.

By taking the time to learn how to control Photoshop to your liking, how to adjust your monitor to display accurate color, and how to increase the power of Photoshop with a pen tablet, you are able to control Photoshop for the wide variety of projects you use it for.

DIFFICULTY LEVEL

In Photoshop CC, you can choose a color scheme for the interface that best suits your editing needs. The preset themes include four shades of gray ranging from light gray to dark gray. Within each theme are additional options for setting the color behind your image to one of these grays, to black, or to a custom color.

Your choice of Color Theme determines your comfort level working with Photoshop during long editing sessions. Black type against a lighter gray background is easier on

the eyes for extended sessions, but the lighter interface can distract you from the image. A darker interface concentrates your attention on the image, but reading small white type against the darkest gray background is hard on the eyes for extended periods.

Choose the interface color that is best for you. Behind your image itself, a dark gray background is best when menus are visible, and black is best with the image full screen.

Note: To better judge the options, first open an image.

1 Click Edit (Photoshop).

2 Click Preferences.

3 Click Interface.

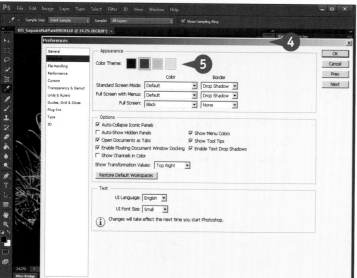

The Interface pane of the Preferences dialog box opens.

4 Click the title bar and drag the Preferences dialog box slightly to the side or down to see the image, tools, and panels.

5 Click each of the four Color Theme boxes to see the changes.

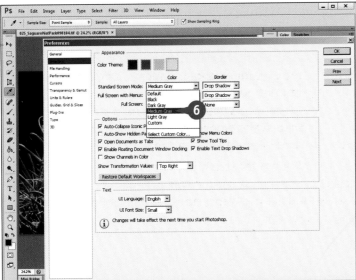

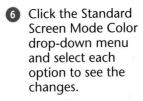

#1

DIFFICULTY LEVEL

Ⓐ The tool and panel menus change color with each theme.

⑥ Click the Standard Screen Mode Color drop-down menu and select each option to see the changes.

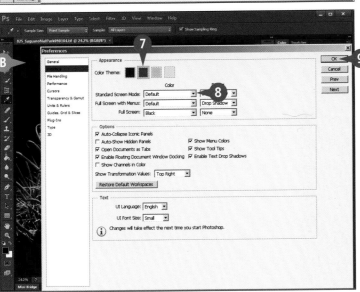

Ⓑ The screen background changes as you select different colors.

⑦ Click the second darkest Color Theme, the default, for the tools and panels.

⑧ Click the Standard Screen Mode Color drop-down menu and select Default if it is not selected.

⑨ Click OK to save your workspace color theme.

TIPS

More Options!
With the default dark gray backgrounds you cannot see the drop shadow that Photoshop must process and create each time. Click the Standard Screen Mode Border and Full Screen with Menus Border drop-down menus and select None.

Did You Know?
Pressing F toggles the screen modes from Standard, to Full Screen with Menus, to Full Screen, and back to Standard. Pressing Shift+F moves you backward through the modes.

Did You Know?
In each of the screen modes you can right-click the background outside of your image to display a pop-up menu of the background color options.

Photoshop includes preset color settings, but you can create your own custom settings. Photoshop is used in many disciplines, each of which has a preferred output color space. Even among photographers there are three color spaces in common use.

Most common is sRGBIEC61966-2.1 because it is the default color space for JPEG captures with digital cameras, the output space most color labs prefer for printing digital images, and the default color space for web pages. It is also the smallest of the three color spaces with the fewest available colors. And sRGB is the default color space in Photoshop.

Photographers who print images on inkjet or high-end lithographic printers prefer the Adobe RGB (1998) color space. This space contains more shades of color than the sRGB space. Adobe RGB (1998) is an option on higher-end digital SLR cameras and a better choice for capturing images than sRGB.

The color space holding the most color values is ProPhoto RGB. If you capture images primarily in RAW format, ProPhoto RGB is the best option.

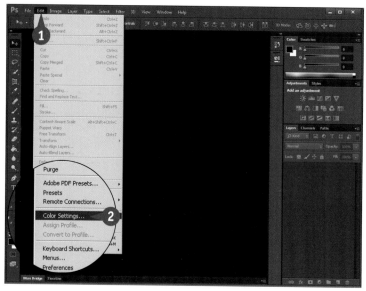

① Click Edit.

② Click Color Settings.

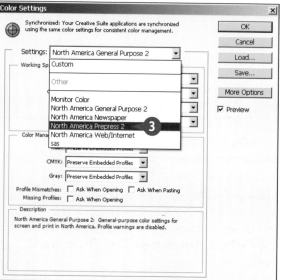

The Color Settings dialog box opens.

③ Click the Settings drop-down menu and select North America Prepress 2.

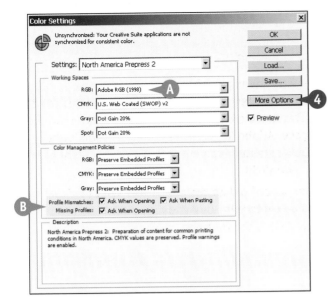

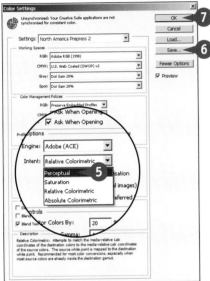

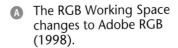
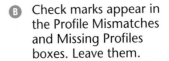

#2

DIFFICULTY LEVEL

Ⓐ The RGB Working Space changes to Adobe RGB (1998).

Ⓑ Check marks appear in the Profile Mismatches and Missing Profiles boxes. Leave them.

④ Click More Options.

The dialog box expands.

⑤ Click the Intent drop-down menu and select Perceptual for photographic projects.

⑥ Click Save and name your custom color settings North America Prepress+Perceptual.

⑦ Click OK.

You have saved your first custom Color Setting.

 TIPS

Try This!

Make a ProPhoto RGB Color Setting. Repeat steps 1 to 4. Click the RGB Working Spaces drop-down menu and select ProPhoto RGB. Click Save and name your new color setting ProPhoto RGB.

Apply It!

When you want to work in a different color space for a session, change your color setting to another saved setting. This also prevents the Profiles Mismatch dialog box from appearing for each image you open in that color space. Click Edit ➪ Color Settings. In the Color Settings dialog box, click Load, and the Load dialog box opens. Select the ProPhoto RGB color setting you made. Click Load and the dialog box closes. The Color Settings dialog box shows the ProPhoto RGB settings. Click OK to use the settings.

The ability to customize Photoshop to your personal working environment is one of the most powerful features of the program. Using Preferences settings you can control the look of the interface and cursors and the way in which files are handled, set units for measuring and type, set default resolution for new documents, set type options, and designate a location other than the default for third-party plug-ins.

Preferences is also the location where you optimize memory usage, choose one or more scratch disks in case you exceed your available RAM, and optimize your graphics processor settings. These options are found in the Performance pane. There is a Description area to help you choose appropriate settings in the Performance pane.

Each option in the Preferences menu opens a pane in the Preferences dialog box with options that customize Photoshop. The choices you make in Preferences determine not only the speed with which Photoshop performs, they also affect the pleasure you have working in the program.

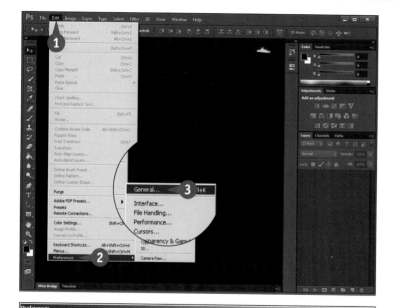

1. Click Edit (Photoshop).
2. Click Preferences.
3. Click General.

The General pane of the Preferences dialog box opens.

4. Click any of the drop-down menus to change your settings.

5. Select the options you want, or deselect the options you do not want (☐ changes to ☑ or ☑ changes to ☐).

   Note: For this task, Enable Flick Panning is deselected.

6. Click Performance in the left pane to adjust the performance settings.

   Note: You can also click Prev or Next to navigate through the Preferences menu.

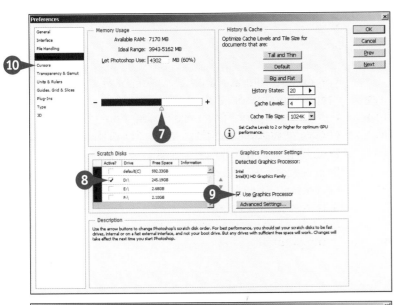

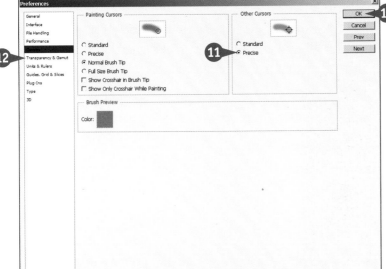

7 Click and drag the slider to adjust the maximum amount of RAM allocated to Photoshop.

Note: Increase the amount of RAM if you work on large image files and only have Photoshop and Bridge open. Decrease the amount of RAM if you generally have several other programs open.

8 Select a different scratch disk other than your boot drive if you have a fast internal or external drive available (☐ changes to ☑).

9 Select Use Graphics Processor if it is available (☐ changes to ☑).

10 Click Cursors or another option from the Preferences menu in the left pane.

11 Select Precise (○ changes to ◉).

12 Make any other changes you prefer in the other Preferences dialog box panes.

13 Click OK.

14 Click File ➪ Exit. On a Mac, click Photoshop ➪ Quit Photoshop.

The next time you open Photoshop, your custom Preferences take effect.

TIPS

Optimize Photoshop Performance!

● Close applications other than Photoshop and Bridge.

● Set the Memory Usage slider closer to the top end of the ideal range.

● Keep open only the Photoshop documents that you are currently using.

● Add more RAM to your computer

Did You Know?

In order for a thumbnail of your PSD or PSB file to automatically display in Lightroom, you must select Always for Maximize PSD and PSB File Compatibility in the File Handling pane of the Preferences dialog box.

Did You Know?

You can open the Preferences dialog box by pressing Ctrl+K (⌘+K).

Create a CUSTOM WORKSPACE

The Photoshop *workspace* refers to the arrangement of tools and panels on your screen. With 26 windows plus the Options bar and Tools panel available, your screen can easily become cluttered with panels you are not using for the current project.

You can create a custom workspace suited for the way you work. Your options for creating a custom workspace are many. You can dock panels together or have individual panels or panel groups float in the workspace or on a second monitor if you have one.

The default Photoshop workspace is Essentials. There are six other prebuilt workspaces available. The one closest to

the project type you are working on is a good starting point to design a custom workspace.

You can design a custom workspace for photography and then alter it for a specific editing task using only those tools that are essential to that task. You can even save custom keyboard shortcuts (see task #5) you have created when you save the workspace. When you alter an existing workspace, the changes are automatically saved. If you do not want to save the changes, you can reset the workspace to its original configuration.

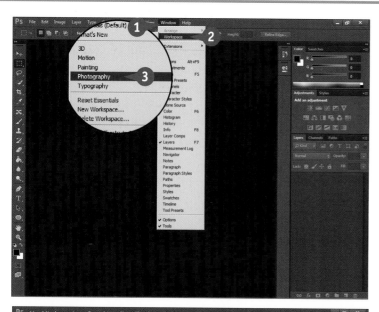

1 Click Window.

2 Click Workspace.

3 Click Photography.

A The preset Photography workspace opens.

4 Click here to drag Mini Bridge to the top of the collapsed panel on the right.

5 Click here to change the width of the Toolbox.

6 Click here to expand the panel groups.

7 Click here to collapse the panel groups to icons.

8 Click here and drag the Info panel to dock with the Histogram and Navigator panels.

9 Click here and drag to dock the Properties panel with the Adjustments panel.

10 Right-click here to close the Clone Source.

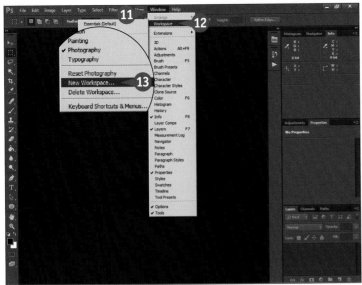

Note: *Continue making changes until you are satisfied with your custom workspace.*

11 Click Window.

12 Click Workspace.

13 Click New Workspace.

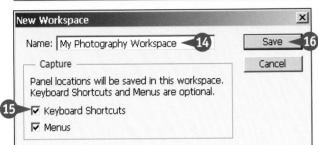

The New Workspace dialog box opens.

14 Type a unique name for your new workspace.

15 Select this option to save the new keyboard shortcut changes if you created any (☐ changes to ☑).

16 Click Save.

Your new workspace is saved and appears in the Window ⇨ Workspace menu.

TIPS

Did You Know?
If you make changes to your custom workspace or any of the prebuilt workspaces while working on a project, you can reset the workspace to its default condition. With the workspace active, click Window ⇨ Workspace ⇨ Reset *Workspace Name*.

Did You Know?
You can delete any workspace you no longer need, including the prebuilt ones. First, select a workspace you do not want to delete and click its name to make it active. Then click Window ⇨ Workspace ⇨ Delete Workspace. Click the Workspace drop-down menu in the Delete Workspace window that appears. Select the name of the workspace to delete and click Delete. Click Yes in the warning box that appears.

ADD A KEYBOARD SHORTCUT
to open an image as a Smart Object

As you become more familiar with Photoshop, you find that keyboard shortcuts are tremendous timesavers. You can use keyboard shortcuts in application menus, panel menus, and to select tools. Photoshop includes many keyboard shortcuts prebuilt into the program, especially for tools in the Toolbox, and these are worth remembering. Photoshop lists many of them to the right of the menu items or as pop-up tool tips when you hover your mouse over a tool.

Even with the many prebuilt keyboard shortcuts, you may find yourself clicking through menus to select an item so often that creating a custom keyboard shortcut is a welcome timesaver.

Not only can you create a keyboard shortcut for an item that lacks one, you can change a prebuilt keyboard shortcut to different keystrokes that you find easier to remember, delete existing keyboard shortcuts, or reassign a prebuilt keyboard shortcut to your item.

A keyboard shortcut to quickly open an image as a Smart Object is very useful. Smart Objects preserve the source content of an image with all its original characteristics, enabling you to perform nondestructive editing to the layer. Smart Objects are discussed in task #48.

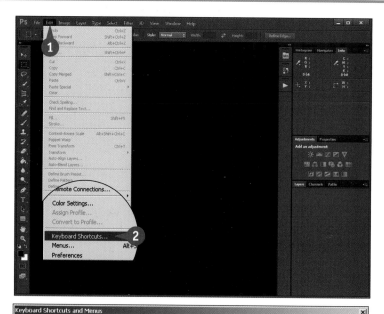

① Click Edit.

② Click Keyboard Shortcuts.

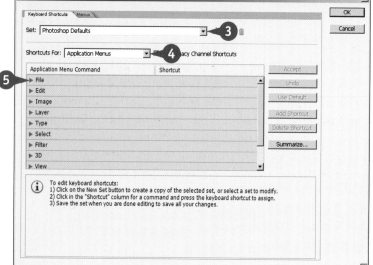

The Keyboard Shortcuts and Menus dialog box opens with the Keyboard Shortcuts tab selected.

③ Click the Set drop-down menu and select Photoshop Defaults.

④ Click the Shortcuts For drop-down menu and select Application Menus if it is not already selected.

⑤ Click the File disclosure triangle.

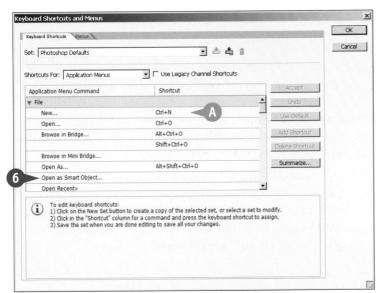

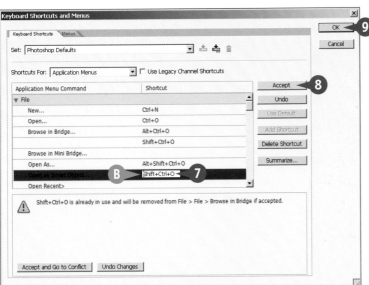

A The File commands are displayed along with any existing keyboard shortcuts.

6 Click Open as Smart Object.

#5

DIFFICULTY LEVEL

B An empty field appears in the Shortcut column.

7 Press Shift+Ctrl+O (Shift+⌘+O).

Note: A warning appears saying this keyboard shortcut is already in use for Browse in Bridge. But because there is an alternate keyboard shortcut for Browse in Bridge, this is not a problem.

8 Click Accept.

9 Click OK.

The Photoshop Defaults set is updated with your new keyboard shortcut.

 TIPS

Preview It!
Check to see that your new keyboard shortcut appears where you wanted it. Click File. The keyboard shortcut is listed in the menu in all of the prebuilt Photoshop workspaces.

Did You Know?
For your custom keyboard shortcuts to appear in your custom workspaces, you must have the workspace active before you begin and you must select the custom workspace in the Set drop-down menu of the Keyboard Shortcuts tab.

Did You Know?
You can access the Keyboard Shortcuts dialog box with a keyboard shortcut. In Windows, press Ctrl+Shift+Alt+K. On a Mac, use ⌘+Shift+Option+K. You can also access the Keyboard Shortcuts dialog box using Window ➪ Workspace ➪ Keyboard Shortcuts and Menus.

There are many times when you work on photos individually in Photoshop, but more often you use the power of Photoshop to composite multiple photos, or combine photos with graphics. These tasks require multiple images to be open or available to be opened quickly.

You can view multiple images several ways in Photoshop. The default setting opens multiple images as individual tabs in one window. You can view each image on its own by clicking the name of the image in its tab. You can also tile the images in different combinations or float them on the screen. When you tile multiple images they all fit together on the screen. When you float them, they overlay each other and you can move each one independently of the others. Even when multiple images are tiled together, you can float one or more of them over the others.

You can also compare multiple photos in various ways. You can view them all at the same zoom level or at the same location in the image or even at the same rotation.

① Click File.

② Click Browse in Bridge.

The screen changes to the Bridge interface.

③ Ctrl+click (⌘+click) images to select them.

Note: Shift+click to select the first and last images if they are consecutive.

④ Click File.

⑤ Click Open With.

⑥ Click Adobe Photoshop CC (default).

The screen changes back to Photoshop.

Note: If Photoshop displays the Embedded Profile Mismatch window before opening an image with Use the Embedded Profile (Instead of the Working Space) selected, click OK.

The images open in the default tab mode.

7️⃣ Click any tab to open another image.

8️⃣ Click Window.

9️⃣ Click Arrange.

🔟 Click 4-up.

The images arrange in a tiled grid.

⓫ Click Window.

⓬ Click Arrange.

⓭ Click Match Zoom.

If you selected one of the images and changed its zoom level and it is the active image, the zoom level of the other images changes to match.

TIPS

More Options!

With multiple images open, click Window ➪ Arrange ➪ Float All in Windows. Photoshop automatically arranges each image in its own floating window.

Try This!

With multiple images floating or tiled, click Window ➪ Arrange ➪ Consolidate All to Tabs. Photoshop automatically arranges the images into the default tabbed configuration.

More Options!

With multiple images tiled, use the Hand tool to drag one image to the top left in its window. Click Window ➪ Arrange ➪ Match Location. Photoshop automatically repositions the remaining images to the top left of their window.

Actions are a way that you can quickly perform a series of repeated steps to an image. An *action* is a series of commands that are recorded once and that you can apply to another image or even folders of images with one click in the future.

Photoshop includes a default set of actions and nine other sets designed to automate specific techniques, including a set of video actions. Even with all of the prebuilt actions, you may not find just the one you need for a task you

perform repeatedly. Virtually everything you can do in Photoshop you can record into an action, including incorporating a plug-in. Actions can even include pauses that allow you to enter specific information before they continue running.

Using the Actions panel, you record the steps and save your new action in your own custom actions set. Fortunately, there is no time limit while you are recording your action. You can take as long as you need.

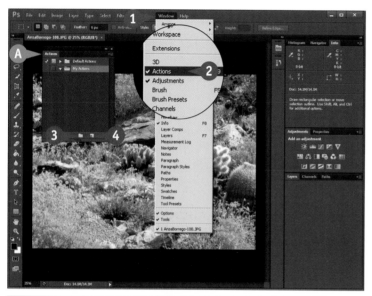

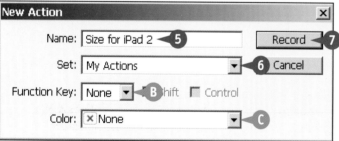

Note: The steps in this task create a simple action for saving an image as a 1024-×-768-pixel document for an iPad 2.

1 With a dSLR image open, click Window.

2 Click Actions.

A The Actions panel opens.

3 Click the Create New Set icon and name the set My Actions in the New Set dialog box.

4 Click the Create New Action icon.

The New Action dialog box opens.

5 Type a descriptive name for your action.

6 Click the Set drop-down menu and select My Actions.

B You can select the Function Key drop-down menu and assign a keyboard shortcut to your action.

C You can select the Color drop-down menu and assign a color to your action.

7 Click Record.

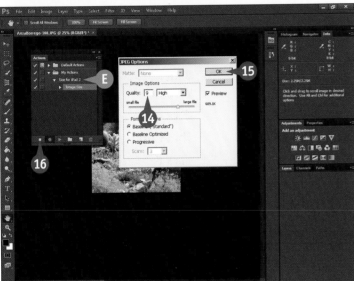

D The Record button in the Actions panel turns red.

Perform the steps that you want to record:

8 Click Image ⇨ Image Size to open the Image Size dialog box.

9 Change the width to 1024 pixels. The height changes to 768 pixels.

10 Click OK.

11 Click File ⇨ Save As.

The Save As dialog box opens.

12 Click the Save In drop-down menu and select a location.

You can click the File Name box and enter a new filename.

13 Click Save.

The JPEG Options dialog box opens.

14 Type **9** in the Quality box. This is a good balance of quality vs. file size.

15 Click OK.

16 Click the Stop Recording button.

E Your custom action is complete and listed in your My Actions set of the Actions panel.

TIPS

Test It!

Test your new action. Open a new image. Open the Actions panel and select your new action. Click the Play button (▶). Navigate to the folder whose location you selected in step 12. Check that the resized image is there.

Try This!

You can apply an action to an entire folder of images, including all of its subfolders. In Photoshop, click File ⇨ Automate ⇨ Batch and select the action and the source folder. In Bridge, click Tools ⇨ Photoshop ⇨ Batch.

Did You Know?

There are hundreds and possibly thousands of Photoshop actions available for download on the web. If you find one that you can use, download it and move it to the Actions folder inside the Presets folder of the Photoshop application folder.

Just as you can customize your interface and your workspace, you can customize many of the tools and panels in Photoshop. By doing so you can work more efficiently on an individual project. You can also set the changes as a default so they are always available. The tools and panels you customize depend on whether you use Photoshop as a photographer, an artist, or as a print or web designer.

The Color Swatches panel is used by all disciplines. It provides a way to save and select colors so that you can

access them quickly. Photoshop also includes prebuilt swatch sets for photographers, artists, and designers. One of the most useful sets for photographers is the set of photographic filter colors. You can use these to simulate the effect of placing a filter over your camera lens.

Other panels include a submenu of prebuilt options and the ability to customize the panel. These include Brush Presets, Styles, and Tool Presets.

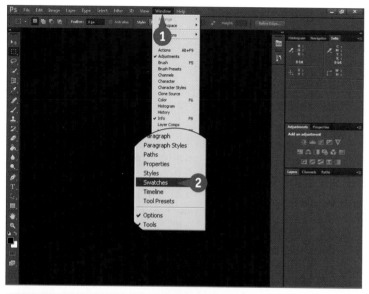

① Click Window.

② Click Swatches.

The Swatches panel opens.

③ Click the panel menu button.

Ⓐ The panel submenu opens.

④ Click Large Thumbnail.

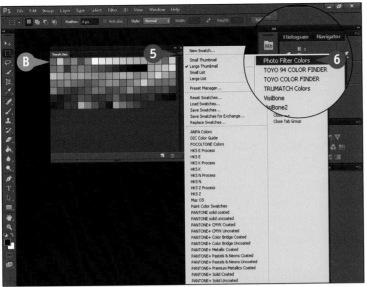

B The swatches are larger.

5 Click the panel menu button.

6 Click Photo Filter Colors.

A dialog box opens asking if you want to replace the current color swatches with the colors from Photo Filter Colors.

7 Click Append.

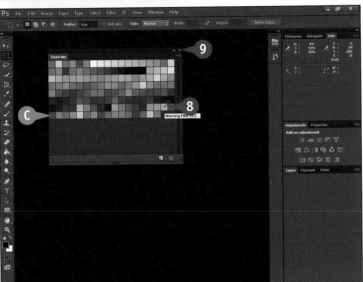

C The Photo Filter Colors are added to the default set.

8 When you hover your cursor over a swatch, the name of the filter appears.

9 Click here to close the Swatches panel.

Your Photo Filter Colors are now a part of the default Swatches panel.

Note: *Rather than closing the Swatches panel, click the title bar and drag it to the right to dock it with other panels.*

TIPS

Remove It!

If you decide that you do not use the photo filter colors often enough to have them be a part of the Swatches panel, open the panel, click the panel menu button, and select Reset Swatches. The color filters and any other filters you added are removed.

Apply It!

With the Photo Filter Colors available in the Color Swatches panel it is easy to quickly warm an image. Open an image taken in the shade. Add a new layer. Open the Swatches panel and click the 81 photo filter. The foreground color changes to the 81 photo filter color. Fill the new layer with the foreground color. Change the blend mode to Soft Light. Adjust the layer opacity to your liking.

As you become more familiar with Photoshop, you try increasingly complex projects, sometimes with other collaborators. After spending time working on a project to achieve just the look you imagine, you wonder if you could ever achieve that same look on a new project. With the help of two Photoshop tools, the History Log and the Notes tool, you can.

With Photoshop's History Log active, you can automatically record every command and setting you select. It is like recording an action, but the History Log

cannot be played back automatically. It is, however, available for you to review when creating a new project.

You activate and set preferences for the History Log in the General pane of the Preferences dialog box. You can view the History Log in the History tab of the File ⇨ File Info window.

The Notes tool allows you to add review comments, cautions, and instructions to an image. The notes appear as small nonprintable icons on the image itself and are associated with a specific area of the image. You can toggle notes on and off by clicking View ⇨ Show ⇨ Notes.

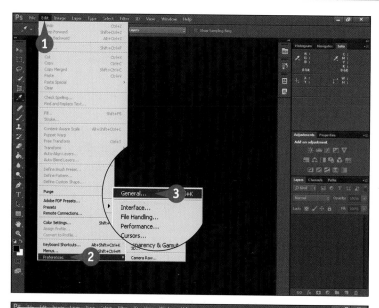

Activate the History Log

1 Click Edit (Photoshop).

2 Click Preferences.

3 Click General.

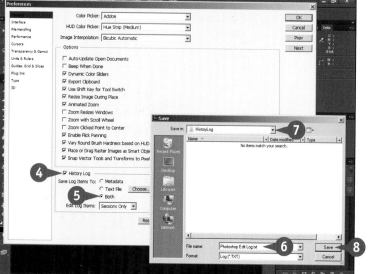

The General pane of the Preferences dialog box opens.

4 Select History Log (☐ changes to ☑).

5 Select Both (○ changes to ◉).

The Save dialog box opens.

6 Accept the default name or type a new name in the dialog box.

7 Navigate to a folder to select a location to store the History Log.

8 Click Save.

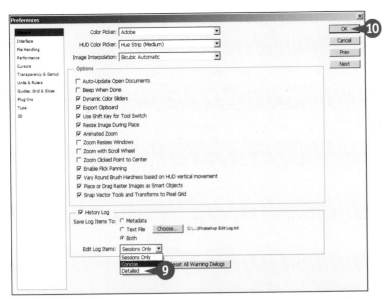

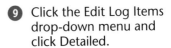

9 Click the Edit Log Items drop-down menu and click Detailed.

10 Click OK.

The History Log is now set to save in both the metadata of the image and in the text file at the location you chose in step 7.

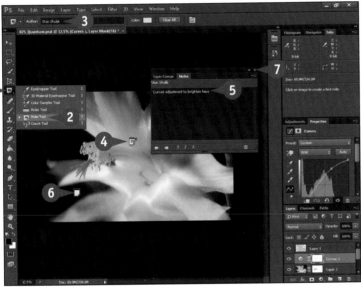

Activate the Notes Tool

1 Click the Eyedropper tool in the Toolbox.

2 Click Note Tool.

The Options bar changes.

3 Type your name as author.

Note: Click the Color box to change the color for your notes, or use the default yellow color.

4 Click in the image where you want the note icon to be placed.

The notes icon (📝) appears and the Notes panel opens.

5 Type a note in the Notes panel.

6 Add other notes in the image.

7 Click here to close the Notes panel.

More Options!

The History Log options can be confusing. When you save log items to **Metadata**, you are saving them within the image file. When you save them to a **Text File**, you are saving them as text at the location you select. The file continuously increases in size with each file you edit with the History Log active until you create a new text file. **Sessions Only** records only the time you opened and saved files, and the time you closed Photoshop. **Concise** records the name of a command you select, but not the settings. **Detailed** records the name of the command and the settings applied. It also records each brush stroke, but not where you applied it.

Try This!

If history logs are important to your workflow, create a separate text file for each project. Use the name of the project as the name of the text file.

All of the color decisions you make when using Photoshop are based on what you are seeing on the screen, so the color accuracy of your monitor is extremely important. New monitors vary widely in color accuracy and all monitors age at different rates depending on their initial quality and the amount of use they see.

Macintosh and Windows both include a software-based color calibration option in the Display panel of their system preferences or control panel. These require highly subjective comparisons to the point of being useless for critical color decisions.

Hardware-based monitor profiling devices are capable of nonsubjectively calibrating your monitor to an established standard and then creating a color profile to interpret image RGB numbers and accurately translate them to colors on your display.

Hardware-based solutions are available at many price points. Even the least expensive do an excellent job of profiling a monitor. More expensive devices increase color accuracy by more accurately measuring more colors during profiling.

The following steps are those used with an X-Rite i1 Photo Pro, i1 Photo Pro 2, and i1 Display. The steps in other devices are similar.

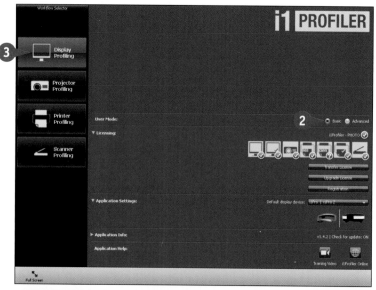

① Install the software that controls the hardware profiling device and connect the device.

② Select Basic (○ changes to ◉).

Note: If Basic and Advanced modes are available, select Basic the first time you use it. Later you can try the Advanced mode.

③ Click Display Profiling.

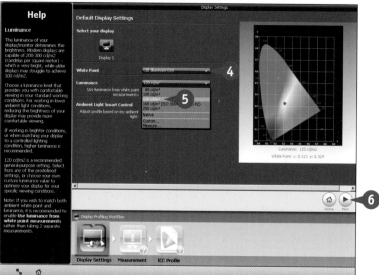

④ Select a white point of D65 or 6500 Kelvin.

⑤ Select a luminance value, which is the brightness of your display, not greater than 120 cd per square meter.

⑥ Click Next.

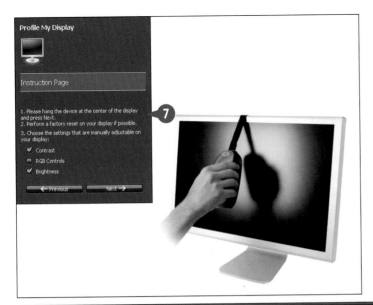

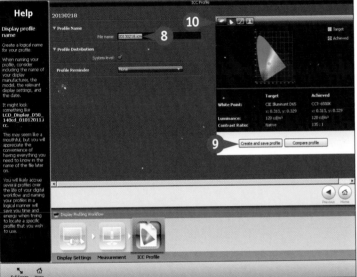

7 Follow the on-screen instructions for placing the profiling device and conducting the profile.

Note: *The profiling procedure involves the control software generating a series of color screens with known color values and reading the color values that your monitor displays. The software then generates a look-up table (LUT) to correct your monitor to display the colors accurately.*

8 When profiling is complete, type a unique name for the profile. It is useful to include the date in the name.

9 Click Create and Save Profile.

10 Click options for before and after views, a display of how accurately the device met profiling targets, and other options.

TIPS

More Options!
Use you monitor's on-screen controls to manually adjust contrast and brightness during the calibration if these controls are available. They are not available on most laptops.

Did You Know?
The color stability of modern LCD screens is very good compared to the old CRT monitors. However, even these monitors should be re-profiled at least monthly. Inexpensive LED monitors are not recommended for photography because they are very difficult to profile accurately for a number of reasons.

Important!
The first time you profile a new monitor you may feel that something went wrong because it may seem dark and the colors may seem too warm. Do not despair! When manufacturers ship monitors and laptops, the brightness is usually set at its maximum and the color temperature to over 9000 Kelvin (very blue).

A mouse, trackball, or touchpad may be an appropriate device for navigating web pages or business documents, but they fall far short of desirable for working in Photoshop.

Any Photoshop tool that uses a brush only reaches its full potential when controlled by a pen and pressure-sensitive tablet. When you paint or retouch with a mouse, you can only paint with the maximum flow or opacity that you have set. When you paint with a pen tablet, you can paint with any flow, roundness, size, or opacity from the barest minimum to the maximum that you have set, and

thousands of degrees in between by adjusting the pen pressure and tilt.

All of the pen tablet controls are built in to Photoshop. But before you activate them, there are some important preferences that you need to make in the tablet window in the Control Panel or System Preferences. Then you are ready to activate settings in Photoshop.

The following steps before reaching Photoshop are shown with a Wacom Intuos4 tablet connected to a USB port. Other tablets have similar settings.

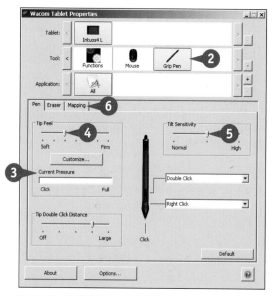

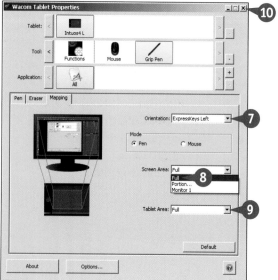

① Open the tablet properties window from the Control Panel (System Preferences) after installing the tablet and software.

The tablet properties window opens.

② Click Grip Pen.

③ Watch the Current Pressure window while you drag the pen tip across the window.

④ Adjust the Tip Feel settings until your maximum pressure makes the bar touch the window's right edge.

⑤ Set the Tilt Sensitivity to the center of the scale.

Note: These are the two important settings in the Pen window. Adjust any of the others that you want.

⑥ Click the Mapping tab.

The Mapping window opens.

⑦ Click the Orientation drop-down menu and select ExpressKeys Left if you are right handed.

⑧ Click Full from the Screen Area drop-down menu.

⑨ Click Full from the Tablet Area drop-down menu.

⑩ Close the tablet properties window.

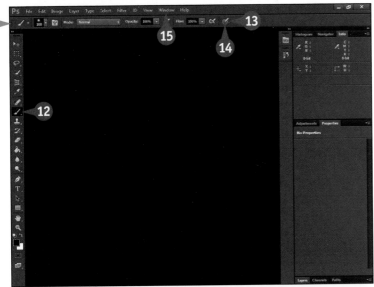

A

① Open Photoshop.

② Click the Brush tool in the Toolbox.

Ⓐ The Options bar changes to brush options.

⑬ Click the Pen button at the far right of the Options bar (🖋 changes to 🖋). This sets pen pressure to control brush size.

⑭ Click the Pen button at the far right of the Options bar (🖋 changes to 🖋). This cancels pen pressure controlling brush size.

⑮ Click Window ➪ Brushes.

The Brush panel opens.

⑯ Select Shape Dynamics (■ changes to ☑).

⑰ Click Pen Pressure in the Control drop-down menu of the Size Jitter subpanel to have it controlled by your pen pressure.

Note: Set any of the Brush Tip Shapes that have a Control setting in a subpanel to Pen Pressure or Pen Tilt.

⑱ Click here to close the Brush panel with your new settings.

#11

DIFFICULTY LEVEL

TIPS

Test It!
Experiment with varying your brush size by varying the pressure you use with your tablet pen. Open a blank document. Click the Brush tool and click the brush size pen button at the far right of the Options bar. Select a color other than white and paint while varying pressure on the pen.

Important!
Becoming comfortable using a pen tablet takes time and is a considerable test of eye/hand coordination. The benefits you gain from a pen tablet in Photoshop far outweigh the learning curve.

Did You Know?
Wacom Intuos pen tablets are available in four sizes. The smallest size is sufficient for many users. The largest size is overkill for all but the most dedicated and precise digital artists.

Chapter 2

Manage Photos with Adobe Bridge and Mini Bridge

Adobe Bridge and Mini Bridge are useful add-ons to Photoshop. Mini Bridge is an application that runs within the Photoshop workspace. Bridge is an independent application that is available as an optional download from the Adobe Cloud. Bridge is the common central hub that ties the Adobe Creative Cloud applications together as well as tying Photoshop to your camera and hard drive.

Bridge is a powerful application that you can use in conjunction with Photoshop to browse, preview, and work with your images. Different workspaces in Bridge allow you to easily import photos and videos, apply keywords, preview and rate photos and videos, and more.

As with Photoshop, you can customize the look of your Bridge workspaces. Bridge offers several workspaces that make working with different Bridge

functions easier. Each workspace can run full screen, making each task easier to perform.

Mini Bridge resides within the Photoshop interface and provides the browsing capabilities of Bridge on a smaller scale, both in function and in screen size. Mini Bridge saves you time spent switching between Photoshop and Bridge when you simply want to locate, sort, and open images.

To work efficiently in Bridge and Mini Bridge they need to be synchronized. Once Bridge and Mini Bridge are in sync, selecting and opening photos and videos is possible in either one.

By using Bridge as the central hub when you are working with images, and Mini Bridge as a quick image browser within Photoshop, you become more productive when working with your projects.

DIFFICULTY LEVEL

As with Photoshop, you can set the color theme for your Bridge workspaces. The settings you select control the colors for all of the workspaces. The four preset themes in Bridge include four shades of gray ranging from light gray to dark gray. There are additional options within each theme for setting the color in the Preview panel to one of these grays, to black, or to white. Additionally, there is an option to choose a custom accent color for the active menu selection.

Because Bridge and Photoshop are designed to work closely together, choosing the same color theme for both makes switching between them easier on the eyes. While four options are offered in both applications, there are differences in the actual gray values between the options in the two programs. Adjusting them to the same values, however, is easy.

Choose the interface color that you prefer for your images in Photoshop first. Then adjust the Bridge interface to match, or not, if you prefer.

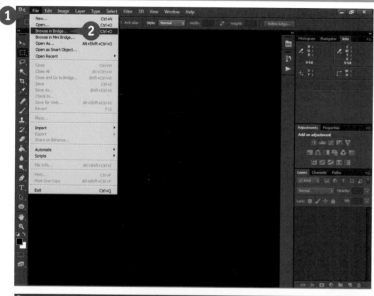

1 With Photoshop open and maximized, and your color scheme set as in task #1, click File.

2 Click Browse in Bridge.

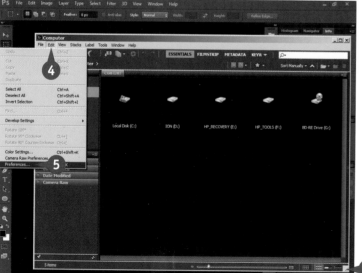

Bridge opens.

3 Resize Bridge and arrange Bridge to see Photoshop behind it.

4 Click Edit (Bridge).

5 Click Preferences.

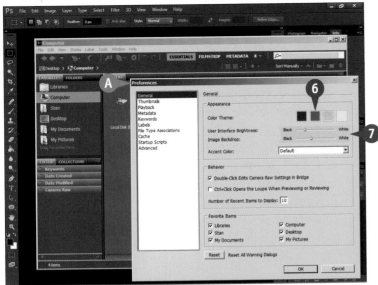

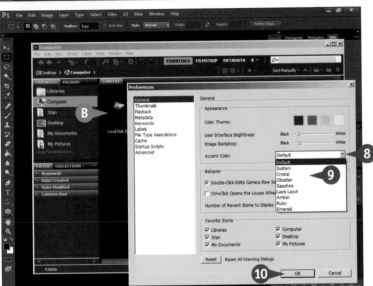

A The General pane of the Preferences dialog box opens.

6 In the Appearance pane, click the Color Theme that is closest to your Photoshop Color Theme.

Note: The grays in the user interface and image backdrop in Bridge and Photoshop do not match.

7 Adjust the User Interface Brightness and Image Backdrop sliders until the grays in the User Interface Brightness and Image Backdrop match as closely as possible.

B The screen changes to the colors you select.

8 Click the Accent Color drop-down menu.

9 Click through the Accent Colors until you find one you like.

10 Click OK to save your Bridge color theme.

TIPS

More Options!
Click through the other Preferences panes in Bridge to familiarize yourself with the options. Change any to suit your project. For example, if you are shooting videos, go to the Playback pane and select Play Video Files Automatically when Previewed (☐ changes to ☑).

Did You Know?
You can navigate to any folder on your hard drives or on a network from the Bridge workspace. Click the Folders tab in the upper-left panel to change from the default Favorites panel to the Folders panel. If you prefer the Folders panel as the default rather than the Favorites panel, leave the panel active when you close Bridge.

Did You Know?
You can select an image in Bridge and press the spacebar to open it full screen in Bridge. Press the spacebar again to return to the thumbnail view.

Change your WORKSPACE VIEW

You can customize each of the seven prebuilt Bridge workspaces to your individual taste or specific project. And once you customize a workspace you can save it for use later. The default Bridge workspace is Essentials. You can also access six other prebuilt workspaces available in Bridge. They are: Filmstrip, Metadata, Keywords, Preview, Light Table, and Folders.

Unlike with Photoshop, where you generally create one custom workspace with the tools and panels you use most often and then remain in it, with Bridge you find yourself

navigating among the prebuilt workspaces. By changing workspaces you maximize the screen space available to use the specialized function of the workspace.

In each custom workspace you can save window locations and the image sort order you select. You can rearrange the way that panels dock together and close panels you do not use. If you customize a prebuilt workspace and close Bridge, Bridge remembers the layout the next time you open it. And you can always reset the prebuilt workspace and delete custom workspaces at any time.

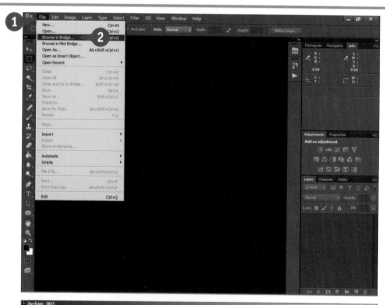

① With Photoshop open, click File.

② Click Browse in Bridge.

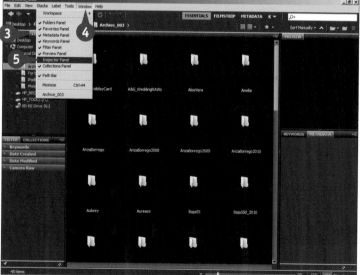

Bridge opens. Maximize Bridge if it is not already.

③ Click the Folders tab.

④ Click Window.

⑤ Uncheck panels you do not use to close them.

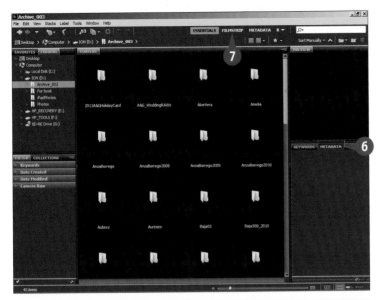

6 Click the Metadata tab, drag it slightly upward until a blue bar appears, and then release the mouse.

Note: The Metadata panel docks above the Keywords panel. The changes are saved to the Essentials workspace.

7 Click Filmstrip.

The Filmstrip workspace appears.

8 Click the Folders tab.

9 Click here and drag upward to enlarge the filmstrip thumbnails.

10 Close Bridge.

Your changes to the Bridge interface are saved.

Did You Know?

You can change the size of image thumbnails in any workspace in which they appear by dragging the slider below the Preview panel. And you can lock the thumbnail grid, and view information in the workspace as details or a list by clicking the icons to the right of the slider.

Did You Know?

You can collapse any Bridge panel to a tab by double-clicking its name in the tab. To enlarge it when collapsed, double-click the tab.

Did You Know?

You can click and drag a workspace name in the Applications bar to reorder the list. Then click and drag the grabber to the left of the list to show only those workspace titles you want to see.

By using the Folders panel in Bridge you can browse photos and videos that already exist on your hard drive. You may have added images to your hard drive in the past by using the software provided by your camera manufacturer, by importing them with a third-party application, or by using your computer's operating system. You can continue to import photos and videos as you have done in the past, but you may miss out on some of the capabilities that Bridge provides during image import.

Before importing images using Bridge you can select just those you want to import by viewing thumbnails of the photos and videos on your camera or camera card. You can choose where to store the imports and where to store a backup copy during import.

During import you can rename files and apply metadata, either basic metadata or more complex metadata from a template you have created. While you can apply metadata using Bridge after importing, often it is simpler to apply it during import if the photos or videos were all taken at a single event.

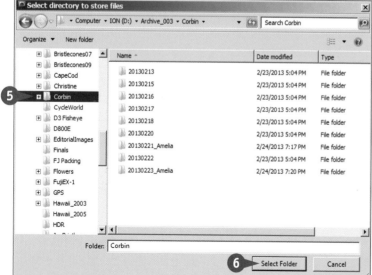

1 With Bridge opened and maximized, click File.

2 Click Get Photos from Camera.

The Adobe Bridge Photo Downloader dialog box opens.

3 Click the Get Photos from drop-down menu and select the drive with your camera or card reader.

A You can click the Create Subfolder(s) drop-down menu to create a subfolder using one of the prebuilt options or a custom subfolder if you want.

B You can click the Rename Files drop-down menu to create a custom name for the files or use one of the prebuilt options if you want.

4 Click Browse.

5 Select a location to store the import.

6 Click Select Folder.

7 In the Adobe Bridge Photo Downloader dialog box, click Advanced Dialog.

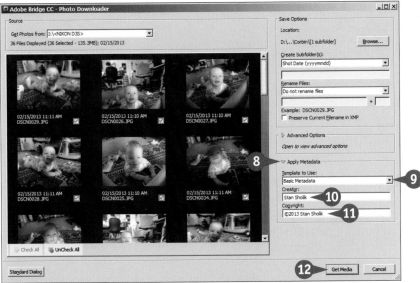

The Advanced dialog box of the Photo Downloader opens.

8 Click the Apply Metadata disclosure triangle.

9 Click the Template to Use drop-down menu and select Basic Metadata.

10 Type a name in the Creator field.

11 Type copyright information.

12 Click Get Media.

C The Copying window opens, Bridge imports the files, and displays the import in the Content panel.

13 View the files in Bridge.

TIPS

Did You Know?

You can click the camera icon (📷) in the Applications bar to open the Adobe Bridge Photo Downloader dialog box.

Try This!

If none of the prebuilt auto-naming choices seem right in the Rename Files drop-down menu, click the Advanced Rename preset at the very bottom. Here you can create your own naming convention for the import from a wide range of possibilities. Choose from the many options to create your custom file renaming template.

Caution!

Leave the Delete Original Files check box unchecked in the Bridge Photo Downloader dialog box. If there is a problem during download, the files remain on the card and you can download them again.

Many Photoshop users initially find adding keywords to images a time-consuming and virtually pointless operation. After all, you can just open Bridge, navigate through the folders, and find the image you are looking for.

But as the size of your image library grows, the time-consuming operation becomes navigating through folders looking for an image. At that point, you wish you had started adding keywords long before, when you first started adding images to your library. Using Bridge, you can add keywords and hierarchies of keywords to find photos in your library.

Stock photographers often add multiple keywords to images, while wedding and event photographers may add only the name and date of the assignment. While other software such as Adobe Lightroom allows you to enter keywords during import, Bridge does not. In Bridge you add keywords in either the Keyword panel of the Essentials workspace, or in the Keyword workspace.

When keywords are available, both Bridge and Mini Bridge provide complex search and filtering options for finding images. With keywords you can easily find the images you need for compositing or other projects.

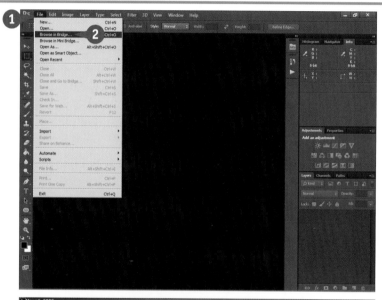

① With Photoshop open and maximized, click File.

② Click Browse in Bridge.

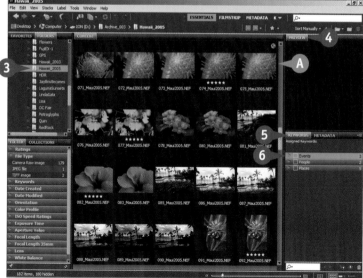

Bridge opens. Maximize it if it is not full screen.

③ Click a folder that holds images you want to keyword.

Ⓐ The image thumbnails open in the Content panel.

④ Double-click the Preview tab.

The Preview panel closes to a tab.

⑤ Click the Keywords tab.

The Keywords panel opens.

⑥ Click the disclosure triangles next to Events, People, and Places.

B The prebuilt Events, People, and Places panels open.

7 Click in the Events title bar.

Note: The Events title bar is highlighted.

8 Click the panel menu button.

9 Click Delete.

Note: If you feel that the Events keyword set would be of use, do not delete it.

The Adobe Bridge dialog box opens asking if you are sure you want to remove the Events keyword set.

10 Click Yes.

11 Repeat steps 7 to 10 for the People and Places keyword sets.

Note: If you feel that these keyword sets would be of use, do not delete them.

12 Click an image to select it.

13 Click the New Keyword icon to add a new keyword.

C A text entry box opens in the Keywords panel.

14 Type your keyword and press Enter (Return).

TIPS

Did You Know?

You can create a keyword in any image folder and apply it to images in any other folder. The keywords you create remain in the Keywords panel when you change to another folder.

Did You Know?

If you misspell a keyword and press Enter (Return) without noticing the misspelling, you can correct the spelling. Click the misspelled keyword to select it and click the Keyword panel menu button. Select Rename and correct the spelling.

More Options!

You can quickly delete a keyword or keyword set by clicking and dragging it to the trash icon at the bottom of the panel.

Once you create a keyword, you can add that keyword to multiple images in the same folder. You can select all of the images in the folder and apply the same keyword, or you can navigate through the images and select any number of them and apply the keyword to them.

You can also create a hierarchy of keywords. If you want to search for a specific type of flower, you do not want to have to look through all of the images you have keyworded "Flower." By creating subcategories to as

many sublevels as you need, you can narrow your search to the specific images you want to see. An image can have as many keywords as you want to assign to it. Adding about five keywords to each image should be your goal.

Keywording allows you to take advantage of the powerful search capabilities in Bridge and Mini Bridge. As your image library grows, you come to appreciate the time you spent adding keywords.

⑮ Select other images in the folder that need the same keyword.

⑯ Select this option to add the keyword to the selected images (☐ changes to ☑).

⑰ Select another image or images.

Note: Other images you select can already have a keyword.

⑱ Click the New Keyword icon to add the new keyword.

Ⓐ A new text entry box appears in the Keywords panel.

⑲ Type your new keyword and press Enter (Return).

⑳ Select this option to add the keyword to the selected images (☐ changes to ☑).

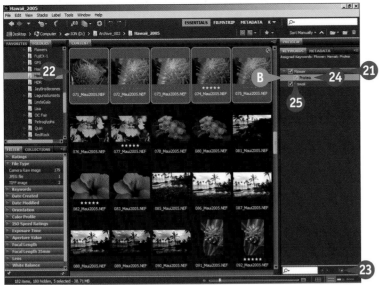

21 Select a keyword set.

Note: *When you add subcategories, the top keyword set is called the "parent" and the subcategory is called the "child."*

22 Select images in a keyword set that are the same, but different from other images in the set.

23 Click the New Sub Keyword icon to add a subcategory to the keyword set.

Ⓑ A text entry box opens below the keyword set name.

24 Type a subcategory keyword and then press Enter (Return).

25 Select this option to add the subcategory keyword to the selected images (■ changes to ☑).

26 Select the same parent keyword set you selected in step 21.

27 Select different images in the set that are the same.

28 Click the New Sub Keyword icon to add a new subcategory.

29 Type a new subcategory name in the new text entry box and then press Enter (Return).

30 Select this option to add the subcategory keyword to the selected images (■ changes to ☑).

TIPS

Test It!

Test your new keyword. Click Window ➪ Workspace to open the Workspace drop-down menu. Click Keywords. The keyword workspace opens. Navigate to any of the images to which you added keywords and check that the keywords are there.

Try This!

You do not need to have an image selected to add a keyword. Just click in the gray area of the Keyword panel so that no keyword sets are highlighted. Then click the New Keyword icon (⊞) to add a keyword.

Apply It!

Use the Keyword panel to find images with a specific keyword. Right-click a keyword you created and click Find. The Find dialog box opens. Make selections for Source, Criteria, and Results. Click Find and Bridge finds and displays images matching your criteria.

REVIEW AND RATE images

Now that you are capturing images with a digital camera, the number of images you capture each time you shoot is far higher than it would have been if you were shooting with a film camera. Bridge provides tools that you can use to easily review and rate the images you capture. Reviewing the images in your shoot and deciding which of those images are your favorites can be a time-consuming task if you do this with thumbnails in the Content panel. Bridge offers a review mode to make the task easier.

In the Review Mode screen, your entire take is presented as a carousel of images. You can navigate forward and backward through them to see similar images and select your favorites. Once you select your favorites, you can rate them from least favorite to most favorite using stars. You can then filter your selects to show those you rated.

By reviewing and rating images, you can return to the take later and concentrate only on those images that you decided were the best.

1. With Bridge open and maximized, select a folder of images from the Folders tab.

2. Click View.

3. Click Review Mode.

The Review Mode screen opens.

4. Click here to move forward in the stack.

5. Click here to move backward in the stack.

6. Click here to reject a photo that is not one of your favorites.

7. Click here to open the 100% loupe view.

   Note: The loupe view is open to check sharpness of the helmet of the rider.

8. Click here to exit review mode.

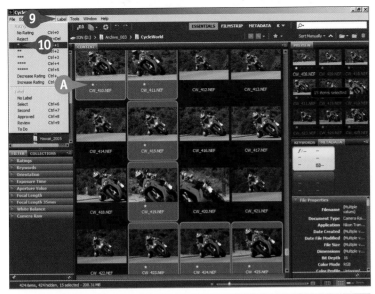

The Essentials workspace appears. The rejected images are not highlighted.

9 Click Label.

10 Click *.

A One star is added to the images you did not reject.

11 Click the Filter tab.

12 Click the Ratings disclosure triangle.

The Ratings subpanel opens.

13 Click to the left of the one star (■ changes to ☑).

B The images rated with one star appear in the Content panel.

TIPS

Did You Know?
In review mode, if you accidently reject a photo, you can return it to the carousel by pressing the up arrow key. You can only do this immediately after you reject it.

More Options!
In review mode, use the left- and right-arrow keys to navigate through the carousel. Use the down arrow key to reject a photo. Press Esc to exit review mode.

Try This!
Return to review mode with the one-star photos and repeat the steps to rate some of those images higher.

You can use Bridge to select photos to open in Photoshop when you are in Bridge, but if you are in Photoshop you can select them more quickly using Mini Bridge.

Mini Bridge contains much of the functionality of Bridge, and Bridge must run in the background for you to use Mini Bridge. If Bridge is not open when you launch Mini Bridge you must click the Bridge button in Mini Bridge to launch Bridge. With Mini Bridge open, you can browse your computer for images, preview images full screen,

filter images by rating, change the order that you view your images, and even search for images to which you have added a keyword.

Use Bridge to do tasks that are easiest done with a full-screen interface. These include importing photos from your camera or memory card, reviewing and rating images, and adding keywords. Use Mini Bridge to quickly select a photo or group of photos when you are working in Photoshop.

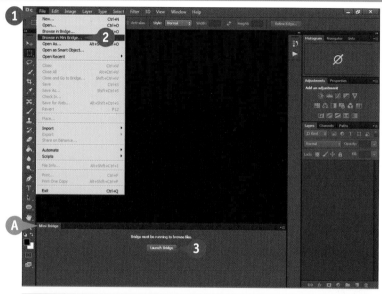

1 Click File.

2 Click Browse in Mini Bridge.

A Mini Bridge opens. You can click and drag Mini Bridge to dock it to the bottom of the preview window.

3 Click Launch Bridge or click Reconnect if you had previously opened Bridge but it is no longer open.

4 Click the Computer drop-down menu to navigate to your image folder.

5 Click a folder to open thumbnails of the images in it.

6 Click here and drag up to enlarge the thumbnails.

7 Click and drag here to scroll through the images.

8 Click the sort drop-down menu to change to a different sort order or criteria.

9 Click here to filter by rating.

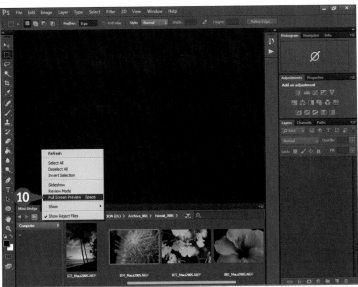

10 Click the View drop-down menu (▦▾) and select Full Screen Preview.

Note: You can optionally press the spacebar to launch the full-screen preview mode.

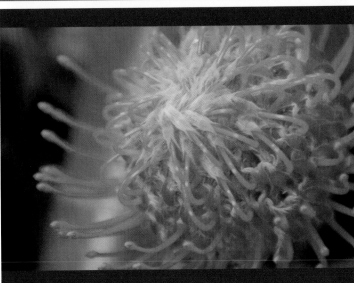

The screen fills with a full-screen view.

11 Press the left- and right-arrow keys to navigate through the images.

12 Press Esc to return to Photoshop.

TIPS

Did You Know?
You can click the symbol (▸) between the names in the navigation bar to display the subfolders in the drive or folder to the left symbol.

Did You Know?
You can synchronize Bridge and Mini Bridge so that the same folder is active in both. In Mini Bridge, click the Reveal in Bridge icon (▣) in the navigation bar. In Bridge, click the boomerang icon (◤) in the Applications bar.

Did You Know?
You can rename a file in Mini Bridge. Right-click an image. Select Rename. Type a new name for the image.

You can use Mini Bridge to open a single image or to open multiple images in Photoshop in a number of ways. The File ➪ Open command in Photoshop is the most inefficient way to open a single or multiple images. With Photoshop open, the most efficient way to open images is through Mini Bridge.

You can open a single image in Photoshop using several techniques, but the result is simply the image opens as a tab in Photoshop. You can also open a single image in

Camera Raw. But with multiple images, your options are open. Depending on what you want to do with the photos in Photoshop, you can open them as individual tabbed images, run an action on them, load the images as Photoshop layers, open the images to merge in HDR Pro, or open them to composite in Photomerge.

Mini Bridge provides all of the options you need to efficiently open images in Photoshop.

1 With Mini Bridge open, navigate to the first file you want to open.

2 Click and drag the image into the Photoshop workspace.

Note: If the Embedded Profile Mismatch dialog box opens, select an option and click OK.

A You can optionally double-click the image thumbnail in Mini Bridge.

B You can also optionally right-click the thumbnail and select Photoshop from the Open With submenu.

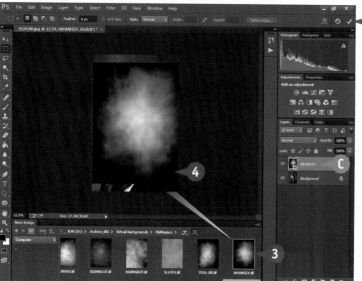

3 Navigate to another photo that you want to open in a layer with the first image.

4 Click and drag the second image on top of the first.

C The second image opens on its own layer.

5 Click the Commit any Current Edits icon in the Applications bar.

The second image opens as a Smart Object.

Note: Smart Objects are discussed in task #48.

Note: If you do not want the second image to open as a layer of the first, drag the second image to the blank area next to a tab in the Tabbed Document bar.

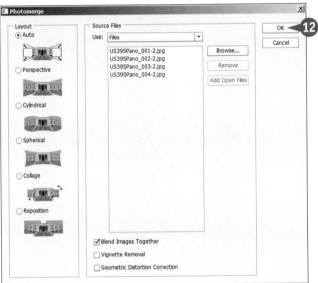

6 Navigate to a folder holding images you want to merge in a panorama.

7 Click the first image.

8 Shift+click the last image.

The images to merge are highlighted with a blue outline.

9 Right-click one of the images.

A submenu appears.

10 Click Photoshop.

Another submenu appears.

11 Click Photomerge.

The Photomerge dialog box opens.

12 Click OK.

Photoshop creates the panorama.

TIPS

Did You Know!

You can click the double arrowheads (⬍) to the right of Computer in Mini Bridge to open a drop-down menu with shortcuts to your documents, the Favorites you set up in Bridge, your recent folders, and your recent files.

Try This!

Find an image on your computer. Click the magnifying glass (🔍) at the far right of the navigation bar. Select Search in Bridge. Bridge opens and the Find dialog box appears. Select your search criteria and click Find.

More Options!

If Mini Bridge is closed, you can also open it from Window ⇨ Extensions ⇨ Mini Bridge.

Chapter 3

Process Photos in Camera Raw

Adobe Camera Raw was originally introduced in Photoshop 7 to allow photographers to open RAW file format images through Photoshop without having to venture too far from the Photoshop workspace. Camera Raw still serves this function, but its capabilities have been expanded far beyond the original version, including the capability to use Camera Raw to process TIFF and JPEG images.

There are many advantages to using Camera Raw as a part of your workflow. The most important of these is the ability of Camera Raw to adjust global characteristics such as exposure and color temperature without affecting the actual pixel information in the image. This is called *nondestructive* editing. The changes are saved as metadata in a small text file called a sidecar XMP file. You can reopen the image file at any later time and undo the adjustments or make further changes to the image.

There are other advantages to using Camera Raw. It is very quick because there is no waiting to render or save each adjustment. There is no increase in the file size of the image no matter how many adjustments you make. You can open multiple images in Camera Raw, adjust one, and apply those adjustments to the other images. And you can even make local adjustments nondestructively without the complex masking often needed in Photoshop.

Camera Raw is automatically installed as a plug-in when you install Photoshop. New in Photoshop CC is the ability to access Camera Raw at any time by choosing Filter ➪ Camera Raw. Use Camera Raw to globally adjust your images and prepare them for pixel-level refinements in Photoshop.

In both Bridge and Photoshop you can set preferences for the way you want to use Camera Raw. Setting the preferences in one sets the same preferences in the other. The default settings work well for most photographers. However, the Camera Raw Preferences dialog box does not make it clear what the effect of selecting a setting other than the default has on your image processing. For example, if you only view the processed Camera Raw image in Bridge or Photoshop, then there is no need to save the adjustments in a sidecar XMP file, the default. This is rarely the case, so the default of saving the adjustments in the sidecar file is better.

You can also use Camera Raw preferences so that TIFF and JPEG files that you previously adjusted in Camera Raw automatically open again in Camera Raw when you select File ➪ Open in Bridge or Photoshop. Or you can turn off Camera Raw support for TIFF and JPEG in the preferences.

And if you convert your RAW files to DNG, Adobe's nonproprietary Digital NeGative RAW file format, you have options to select for handling those files.

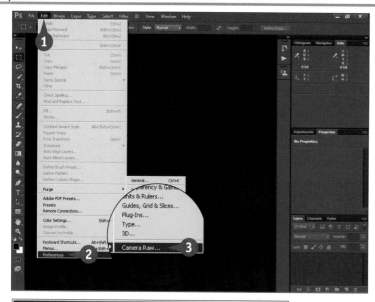

① With Photoshop open, click Edit (Photoshop).

② Click Preferences.

③ Click Camera Raw.

The Camera Raw Preferences dialog box appears.

④ Leave the default settings in the General section.

⑤ In the Default Image Settings section, select the last two options (☐ changes to ☑).

Note: *Leave the default options for the first two options.*

⑥ If you use DNG files, select both options in the DNG File Handling section (☐ changes to ☑).

⑦ Leave the default settings for JPEG and TIFF handling.

⑧ Click OK to save the Camera Raw preferences.

The interface in Camera Raw, like that in Photoshop, can seem confusing with its icons, panels, and sliders. However, unlike with Photoshop, you can achieve a remarkably acceptable set of adjustments to your image with one mouse or tablet pen click in the default opening screen of Camera Raw.

In many cases you may find this automatic correction of exposure, contrast, highlights, shadows, whites, and blacks in your image to be as good as anything you can achieve on your own. Camera Raw makes it easy to see your image before and after the automatic adjustments, and the histogram visually displays what you are seeing in the preview window. The automatic correction generally does an excellent job of preventing shadow areas and highlights from clipping. But it is always a good idea to turn on the clipping warnings just to check.

Even if you decide that you do not like everything about the automatic correction, it provides a starting point you can use to make further adjustments to your liking.

1 Double-click a RAW file in Bridge to open it in Camera Raw.

A Camera Raw opens with the White Balance settings as they were when you shot the photo and the adjustment sliders set to the center of their range.

2 Click the Shadow Clipping Warning triangle. Clipped shadows are displayed in blue.

Note: *There are no clipped shadows in this image.*

3 Click the Highlight Clipping Warning triangle.

Note: *Clipped highlights are displayed in red.*

4 Click Auto.

Camera Raw automatically adjusts the image.

5 Toggle Preview between the automatically adjusted image and the unadjusted original image.

6 Note the changes to the sliders in the adjusted version when you toggle Preview.

7 Click Done to save the image with the adjustments without opening it.

Our emotional response to an image is based on many factors, but the overall color balance of the image largely determines our initial reaction. Using Camera Raw you can adjust the overall white balance of an image, and even shift it to a more, or less, pleasing balance. Once you have the image to a neutral white balance, you can adjust the overall color balance to your taste.

White balance is so important to digital imaging that Camera Raw places the white balance adjustment at the top of its Basic panel and provides three paths to adjust overall color balance. Which path you choose depends on the image.

If the white balance is off because of the wrong choice set in your camera, there is one easy fix. If there is an object in the scene that you know is neutral, there is another technique. And if neither of these two is appropriate, there is a third way. Most often a combination of the white balance methods yields the most pleasing result.

Note: This image and others from the book are available for download from www.wiley.com/ go/photoshopcctop100. The images on the companion website are small, low-resolution images for you to practice the steps. You will get better results and learn more when you use your own photographs.

Adjust White Balance with the White Balance Menu

1 With a RAW file open in Camera Raw, find the White Balance drop-down menu.

Note: Only RAW images show the white balance settings from your camera. If you have never adjusted the white balance, the window reads "As Shot."

2 Note the setting in the Temperature box.

3 Note the setting in the Tint box.

4 Click the White Balance drop-down menu.

5 Click the white balance options to find the correct one for the image.

Note: Shade is selected for this task. The image was incorrectly captured as Daylight.

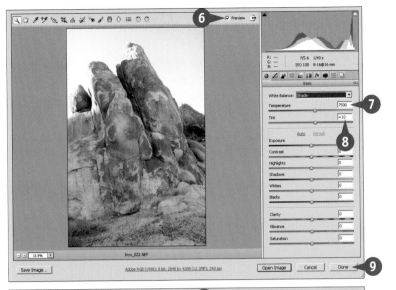

The white balance of the image changes.

6 Toggle Preview to see before and after views.

7 Note the new setting in the Temperature box.

8 Note the new setting in the Tint box.

9 Click Done.

Your new white balance is saved with the image.

Adjust White Balance with a Neutral Object

1 With an image open containing an object that you know is neutral, click the White Balance tool.

Note: A white balance card held in the lighting that falls on the subject is ideal.

2 Select Preview if it is not already selected (☐ changes to ☑).

3 Hover the eyedropper over the area that should be neutral.

4 Note the RGB values of the area that should be neutral. For the area to be neutral, all three numbers should be identical.

5 Click in the neutral area if the RGB numbers are not identical.

6 Note that the RGB values are identical.

A The White Balance drop-down menu box changes to Custom.

7 Note the new Temperature value.

8 Note the new Tint value.

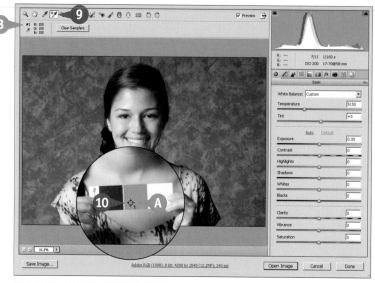

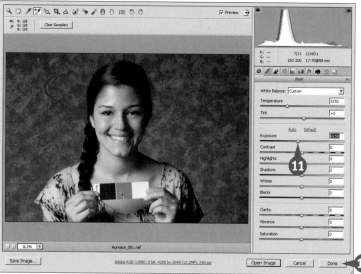

9 Select the Color Sampler tool if you have a white balance card in the scene.

10 Click in the gray area of the white balance card with the Color Sampler Tool.

Ⓐ A color sample icon appears with the number 1 to indicate it is your first color sample in the image.

Ⓑ The Color Sampler panel opens. The panel displays the RGB values under the color sample icon on the gray card.

Note: The gray patch of a white balance card is the middle tone of gray. The RGB values should read 127,127,127.

11 Click and drag the Exposure slider while you watch the RGB values change in the Color Sampler panel. Stop dragging and release the mouse when the values are as close to 127,127,127 as you can make them.

12 Click Done.

You have corrected the white balance and adjusted the gray value to the correct level.

Adjust White Balance with Temperature and Tint

1 With a RAW file that has no large neutral area open, select Preview if it is not already selected (☐ changes to ☑).

2 Click the White Balance drop-down menu.

3 Click each of the white balance options, selecting the white balance option that is close to the way you visualize the final image.

Note: When there is no flesh tone or large area that should be neutral, you have a wide range of options for white balance. For this task, Cloudy is selected to add warmth to the stuffed animals and enhance the feeling of dusk.

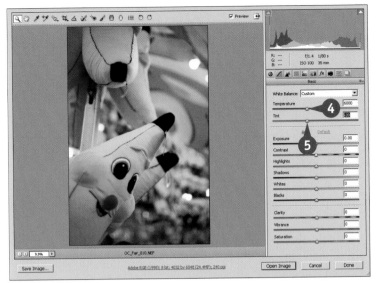

④ Click and drag the Temperature slider to the left to add blue to the image. This gives it a cooler feeling.

⑤ Click and drag the Tint slider to the left to add green to the image.

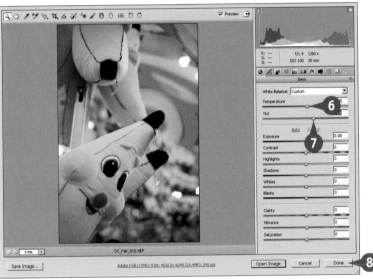

⑥ Click and drag the Temperature slider to the right to remove blue from the image. This gives it a warmer feeling.

⑦ Click and drag the Tint slider to the right to remove green from the image.

Note: Continue adjusting the Temperature and Tint sliders until you are happy with the look of the image.

⑧ Click Done.

You have used the white balance adjustments to add a mood to your image.

TIPS

Did You Know?
You can select the White Balance tool in Camera Raw by pressing I. To quickly reset your white balance to As Shot, double-click the White Balance tool (✐).

Try This!
Adjust the Temperature and Tint sliders with the scrubby slider. Hover your mouse anywhere over the Temperature or Tint sliders until the cursor changes to a hand with a double-headed arrow. Press and hold the right mouse button and drag left and right to adjust the slider.

Did You Know?
You can enlarge the Camera Raw workspace to full screen by clicking the Toggle full screen mode icon (⊡). Click it again to reduce it to its original size. The keyboard shortcut to toggle the full screen mode is F.

#21

The difference between the brightest and darkest areas in a scene is called the *dynamic range* of the scene. Your digital camera does its best to capture the dynamic range of the scene, but the dynamic range may still be greater than your monitor or a print can display. This results in blown-out highlights or shadow areas without information. You can recover the highlight and shadow information using Camera Raw.

You can see the blown-out highlights in Camera Raw by clicking the Highlight Clipping Warning triangle in the

histogram. Blown-out or clipped highlights display in red. When you click the Shadow Clipping Warning triangle, lost shadow information displays in blue.

You can adjust the dynamic range of your image using the sliders in Camera Raw. If necessary, use the Exposure slider to adjust the midtones and the Contrast slider to adjust overall scene contrast. Then use the sliders below the Contrast slider to first recover clipped highlights. Then you can recover and open up shadow areas.

Recover Highlight Information

1. With an image open in Camera Raw, click and drag the Exposure slider to set the midtone values.

   Note: RAW file format images contain more information in the highlights and shadows than TIFF and JPEG images. Highlight and shadow recovery works best with RAW files, but you can use it with TIFFs and JPEGs, also.

2. Click and drag the Contrast slider to adjust overall image contrast.

3. Click the Highlight Clipping Warning triangle to view the clipped highlights.

   Clipped highlights display in red.

4. Click and drag the Highlights slider to the left to recover clipped highlights.

5. Stop dragging when the Highlight Clipping Warning triangle turns black.

A. Watch the histogram as you drag. The right side of the histogram moves to the left as you drag.

6 Click and drag the Whites slider to the left to recover additional information in the white and upper midtones.

7 Stop dragging when you feel there is enough detail in the whites.

B Watch the histogram as you drag. The farthest right does not move. The section of the curve between the farthest right and the middle shifts to the left.

8 Click and drag the Highlights slider to the right.

9 Stop dragging when the Highlight Warning triangle is no longer black.

10 Drag the Highlight slider to the left until the Highlight Warning triangle is black again. You have recovered clipped highlights and recovered additional image information in the upper midrange.

You can recover shadow information similarly to how you recover highlight information. Unless there are large areas of gross underexposure, it can be difficult to see clipped shadows. When this is the case, watching the histogram and the Shadow Recovery triangle is very important. It is often helpful to zoom the image preview to 100% and pan through it by pressing and holding the spacebar, and clicking and dragging the cursor in the image to find areas highlighted in blue.

When the highlighted area does not contain image information you want to recover, or it is very small, you can decide to leave it clipped. A few areas of rich deep black add depth and dimension to an image.

Using the Shadow slider to open up shadow information is important, but entirely subjective. As with using the Whites slider for upper midtones, the amount of correction you make with the Shadows slider to the lower midtones depends on your vision for the image.

Recover Shadow Information

1 Repeat steps 1 and 2 from the previous subsection, "Recover Highlight Information," with a new image, or continue with the same image you used to recover highlights.

2 Click the Shadow Clipping Warning triangle to view the clipped shadows.

Note: If the Shadow clipping triangle is not black, there are clipped highlights although they may not be obvious.

3 Click and drag the Blacks slider to the left. This makes the areas with clipped shadows appear clearly.

A The areas with clipped shadows are highlighted in blue.

4 Click and drag the Blacks slider to the right to recover clipped shadows.

5 Stop dragging when the bright blue areas disappear.

B Watch the histogram as you drag. The left side of the histogram moves to the right as you drag.

Note: In this image, some blacks are still clipped. These areas are under rocks and should be black.

6 Click and drag the Shadows slider to the right to recover additional information in the shadows and lower midtones.

7 Stop dragging when you feel there is enough detail in the lower midtones.

C Watch the histogram as you drag. The farthest left does not move. The section of the curve between the farthest left and the middle shifts to the right.

8 Click the zoom level menu.

9 Click 100%.

The image preview zooms to 100%.

10 Click the Hand tool.

D Click and drag in the preview window to see if the shadow areas contain the information you envision.

11 Click Done to save the image with the Camera Raw adjustments.

#22

TIPS

Important!

When you recover shadow information and zoom to 100%, you may see noise, which appears stronger in the shadows than in the highlights. You can decrease the amount of noise in the shadows. Follow the steps in task #29.

Did You Know?

You can use keyboard shortcuts to toggle the highlight and shadow clipping highlights on and off. The keyboard shortcut to show highlight clipping is O. To show shadow clipping, press U. These are easy to remember if you associate O with overexposure and U with underexposure.

Did You Know?

The Highlight and Clipping Shadow Warning triangles change color to indicate what colors are being clipped. A white triangle means all colors are clipped. A black triangle means no colors are clipped. A red, yellow, blue, or other color triangle means those colors are clipped.

The latest camera lens designs attempt to defy the laws of optics and reduce lens faults, which are called *aberrations*, to the absolute minimum. Yet some still remain in even the most expensive lenses. You can remove the remaining aberrations from your images by using Camera Raw.

Each version of Camera Raw ships with an enormous database of cameras and lenses. The database is updated a number of times during the version cycle of each Camera Raw release. You can access and use the prebuilt database from the Profile and Color subpanels of the Lens Corrections panel to automatically correct lens distortion, vignetting, and chromatic aberration if you own one of the camera and lens combinations included.

The Profiles and Color subpanels also allow some manual control over corrections. But you can exercise greater control over lens distortion and many aspects of camera perspective using the Manual subpanel. The controls in the Lens Distortion panel work with each other. You can make automatic corrections first and then additional changes with manual corrections. You can even use Lens Corrections creatively to add distortions, perspective changes, and vignetting.

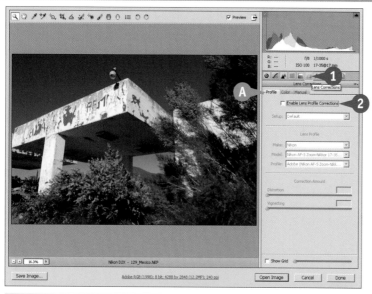

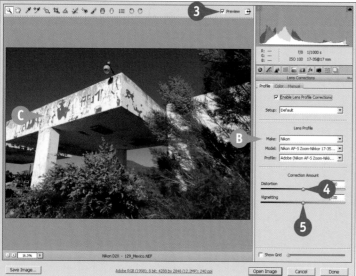

1 With an image open and adjusted in the Basic panel of Camera Raw, click the Lens Correction button.

A The Lens Corrections panel opens with the Profile subpanel open.

2 Select the Enable Lens Profile Corrections check box (☐ changes to ☑).

B The lens make, model, and profile appear in the drop-down boxes of the Lens Profile area of the Profile subpanel.

Note: If the drop-down boxes remain blank or grayed out, your lens does not have a prebuilt lens profile. Proceed to step 6.

C The preview image changes to show the adjusted image with lens distortion removed.

3 Toggle the Preview check box to view before and after views (☐ toggles to ☑ and back).

4 Click and drag the Distortion slider to the left to remove some of the prebuilt distortion correction or to the right to increase the distortion correction.

5 Click and drag the Vignetting slider to the left to add vignetting to the prebuilt profile or to the right to remove any remaining vignetting.

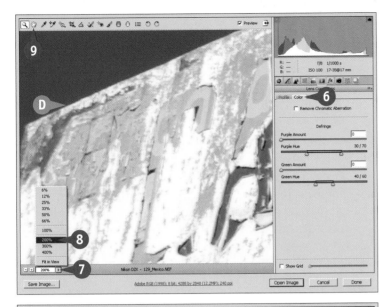

6 Click the Color button.

The Color subpanel opens.

7 Click the zoom level menu.

8 Click 200% or more.

9 Click the Hand tool.

D Click and drag in the preview window to a corner or edge of the image. Look for purple and green fringing at edges with high contrast.

10 Select the Remove Chromatic Aberration check box (☐ changes to ☑).

E The color fringing is removed.

11 Click and drag the Purple Amount slider to remove any last trace of purple fringing.

12 Click and drag the Green Amount slider to remove any last trace of green fringing.

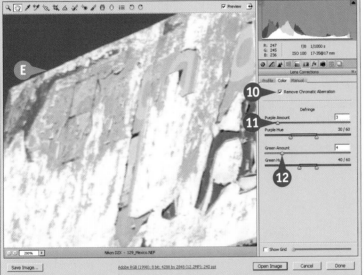

13 Click the zoom level menu.

14 Click Fit in View.

Automatic lens corrections provide a quick and easy way to remove lens aberrations. But you can also correct lens distortion and vignetting manually. This is necessary if your lens is not listed in the lens profile database. Your lens may be an older model, a third-party lens, or a newer lens that has yet to be profiled. But you can also use the manual corrections to fine-tune your image after applying the automatic corrections.

You can use the manual controls to transform your image, both automatically and manually. You can correct verticals partially or completely for a building you photographed

with a wide-angle lens pointed upward. You can do the same for horizontal perspective to make horizontal lines appear more horizontal.

With manual lens corrections, you can also rotate, scale, and change the aspect ratio of the image vertically and horizontally. A grid overlay is available to help with your alignments. While these adjustments are designed to correct lens aberrations and perspective issues, you can also use manual corrections to creatively alter your images by adding a vignette.

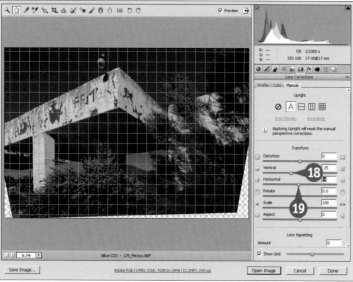

⓯ Click the Manual button.

The Manual panel opens.

⓰ Select Show Grid (☐ changes to ☑). A grid opens on the image.

⓱ Click the Applied Balanced Perspective icon. The image perspective corrects so that vertical lines in the center of the image are vertical and a horizontal correction is applied to balance this.

Ⓐ An automatic scale correction is applied to remove any areas without image information.

⓲ Click and drag the Vertical slider in the Transform subpanel to the left to align a vertical line of the image with a vertical line of the grid. Drag to the right to create a more dramatic perspective.

⓳ Click and drag the Horizontal slider in the Transform subpanel. Drag to the left to make the horizontals on the left of the image more horizontal. Drag to the right to do the same to the lines on the right.

Note: The checkerboard pattern indicates areas in the original image area where there no longer is image information.

#23

20 Click the Scale slider in the Transform subpanel. Drag to the right until you cannot see the checkerboard pattern around the image.

21 Deselect the Show Grid check box (☑ changes to ☐).

The grid overlay disappears.

22 Click and drag the Amount slider in the Lens Vignetting subpanel to the left to add a creative vignette to draw the viewer's eye to the center of the image.

23 Click and drag the Midpoint slider in the Lens Vignetting subpanel to the left to increase the area the vignetting covers, or to the right to decrease it.

24 Click Done to save your lens correction adjustments and vignette.

TIPS

Did You Know?
You can create your own custom lens correction using an application Adobe created. Download the application from http://labs.adobe.com/technologies/lensprofile_creator. Lens profiles created by users are also available online.

Did You Know?
You can reset all of the adjustments you make in the Lens Corrections panels by pressing and holding Alt (Option). The Cancel button changes to a Reset button. Click the Reset button.

Try This!
You can automatically remove chromatic aberrations from every image you open in Camera Raw. Open an image and open the Color panel. Select Remove Chromatic Aberration (☐ changes to ☑). Click the Lens Corrections panel menu button (≡▲) and select Save New Camera Raw Defaults. Close the image.

You can use the Spot Removal tool in Camera Raw to remove blemishes, moles, freckles, or other small skin imperfections nondestructively. Should you or your subject decide later that the freckles should really be there, you can return to Camera Raw and delete or adjust your retouching. Using Camera Raw rather than Photoshop saves you time, the need for layers, and the associated increase in file size.

The Spot Removal tool in Camera Raw was originally designed to remove sensor dust from captures. The latest refinements to the tool make it ideal for removing skin blemishes.

The Spot Removal tool has two options, Clone and Heal. Using the Clone option, you replace the blemish with an exact duplicate of another area. In most cases, this results in an improvement, but not an exact match. The better choice is the Heal option. Heal adjusts the tonality and color of the area that will heal the blemish to the area around the blemish. In most cases the match is perfect. If not, you can adjust the spot that is cloned over the blemish until the match is perfect.

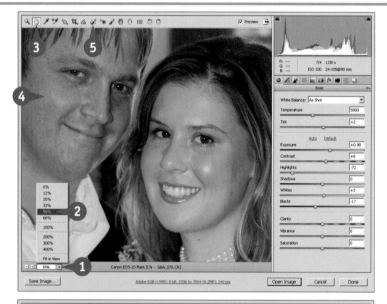

1. With a portrait image open in Camera Raw, click the zoom level menu.

2. Click a zoom level so that the portrait is large in the preview window.

3. Click the Hand tool.

4. Click and drag in the image to center the portrait.

5. Click the Spot Removal tool.

The Spot Removal panel appears.

6. Click the Type drop-down menu and click Heal.

7. Select Show Overlay (☐ changes to ☑).

8. Select Visualize Spots (☐ changes to ☑).

The preview window changes to a black-and-white overlay.

9. Click and drag the Visualize Spots slider to see where blemishes and other problems are.

10. Deselect Visualize Spots (☑ changes to ☐).

Note: You can remove spots in the Visualize Spots preview if you wish.

The preview image returns to color.

⑪ Click and drag the Size slider to 1.

⑫ Click and drag the Opacity slider to 100.

⑬ Position the cursor over a blemish and then press and hold Ctrl (⌘).

⑭ Click and drag a circle until it is just larger than the blemish and release the mouse button and Ctrl (⌘).

Note: You can draw an irregular outline for the Heal tool if you do not press and hold Ctrl (⌘).

A red circle appears where the blemish was. A green circle appears to indicate the area Camera Raw chose to heal over the blemish.

Note: Adjust the Opacity slider if you do not want to remove the entire blemish. The Opacity slider is specific to the spot you are working on.

⑮ Continue until you have removed all of the blemishes.

Ⓐ You can click and drag inside the green circle to reposition it if needed.

Ⓑ You can position the cursor over the outline of one of the circles, and click and drag to change the size of the circle.

⑯ Click Done to save your retouching.

#24

DIFFICULTY LEVEL

● ● ● ◡

Did You Know?

You can use keyboard shortcuts in Camera Raw to speed your retouching. Press B to open the Spot Removal panel. Press V to hide and show the overlays. Press P to see before and after previews.

Remove It!

You can remove the retouching as easily as adding it. Nothing is worse than a portrait that looks overly retouched. If you or your subject wants to add back in any of the freckles or moles, reopen the image in Camera Raw. Toggle P to preview the image before and after retouching. Click the spot you want to bring back. Click and drag the Opacity slider to bring it partially back. Press Backspace (Delete) to remove the retouching entirely on the selected spot.

There are a number of ways you can adjust image contrast in Camera Raw. The Basic panel provides a slider that you can click and drag to the right to increase contrast, or to the left to decrease it. But if you watch the histogram as you drag the slider, you see that what you are doing is simply dragging the left and the right sides of the curve away from or toward the center. This increases contrast, but only in the grossest possible way.

The better tool to use is the Tone Curve. But the Tone Curve can be daunting to use with its two different curves,

Point and Parametric, and a histogram shape as well as a straight line in each of the curves.

Until you become familiar with these curves, there is another tool that makes working with contrast easier and more visual. It is the Targeted Adjustment tool. And you can use the Targeted Adjustment tool with other tools to target the adjustments to specific colors or values without creating masks.

1 With an image open in Camera Raw, make needed adjustments in the Basic panel to any sliders.

2 Leave the Contrast slider unadjusted.

3 Click the Tone Curve button.

The Tone Curve panel opens.

4 Click the Targeted Adjustment tool.

5 Click the Parametric tab.

The parametric curve subpanel opens.

Note: The Targeted Adjustment tool works with both the Point and Parametric curves. The adjustments are more apparent on the sliders in the Parametric subpanel.

6 Click an area in the image that you want lighter and drag slowly upward. Release the mouse when the area is light enough.

The area is lighter and the sliders move to new positions.

⑦ Click an area in the image you want darker and drag slowly downward. Release the mouse when the area is dark enough.

The area is darker and image contrast is increased.

⑧ Repeat steps 6 and 7 in other areas of the image.

⑨ Click the Highlight Clipping Warning.

⑩ Click and drag the Highlights slider to remove any highlight clipping.

⑪ Depending on your image, click Done or OK to save your adjustments.

Note: This image is originally a JPEG, so the choice is OK to close it.

Important!
You can easily push highlights and shadows into clipping using the Targeted Adjustment tool, particularly with a JPEG photo. Some shadow clipping may be acceptable, but always check for highlight clipping.

Did You Know?
You are adjusting more tones than the tone directly under the Targeted Adjustment tool when you click and drag it in the image. The Targeted Adjustment tool adjusts the curve around the targeted tone, so other tones also change. To target a tone more exactly, use the Point curve without the Targeted Adjustment tool.

Did You Know?
The keyboard shortcut for the Targeted Adjustment tool is T. Press P to see before and after views of the adjustments you make with the Targeted Adjustment tool.

You can re-create the look of traditional on-lens graduated filters in Camera Raw. These traditional filters have an area of neutral density or color on one end that graduate down until they are completely transparent. Landscape photographers use these filters on their lenses to more closely match the exposure in the sky to the exposure of the foreground.

Using the Graduated Filter in Camera Raw, you can re-create the on-lens graduated filter effect and apply other adjustments to the same area at the same time.

Along with the density and color, you can change the white balance, contrast, and tonal relationships, apply or remove clarity, sharpness, and noise reduction, reduce moiré, and defringe chromatic aberrations.

And you can create multiple graduated filter adjustments in an image. You can stack them on each other and the effects add or subtract from one other. The Graduated Filter is far more of a graduated filter tool than simply a graduated filter.

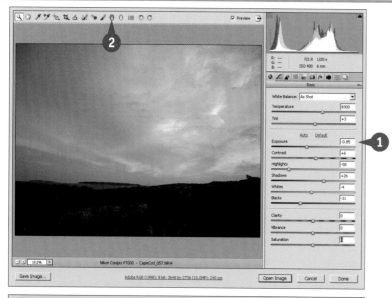

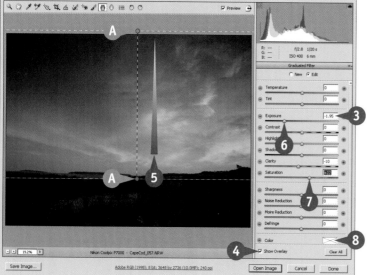

① With an image containing a large area of sky open in Camera Raw, make needed adjustments in the Basic panel to any sliders.

② Click the Graduated Filter button.

The Graduated Filter panel appears in the right panel.

③ Type –1 in the Exposure slider text entry box.

Note: You must have an adjustment preloaded to a nonzero amount to use the Graduated Filter.

④ Select Show Overlay (☐ changes to ☑).

⑤ Shift+click and drag from the top of the image to just below the bottom of the sky and then release the mouse.

Ⓐ The Graduated Filter overlay appears with a green pin showing the origin of the filter and a red pin showing the end.

⑥ Click and drag the Exposure slider to adjust the sky exposure.

⑦ Click and drag other sliders as needed to correct the sky.

⑧ Click the Color box.

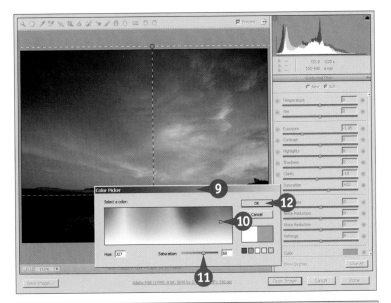

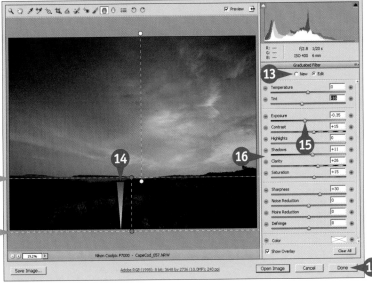

The Color Picker appears.

9 Click the Color Picker panel and drag it away from the sky.

10 Click a color to add to the Graduated Filter.

11 Click and drag the Saturation slider to adjust the color saturation.

12 Click OK.

13 Select New (○ changes to ●).

14 Shift+click and drag from the bottom of the image to just above the bottom of the sky and then release the mouse.

Ⓑ The Graduated Filter overlay appears over the foreground.

15 Click and drag the Exposure slider to adjust the foreground exposure.

16 Click and drag other sliders as needed.

17 Click Done.

TIPS

Try This!

After you make multiple adjustments with the Graduated Filter, you can go back and edit an adjustment. Make sure that Show Overlay is selected (☐ changes to ☑). Click the Graduated Filter pin you want to edit and make your changes.

Did You Know?

You can reset all of the Graduated Filter adjustments to zero and preload the adjustment you want to make with a small change by clicking the plus or minus icons on opposite ends of the adjustment slider for the adjustment you want to make.

Try This!

You can more easily see the gradient as you create it if you click and drag the Exposure slider all the way to the left. When your gradient is set, adjust the Exposure slider to the right.

Brush on LOCAL ADJUSTMENTS

While local adjustments are traditionally one of the greatest strengths of Photoshop, you can apply many local adjustments in Camera Raw, and in many ways it is quicker and easier to do so.

You can brush on the same adjustments that are available with the Graduated Filter. Exposure correction leads the list. Brushing on an exposure adjustment is the equivalent of local dodge and burn controls, but in Camera Raw you can change the amount of adjustment at any time. Along with exposure, you can change the white balance,

contrast, and tonal relationships; apply or remove clarity, sharpness, and noise reduction; reduce moiré, and defringe chromatic aberrations.

There is only one brush available, but you can adjust it many ways, and change it into an eraser if you need one. Best of all, there is an automatic masking option that looks for edges. Used carefully, Auto Mask allows you to paint in adjustments without creating a selection, as you must in Photoshop.

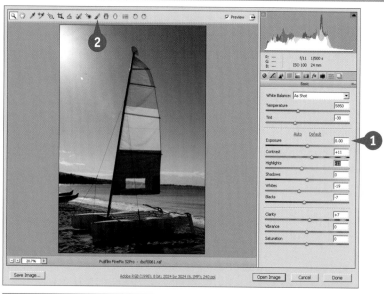

1 With an image open in Camera Raw, make needed adjustments in the Basic panel to any sliders.

2 Click the Adjustment Brush tool.

The Adjustment Brush panel appears below the histogram.

3 Click the minus icon next to the Exposure slider to set all of the sliders to zero other than the Exposure slider.

Note: You must have an adjustment preloaded to a nonzero amount to use the Adjustment Brush.

4 Click and drag the Exposure slider all the way to the left.

5 Scroll to the bottom of the Adjustment Brush panel.

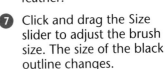

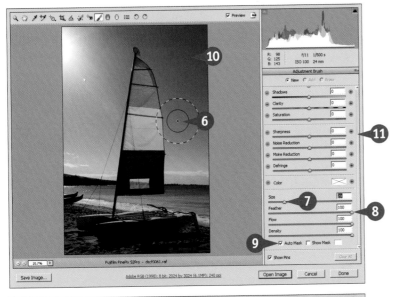

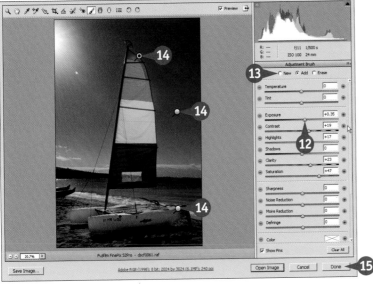

#27

DIFFICULTY LEVEL

⬤ ⬤ ○ ○

6 Move your cursor over the image.

The cursor changes to a brush. The black outline is the brush size. The dotted outline is the edge of the feather.

7 Click and drag the Size slider to adjust the brush size. The size of the black outline changes.

8 Click and drag the Feather slider to adjust the brush feather. The size of the dotted outline changes.

9 Select Auto Mask (☐ changes to ☑).

Note: When you paint near an edge, keep the edge between the black outline and the dotted outline. The correction will automatically stop at the edge.

10 Paint in the image.

11 Scroll to the top of the Adjustment Brush panel when you finish brushing on the adjustment.

12 Click and drag the adjustment sliders to create the adjustment you want.

13 Select New (○ changes to ◉).

14 Repeat steps 3 to 12 to adjust a new area as many times as needed to adjust the image locally.

Each new local adjustment has its own pin.

15 Click Done.

TIPS

Delete It!

You can delete any part of the local adjustment if it extends into an area where you do not want it. Click the Erase tool (0), adjust the brush size, and feather and paint. The settings for the brush to paint on local adjustments are independent of the settings for the erase brush. Be careful when you switch back and forth to check the settings and to set the size and feather for the operation you want to perform.

Try This!

You can adjust the size and feather of the brush with keyboard shortcuts. Press the left bracket key to decrease the size of the brush. Press the right bracket key to increase the size. To decrease the amount of feather, press Shift while you press the left bracket key. To increase the amount of feather, press Shift while you press the right bracket key.

You can apply adjustments to multiple images in Camera Raw. Often you capture a number of images under identical conditions during a photos session that need identical adjustments. To increase your productivity, rather than opening and adjusting the images individually, you can open multiple images in Camera Raw and adjust them as a group. Only a few adjustments cannot be applied this way.

There are actually two ways of applying adjustments to multiple photos. Neither is right nor wrong, and you should investigate both. The first method is to adjust one

image, select the rest of the images, click the Synchronize button, and then select the adjustments you made and paste those adjustments into the others. Unfortunately, Camera Raw is unable to remember what settings you adjusted and what settings you did not. That is left up to you.

With the method in this task, you select all of the images first. As you apply changes to one image, the same settings are automatically applied to the others. No additional clicks, nor the need to memorize what you changed and what you did not.

1 Select multiple images in Bridge.

2 Click File.

3 Click Open in Camera Raw.

Camera Raw opens.

The images are displayed in a filmstrip in the left panel.

The first image you selected in Bridge is highlighted and has a blue border.

4 Click Select All.

All images in the filmstrip are highlighted.

5 Adjust the image in the preview window using the sliders in the Basic panel.

6 Apply adjustments in other panels. The thumbnails in the filmstrip update instantly as you apply the adjustments.

7 Click each of the thumbnails to see if the adjustments are what you expect.

8 Apply further adjustments to any individual image that needs it.

9 Click Select All.

10 Click Done.

TIPS

Did You Know?

You cannot apply the Graduated Filter, the Radial Filter, or Red Eye Removal to multiple images. These must be applied in step 8.

Important!

If you select a single image and attempt to reset its adjustments by pressing Alt (Option) and clicking Reset, you will reset all of the adjustments of all of the images, including those that are not selected. A dialog box appears to remind you of this.

Did You Know?

You can page through the images in the filmstrip at any time by pressing the left or right arrow keys. This works regardless of whether they are selected.

There is sensor noise in every digital capture, but until you shoot at higher ISO settings and look into the shadows, that noise is not obvious. You can eliminate sensor noise in Camera Raw using the Detail panel.

It is important to perform image adjustments in the Basic and Tone Curve panels before you work in the Detail panel. The changes you make in the other panels affect the amount of adjustment you make in the Detail panel. Increasing contrast, for example, makes noise more apparent, and more objectionable.

You can reduce both *luminance noise* and *color noise* in Camera Raw. Luminance noise looks like an overlay of fine grain in the image. Color noise looks like tiny colored dots. The noise reduction subpanel provides sliders to minimize both, and a keyboard trick to view the effects. The process of eliminating noise tends to soften an image by eliminating details. The Detail panel includes a sharpening subpanel, also. Use sharpening to recover some of the lost sharpness.

1 With a RAW image file open in Camera Raw, make the needed adjustments in the Basic and Tone Curve panels.

2 Click the zoom level menu.

3 Click 100%.

   Note: *If you cannot see noise at 100%, select a higher zoom level.*

The photo appears at 100% zoom level.

4 Press the spacebar and click and drag in the image to an area where noise is obvious.

5 Click the Detail button.

   The Detail panel appears.

6 Click and drag the Luminance slider until you eliminate the black dots of the luminance noise.

   Note: *Leave some noise in the lower midtones if you must drag the Luminance slider so far to the right that the image becomes very soft.*

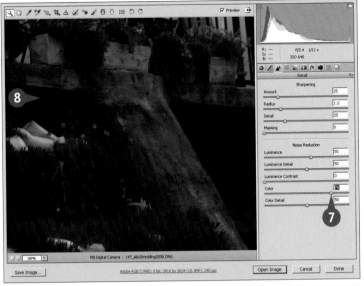

7 Click and drag the Color slider until you eliminate the random colored dots.

8 Press the spacebar and click and drag through the image to see that noise is decreased or eliminated.

9 Press Alt (Option) and click and drag the Masking slider until only the edges of objects are white.

Note: The Masking slider overlays a black-and-white mask on the image as you drag it to the right. White areas are sharpened. Black areas are protected from sharpening.

10 Click and drag the Amount slider in the Sharpening subpanel to recover sharpness lost with noise reduction.

Note: Use only a small amount of RAW file presharpening if you intend to work on the image in Photoshop. Use more sharpening if you intend to output a final image from Camera Raw.

11 Click Done to save your adjustments and close the image.

Note: You can click Save Image if you intend to save the image for output without further work in Photoshop.

TIPS

More Options!

Press and hold Alt (Option) as you drag any of the Luminance sliders in the Sharpening subpanel. A gray mask appears over the image to help you visualize the areas that you are adjusting. Press and hold Alt (Option) as you drag the Amount, Radius, and Detail sliders in the Sharpening subpanel to visualize their adjustments.

Did You Know?

If you use this camera often at this ISO setting, you can save the noise reduction and sharpening settings and use them in the future. Click the Detail panel menu button and select Save Settings. Select Sharpening ⇨ Luminance Noise Reduction ⇨ Color Noise Reduction. Click Save. Name the settings and click Save. To use them in the future, click the Detail panel menu button and select Load Settings.

When you complete your overall and local adjustments in Camera Raw, you can open your image directly into Photoshop to work on it at the pixel level. In Camera Raw you set the color space, color depth, image size and resolution, and sharpening for the image to open with in the Workflow Options dialog box.

To maximize your image quality as you edit in Photoshop, but still keep file size reasonable, you can set the options as shown in this task. However, your settings may differ if your workflow in Photoshop customarily ends by saving the file as a JPEG and uploading it to a photo lab for

printing, for example, or to a designer for a website. You can always change the export options for a specific project.

The Workflow Options dialog box also has an option to open the image as a *Smart Object*. You can reopen images saved as Smart Objects in Camera Raw with all of the adjustments available for further nondestructive adjusting. Saving an image as a Smart Object increases its file size. Saving every image as a Smart Object is not recommended for this reason.

1 With a RAW image open and adjusted in Camera Raw, click the blue underlined output parameters description below the preview.

Note: *This is the link to the Workflow Options dialog box.*

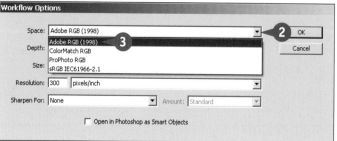

The Workflow Options dialog box appears.

2 Click the Space drop-down menu.

3 Select Adobe RGB (1998).

Note: *If you selected a different color space in task #2, select that color space.*

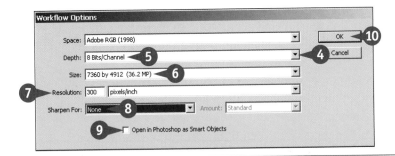

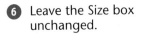

4 Click the Depth drop-down menu.

5 Select 8 Bits/Channel.

Note: *Unless you need to do some major Curves adjustment in Photoshop, this setting allows you to use all of the tools in Photoshop.*

6 Leave the Size box unchanged.

Note: *The default pixel dimensions displayed are the native dimensions of the image.*

7 Type 300 in the Resolution text entry box if your work generally is output to print. Otherwise leave 240.

8 Leave Sharpen For set to None.

9 Leave Open in Photoshop as Smart Objects unchecked.

10 Click OK.

A The Workflow Options dialog box closes and the new default settings appear in blue below the preview.

11 Click Open Image.

The file opens in Photoshop.

TIPS

Did You Know?
You can open any Camera Raw file as a Smart Object without selecting the Open in Photoshop as Smart Objects check box in the Workflow Options dialog box. Simply press and hold Shift when you click Open Image. The image opens as a Smart Object in Photoshop.

Did You Know?
The changes you made in the Workflow Options dialog box are now the default output settings for all images in Camera Raw.

More Options!
You can use different settings in the Workflow Options dialog box to maximize image quality when working in Photoshop. Set Space to ProPhoto RGB and Depth to 16 Bits/Channel. Doing either or both of these doubles the file size.

Fix Common Problems

Using Camera Raw, you can quickly make many of the global adjustments you may be accustomed to making in Photoshop. But Camera Raw can only take you so far with the precise local adjustments needed to fix many common problems. For these problems you need pixel-level corrections. You can make these pixel-level corrections in Photoshop to fix common problems.

Photos of people are one source of common problems. A portrait captures all of the skin blemishes that we rarely seem to see when looking at a person. You can minimize or remove these in Photoshop using a variety of tools. The object is to dial back reality by removing temporary blemishes while leaving permanent facial features. You can also remove some of the weight that photography

adds to a portrait, but again, a light touch is better than overdoing it. Working on new empty layers where you can dial back the opacity is essential. And with a little effort, you can remove reflections in the subject's glasses.

You can also save a badly backlit photo and salvage a group shot so that everyone looks good. You can even reposition objects in a scene or eliminate unwanted objects for a better composition. While Camera Raw gives you some simple ways to improve the sky in an image, you have many more options and tighter control in Photoshop. And if you did not hold the camera quite steady during the exposure, the new Shake Reduction filter can sharpen the image.

REMOVE SPOTS AND SKIN BLEMISHES *two ways*

Many skin defects come and go over time. Yet a photograph of someone records in sharp detail all of the spots and blemishes present at a certain instant in time, both permanent and passing ones. You can dial back reality to remove these impermanent spots and blemishes, and minimize the permanent ones in Photoshop.

As with many techniques in Photoshop, you can use a variety of tools to do this. The best tool depends on the area you are retouching and the effect you aim to achieve.

In many cases, the Spot Healing Brush tool in Content-Aware mode gives the best results for small blemishes. The Spot Healing Brush automatically samples the area around the area to be healed and blends color and luminosity for a perfect match.

At other times, the Healing Brush tool or the Patch tool is a better choice. You can also use the Clone tool, which copies and pastes one area to another, but it is seldom the best choice for this task.

Remove Blemishes with the Spot Healing Brush Tool

1 With the image open in Photoshop, click the Zoom tool.

2 Select Resize Window to Fit (☐ changes to ☑).

3 Click and drag over the area to retouch.

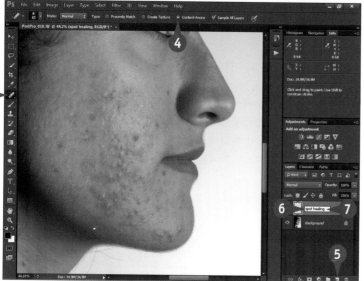

The image zooms to fill the screen.

3 Click the Spot Healing Brush tool.

4 Select Content-Aware (◉ changes to ◉).

5 Click the New Layer button.

6 Double-click the default layer name.

7 Type **spot healing** in the text box.

8 Press Enter (Return).

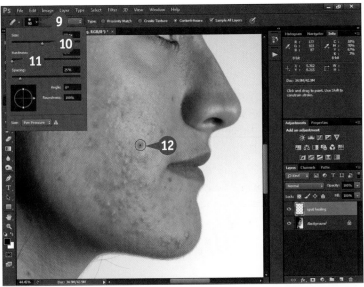

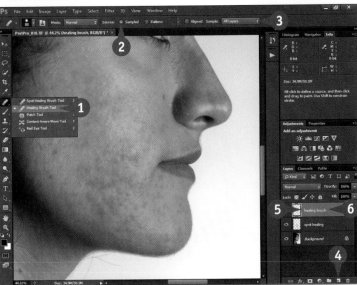

9 Click the Brush Preset drop-down menu.

10 Click and drag the Size slider to create a brush slightly larger than the spot.

11 Click and drag the Hardness slider to 0%.

12 Click each of the spots that you want to remove.

31

DIFFICULTY LEVEL

Photoshop removes the spots and skin blemishes and blends the area into the surrounding skin.

Remove Blemishes with the Healing Brush Tool

Note: In some areas, the Spot Healing Brush does not completely hide the blemish.

1 Click the Healing Brush tool.

2 Select Sampled (⬤ changes to ⬤).

3 Click All Layers from the Sample drop-down menu.

4 Click the New Layer button.

5 Double-click the default layer name.

6 Type **healing brush** in the text entry box.

7 Press Enter (Return).

TIPS

Did You Know?

You can change the size of the Spot Healing Brush with keyboard shortcuts. With the brush selected and in the preview window, press the left bracket key to make the brush smaller. To make it larger, press the right bracket key.

More Options!

Press Tab to close the Toolbox and the right panels. You can concentrate on the retouching more easily. Press Tab to restore the Toolbox and right panels.

Remove It!

You can get carried away with the Spot Healing Brush and remove a mole by mistake. To restore anything you removed, press E to select the Eraser tool and brush back the area you removed. Click the Spot Healing Brush tool to return to its use.

With the Spot Healing Brush, you can click a spot, but Photoshop controls the area that is sampled to fill the spot. This is actually less control than you have with the Spot Removal tool in Camera Raw.

You can control the area where the healing sample is coming from with the Healing Brush. You set the size and feather of the sampled area as well as the area you want to heal when you set the brush size. Then you select a sample area and heal the area over the skin problem. The Healing Brush has the advantage of displaying the sampled area within the tool to help you decide if you chose a good sample. You can use the Healing Brush on separate layers, one to heal in the highlights, and one to heal in the shadow. You can adjust the opacity of each layer for the best match.

The Healing Brush is also an excellent tool to use to remove tattoos. You can work on small areas at a time until you completely remove the tattoo.

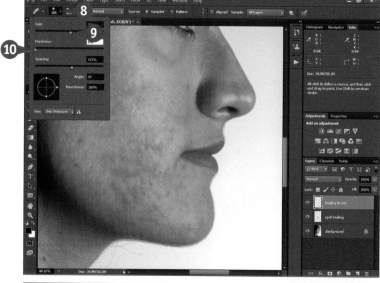

8 Click the Brush Preset drop-down menu.

9 Click and drag the Size slider to create a brush slightly larger than the area you want to heal.

10 Click and drag the Hardness slider to 0%.

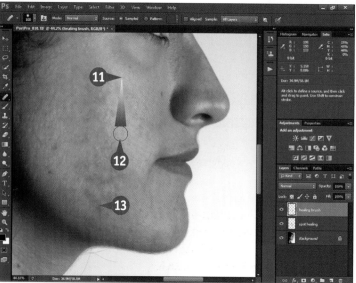

11 Press Alt (Option) and select an area in the upper midtones to clone into a problem area in the upper midtones.

12 Drag the selection over the problem area and release the mouse.

Photoshop uses information from your selection to heal the problem area.

13 Continue Alt+clicking (Option+clicking) to heal highlights and upper midtones.

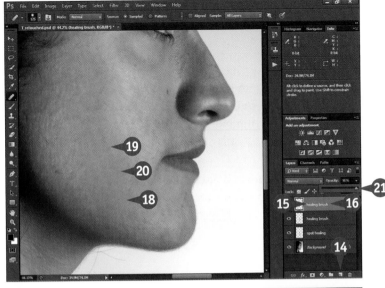

14 Click the New Layer button.

15 Double-click the default layer name.

16 Type **healing brush** in the text entry box.

17 Press Enter (Return).

18 Press Alt (Option) and select an area in the lower midtones to clone into a problem area in the lower midtones.

19 Drag the selection over the problem area and release the mouse.

20 Continue Alt+clicking (Option+clicking) to heal shadows and lower midtones.

21 Adjust the opacity of the layer to improve the blending.

22 Deselect the layer visibility eye icons to see before and after views of your retouching.

23 Click File.

24 Click Save As.

25 Type a name in the File Name text entry box.

26 Select Photoshop (*.PSD, *.PDD) from the Save as type drop-down menu.

Note: Always save layered files as Photoshop (PSD, PDD) files. Use the TIFF file extension for single-layer TIFF files.

27 Click Save.

#31

TIPS

Did You Know?

If you are using a tablet, you can adjust the size of the brush by controlling the pressure you exert with your tablet pen. More pressure gives a larger brush. In the Brush Preset drop-down menu, select Pen Pressure from the Size drop-down menu. If you are using a tablet mouse, you can set the scrolling mouse wheel to adjust the brush size from the same drop-down menu.

Did You Know?

You can deselect all of the layers more quickly than clicking the layer visibility eye icon of each layer. Position your cursor over the eye icon of the top or bottom layer of those you want to deselect. Press Shift and drag your cursor through the eye icons. You can select continuous layers in the same way.

More Options!

You can use keyboard shortcuts to switch between tools that are stacked together in the Toolbox. To switch from the Spot Healing Brush tool to the Healing Brush, press Shift+J.

RETOUCH WRINKLES with the
Healing Brush and Patch Tools

You can soften and even eliminate wrinkles with a combination of the Healing Brush tool and the Patch tool. Wrinkles give character to a face, and eliminating all wrinkles results in a bizarre portrait. Strive to eliminate wrinkles only to the point where the result looks appropriate for the age and expression of the subject. Complete your retouching for spots and skin blemishes before retouching wrinkles.

Removing wrinkles completely is most easily accomplished with the Patch tool. You can now do this on an empty

layer with the Content-Aware option and Sample All Layers. This allows you to reduce the opacity of the Patch tool correction if you later decide that you should not have completely eliminated the wrinkles.

You can use the Healing Brush tool to soften wrinkles. Use it on different layers for different areas of the face. You can then adjust the opacity of each layer to dial in the precise amount of retouching that is appropriate.

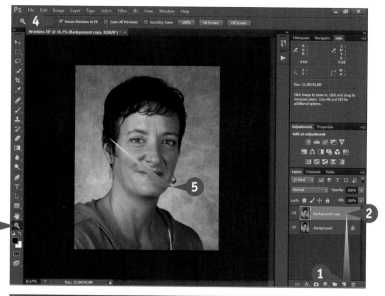

① With an image open, click and drag the Background layer to the New Layer icon.

Photoshop makes a copy of the background layer on a new layer.

② Double-click the default layer name, type **patch tool** in the text entry box, and press Enter (Return).

③ Click the Zoom tool.

④ Select Resize Windows to Fit (☐ changes to ☑).

⑤ Click and drag over the area to retouch.

The image zooms to fill the screen.

⑥ Select the Patch tool.

⑦ Select Content-Aware from the Patch drop-down menu.

⑧ Select Sample All Layers (☐ changes to ☑).

⑨ Draw around the area you want to patch.

Note: The patch outline draws from the tip of the arrowhead.

⑩ Drag the area to a wrinkle-free area and release the mouse button.

Photoshop fills the patch with the new area.

⑪ Adjust the layer opacity as needed.

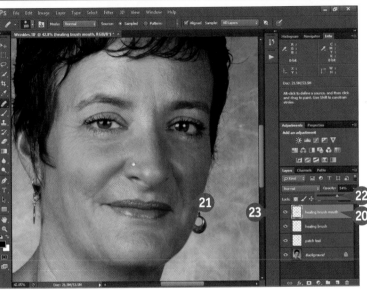

⑫ Click the New Layer button.

⑬ Double-click the default layer name, type **healing brush** in the text entry box, and press Enter (Return).

⑭ Press Shift+J to select the Healing Brush tool.

⑮ Select Sampled (⬤ changes to ◉).

⑯ Click All Layers from the Sample drop-down menu.

⑰ Press the left bracket key to reduce the brush size or the right bracket key to increase brush size until it is just larger than the wrinkle.

⑱ Press Alt (Option) and select a source area. Release Alt (Option) and the mouse button.

⑲ Click and drag over the wrinkle.

⑳ Create new layers for other areas.

㉑ Repeat steps 17 to 19 for all similar wrinkles in those areas.

㉒ Adjust the opacity of the healing brush layers.

㉓ Press Shift and drag through the eye icons for the retouching layers to see the before view. Drag through them again to see the retouched view.

㉔ Save the image with layers as a PSD file.

Try This!

You can save your wrinkle-removing brushes as brush presets for the tools you use. Click the Tool Preset picker drop-down menu next to the tool icon in the Options bar. Click the New tool preset button (🔲). Type a name in the text entry box. Click OK. The next time you retouch with that tool, click the Tool Preset picker and the brush is available.

More Options!

You can change the healing brush cursor to a precise brush. Press and release Shift. The cursor changes to the precise brush cross hair. This may make it easier to paint the healing over a wrinkle. To toggle back to the default brush cursor, press Shift again.

Try This!

To decide the amount of layer opacity to use, start at 0% rather than 100%. Drag to the right from 0% to set the opacity.

SLIM A PORTRAIT by removing the weight the camera adds

It is not your imagination. A photo makes its subject look heavier. This is particularly noticeable in portraits. You can remove this added weight using the Liquify filter.

The Liquify cursor is a circle with a crosshair at the center if you have your cursor preferences set to Show Crosshair in Brush Tip. An invisible circle surrounding the cross hair is the extent of the full Liquify filter. Between this invisible circle and the visible circle, the liquify effect diminishes to zero. It is usually best to use a large brush size and many very small nudges with the Liquify tool. This creates a smoother edge and a smoother transition from the full liquify effect to no effect.

It is easy to go too far with the Liquify filter, and slim the face, neck and arms so much that they end up looking unnatural. Use it on a copy of the background layer, and be subtle. And you must be careful when you are using the Liquify filter that you do not noticeably distort the background.

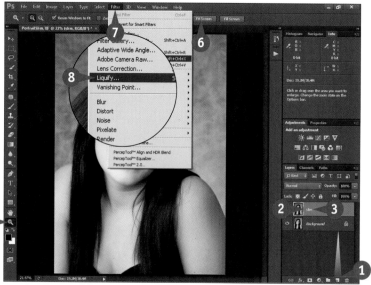

1. With an image open, drag the background layer to the new layer icon.

   Photoshop creates a copy of the background layer.

2. Double-click the default layer name.

3. Type **slim** in the text entry box.

4. Press Enter (Return).

5. Click the Zoom tool.

6. Click Fit Screen in the Options bar.

7. Click Filter.

8. Click Liquify.

   The Liquify filter panel opens.

9. Click the Brush Size menu in the Tool Options subpanel.

10. Drag the cursor to create a large brush.

    Note: The size of your brush depends on the resolution and zoom level of your image.

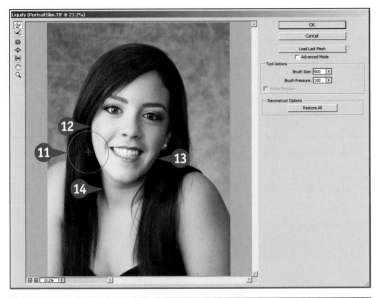

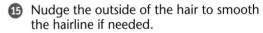

11. Press the mouse button and nudge her right cheek in slightly.

12. Click and nudge adjacent parts of the cheek until the cheek line is smooth.

   Note: Click the zoom level menu and zoom into the image if necessary.

13. Repeat steps 9 to 12 on her left cheek.

   Note: Adjust the brush size as needed.

14. Repeat steps 9 to 12 to thin the right side of her neck.

15. Nudge the outside of the hair to smooth the hairline if needed.

16. Press the left bracket key to reduce the brush size.

17. Position the brush inside the hairline and click along the hairline.

   The volume of the hair increases, which might be appreciated by some portrait subjects.

18. Click OK.

   The face and neck are slimmed to a more natural shape. The hair is smoother and fuller.

TIPS

Did You Know?

You do not need to drag a layer to the New Layer button to duplicate it. You can select the layer and use the keyboard shortcut Ctrl+J (⌘+J) instead.

Try This!

Outdoor portraits often suffer from hair blowing in the wind and swept to one side, or to the front or back. You can fix all of these situations and create a smooth hairline with the Liquify filter. Drag the Liquify brush inward from outside the hair to eliminate the windswept look. Drag from inside the hair outward to increase the volume of hair that was swept in by the wind.

Important!

You should leave enough room in the frame around your subject when you are shooting if you anticipate using the Liquify brush. If the subject is too close to the edge of the frame, the Liquify brush drags in the frame edge when you nudge inward. A checkerboard background appears.

REMOVE REFLECTIONS in eyeglasses

Light sources reflected in eyeglasses are one of the most common problems in the studio for portrait photographers and on location for everyone. The best solution is to take two photos with the subject in the same position, one with the glasses on and one with them off. Then you can move eyes from the glare-free image to the eyeglasses image using layers. But if you only have one image, you can remove the glare in Photoshop.

Unfortunately, Photoshop provides no easy, automated way to remove reflections in eyeglasses. You must work manually. You must zoom into the area and use the Clone Stamp tool to slowly work on the reflection until you eliminate it. Even when you eliminate it, the result usually needs more work with the Dodge and Burn tools to blend the retouching smoothly.

1 With an image open, press Ctrl+J (⌘+J) to make a copy of the Background layer.

2 Click the New Layer button.

3 Double-click the default layer name, type **left eye** in the text entry box, and press Enter (Return).

4 Click the Clone Stamp tool.

5 Click the Brush Preset drop-down menu and select a small brush with zero hardness.

6 Set the Mode to Darken.

7 Set the Opacity to 50%.

8 Set the Flow to 100%.

9 Select Aligned (☐ changes to ☑).

10 Set Sample to All Layers.

11 Click the Zoom tool.

12 Click the left eye of the subject to zoom in.

The left eye area enlarges.

13 Alt (Option)+click one side of the reflection.

14 Click in the reflection.

15 Repeat steps 13 and 14 until the reflection is gone from the eye.

16 Repeat steps 13 and 14 to remove any glare from the eyeglass frame.

17 Press the spacebar to activate the Hand tool and drag the image to the other eye.

18 Click the New Layer button.

19 Double-click the name of the layer and type **right eye**.

20 Press Enter (Return).

21 Click the Clone Stamp tool.

22 Repeat steps 13 and 14 to remove the glare in the right eye and the eyeglass frame.

The reflection and glare are removed.

23 Click the Layer panel menu button (⬛) and select Merge Down to merge the right eye with the layers below.

24 Repeat step 23 to merge the left eye layer.

25 Click the Burn tool.

26 Set Exposure to 20%.

27 Click and drag to paint in cloned areas that need to be darker.

28 Press and hold Alt (Option) to temporarily change to the Dodge tool to lighten areas.

29 Zoom out to inspect your retouching.

30 Click the Layer panel menu button and select Flatten Image when you are satisfied with the retouching.

TIPS

More Options!

Glare and reflections often turn the pupil from black to gray. You can burn the pupil to black while you are burning in the retouching. Add the white catchlight back.

More Options!

Keyboard options speed the process. Press S to select the Clone Stamp tool. Press O to select the Dodge tool. Press Shift+O to select the Burn tool. Press Ctrl+E (⌘+E) to Merge Down a layer.

LIGHTEN A SUBJECT in deep shadow

Every photographer has seen a fleeting moment happen when out shooting. He raises the camera to his eye and captures a frame without regard for exposure. When this happens and the subject is strongly backlit, the result is an underexposed subject, often against a light background. You can save the photo by selecting the subject and then using an adjustment layer to adjust the subject exposure and contrast.

Photoshop provides many tools to make selections. The Quick Selection tool is one of the quickest and easiest to

use. You simply paint over an area and it is selected. The tool opens with the Add to Selection brush automatically selected. You can remove areas of the selection by pressing and holding Alt (Option) as you paint, or using the Subtract from Selection brush.

With your subject selected you can create a Curves adjustment layer with the background masked. After applying a slight feather to the mask to ensure a smooth blending, you can use the On-image adjustment tool to correct the image.

1. With an image open, click the Quick Selection tool.

2. Click the Brush Preset drop-down menu.

   The Brush Preset drop-down menu opens.

3. Click and drag the Size slider to choose a brush size.

4. Click and drag the Hardness slider to 100%.

5. Press Ctrl+J (⌘+J) to create a copy of the Background layer.

   Photoshop creates a copy of the background layer on a new layer.

6. Click and drag inside the part of the image you want to adjust.

   Marching ants appear around the area.

7. Change the brush size and toggle the Quick Selection tool options to add and subtract from the selection until you are satisfied.

8. Click the Adjustments tab in the right panel.

9. Click Curves.

A curves layer opens in the Layers panel with a layer mask of your selection.

10 Click the Add a Layer Mask button in the Properties panel.

The Masks panel appears.

11 Click and drag the Feather slider to a value between 1.0 and 2.0.

12 Click the Curves button in the Properties panel.

The Curves dialog box opens.

13 Click the On-image adjustment tool.

14 Click and drag the On-image adjustment tool in the image.

Note: Keep the tonal value of the subject lower than that of the bright background.

15 Save the image as a layered PSD file.

TIPS

More Options!
You can tone down the curves adjustment at any time. Because it is on its own layer, click the Opacity drop-down menu. Click and drag the Opacity slider to 0% and then drag to the right to a new setting.

Try This!
You can select the Auto-Enhance check box (☐ changes to ☑) in the Options bar before making your selection. Auto-Enhance smooths the selection boundary and extends it in the direction of the edge the Quick Selection tool detects.

More Options!
You can select the Sample All Layers check box (☐ changes to ☑) in the Options bar to select from all of the layers below the currently selected layer rather than just the currently selected layer.

Make a PERFECT GROUP SHOT

The more people you have in an image, the less likely that everyone will look good at the same time. You can create the perfect group shot by combining two or more images where different subjects look good.

If the images are captured in rapid succession, or the camera is mounted on a tripod and the subjects do not move, you can use the Auto-Align Layers command in the Edit menu to help you align the layers. When the camera is handheld or there is significant movement of the subjects, manual alignment is the only option.

You can open both images in Photoshop and drag one onto the other to create a layered document. Using the Move tool and Transform commands, you can manually align the images. You can then use a layer mask to blend the images, erasing unwanted parts of each layer. The flattened result combines the best part of the different images.

1. With the images you want to combine open and tiled, click the Move tool.

2. Press Shift and click and drag the image that you want to use a piece from onto the image that that has most of what you want to keep.

   Note: Using Shift centers one image on the other when you release the mouse.

3. Close the image you dragged.

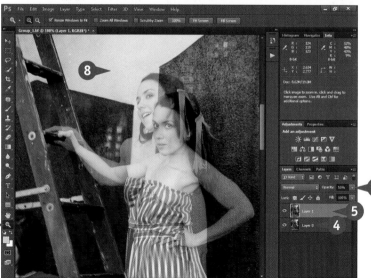

4. Double-click the background layer.

   The New Layer dialog box appears. Click OK to name the layer with the default name.

5. Click Layer 1.

6. Click the Opacity drop-down menu and lower the opacity to 50%.

7. Click the Zoom tool.

8. Click and drag in the image to the area of interest.

#36

DIFFICULTY LEVEL

9. Click the Move tool.

10. Click and drag Layer 1 to align it with Layer 0.

11. With Layer 1 selected, press Alt (Option) and click the Add Layer Mask button.

    A layer mask filled with black appears. Layer 0 disappears.

12. Drag the Layer 1 Opacity slider to 100%.

13. Click the Brush tool.

14. Click the Brush Preset drop-down menu and select an appropriate brush size with 50% Hardness.

15. Click the Default Foreground and Background Colors icon to set the default colors.

16. Click the Switch Foreground and Background Colors icon to set the foreground color to white.

17. Paint with white in the Layer 1 layer mask to replace the head in Layer 0 with the head in Layer 1.

18. Press X to toggle the foreground color from white to black.

19. Paint with black in the mask if you reveal too much of Layer 0.

20. Zoom out.

21. Click Layer ➪ Flatten Image.

22. Save the composed image.

TIPS

More Options!
You can zoom in and out using keyboard shortcuts and your mouse. To zoom in, press Ctrl+spacebar (⌘+spacebar) and click. Press Alt+spacebar (Option+spacebar) and click to zoom out.

Did You Know?
You can press D to select the default foreground and background colors of black and white.

Important!
Pay attention to the Layer panel icons. The layer or layer mask on which you are about to paint has a white border. Make sure that the layer mask of the top layer in this task is selected before you begin painting with white to reveal its contents.

You can remove unwanted objects in your photos with a variety of tools in Photoshop. The Spot Healing Brush, the Healing Brush, the Patch tool, and the Clone Stamp all have a place. But these tools are generally used for small areas or for touch up.

When you have a large object to remove, you can let Photoshop do most of the work by using the Content-Aware fill tool. Using this tool, the result may be perfect with no further work needed. At other times, you may need to use one or more of the other tools to heal or clone the area after using Content-Aware fill.

The Content-Aware fill tool is fairly deeply buried in Photoshop drop-down menus. And even when you find it, it most likely is grayed out, meaning you cannot use it. To be able to select Content-Aware fill, you must first have an active selection. Once you make a selection, the tool is no longer grayed out. You can select it and proceed.

1 With an image open, click and drag the Background layer to the New Layer icon.

Note: Alternatively, press Ctrl+J (⌘+J) to duplicate the layer.

2 Double-click the default name of the new layer.

3 Type **remove** in the text entry box.

4 Press Enter (Return).

5 Click the Zoom tool.

6 Click and drag the Zoom tool around the object you want to remove.

The image zooms in.

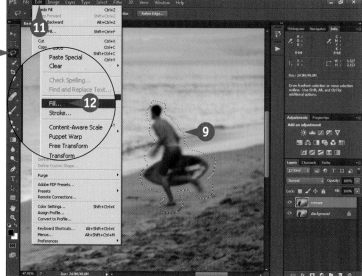

7 Click the Lasso tool.

8 Click the New Selection button (■) in the Options bar.

9 Click and draw a selection around the object.

10 Release the mouse.

The selection outline becomes marching ants.

11 Click Edit.

12 Click Fill.

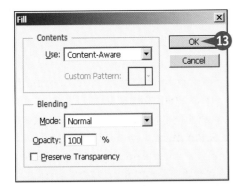

The Fill dialog box opens.

Content-Aware appears in the Use drop-down menu.

⑬ Click OK.

The object disappears leaving the marching ants.

⑭ Click Select.

⑮ Click Deselect.

The marching ants disappear.

⑯ Inspect the area where the Content-Aware fill tool removed the object.

⑰ Use any of the other healing or clone tools if needed.

Note: *No other work was needed on this image.*

⑱ Save the image.

TIPS

More Options!

Press L to select the Lasso tool. Press Shift+L to cycle through the lasso selection tools. Press Ctrl+D (⌘+D) to deselect the marching ants.

Did You Know?

You can add to a selection or remove part of the selection if you make a mistake selecting the object. Click the Add to Selection button (▦) and draw around the area to add. To remove part of a selection, click the Subtract from Selection button (▦) and draw around the area to remove.

Important!

If the object you are removing covers a line in the image that runs behind it, you can remove the object with Content-Aware fill, but you need to fill the break in the line with the Clone Stamp tool after you remove the object.

Unfortunately, every photo you take may not be composed the way you prefer. You may discover this while you are shooting, but be unable to do anything about it. Or you may not think of it until you see the photo on your monitor. In either case, you can recompose the image by moving elements without leaving a hole using the Content-Aware Move tool.

The Content-Aware Move tool works best when the background behind the subject you move is an even tone or repeating pattern. Photoshop always fills the

background with its best guess of what should be there. To do this, Photoshop first analyzes your image, and a progress bar appears on your screen to indicate this. Then Photoshop moves your subject to its new location and fills the background based on its analysis. With a simple background behind the subject, the result is generally perfect and no further work is needed. With a complex background, you can be sure that you need to use other healing tools or the Clone Stamp to clean up areas.

① With an image open, press Ctrl+J (⌘+J) to duplicate the layer.

② Double-click the default name of the new layer.

③ Type **move shadow** in the text entry box.

④ Press Enter (Return).

⑤ Click the Lasso tool.

⑥ Click the New Selection button in the Options bar.

⑦ Click and draw a selection around the object as close as possible.

⑧ Release the mouse.

The selection outline becomes marching ants.

⑨ Click Add to Selection and drag another selection in an area where you came too close to the subject.

⑩ Click Subtract from Selection and drag around an area that contains too much background.

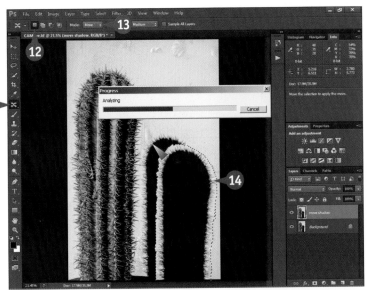

⑪ Click the Content-Aware Move tool.

⑫ Click the New Selection button in the Options bar.

⑬ Select Move from the Mode drop-down menu.

⑭ Click and drag the selection to a new position.

Note: The Analyzing progress panel appears and the progress bar moves while Photoshop analyzes the image.

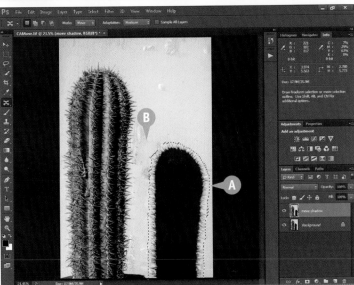

Ⓐ The selection moves to the new position with marching ants surrounding it.

Ⓑ The empty background fills with image information.

You can press Ctrl+D (⌘+D) to deselect the marching ants.

Important!

Remember to move the shadow along with the subject. If you are moving a subject and the shadow of the subject is visible in the original image, select the shadow along with the subject before you move the subject to its new location. Photoshop moves both, and fills the subject hole and the shadow hole with new information.

Did You Know?

You can prevent Photoshop from using a part of your image when it analyzes the image. This prevents that part of the image from appearing in the patch over the hole. Select the area you do not want Photoshop to use before you select your subject. Click Select ⇨ Save Selection. Click OK. Proceed with step 5 and subsequent steps.

BRIGHTEN THE EYES using curves and layers

The eyes are the most important element in a portrait. Retouchers spend more time working on the eyes than any other part of the face. You can brighten the eyes in your portraits to draw attention to them and make your subject appear more alert and attractive. Some fashion and beauty retouchers go so far as to enlarge the eyes in order to draw more attention to them.

Brightening the eyes is a two-step process. In one step you remove any imperfections in the whites of the eyes and then lighten them using a Curves adjustment layer. In the other, you lighten the iris areas of the eyes with a nondestructive dodge and burn technique on a new layer. The iris generally photographs darker than it appears in real life. It is easy to overdo both of these steps when you are working on a zoomed in image. It is important to do each step on a separate layer and then zoom out and adjust the opacity of the layer until the eyes look brighter, but still look natural.

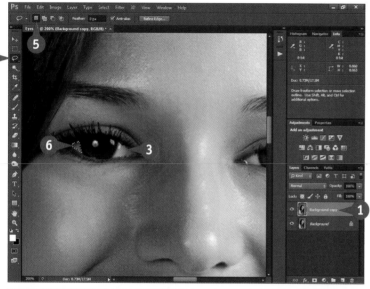

① With an image open, press Ctrl+J (⌘+J) to duplicate the Background layer.

② Press and hold Ctrl+spacebar (⌘+spacebar) to activate the Zoom tool.

③ Click one eye repeatedly to zoom in.

④ Click the Lasso tool.

⑤ Click the New Selection button.

⑥ Draw a selection of one of the white areas of the eye.

Marching ants surround the selection.

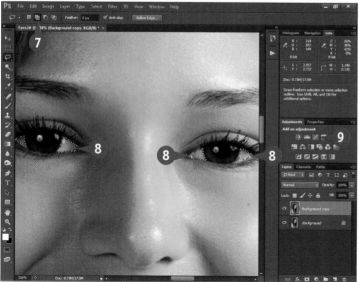

⑦ Click the Add to Selection button.

⑧ Draw a selection in the other white areas in both eyes.

⑨ Click the Curves adjustment in the Adjustments panel.

The Curves panel opens in the Properties panel.

A new layer appears in the Layers panel.

⑩ Double-click the default name of the layer.

⑪ Type **whites** in the text box.

⑫ Press Enter (Return).

⑬ Click and drag the center of the curve upward until the whites are much too bright.

⑭ Click and drag the center of the curve downward until the whites seem the correct brightness.

⑮ Click the Add a Layer Mask button in the Properties panel.

The Masks panel opens.

⑯ Click the mask in the whites layer of the Layer panel.

⑰ Click and drag the Feather slider in the Masks panel to between 1.0 and 2.0 pixels to soften and blend the edges of the whitening.

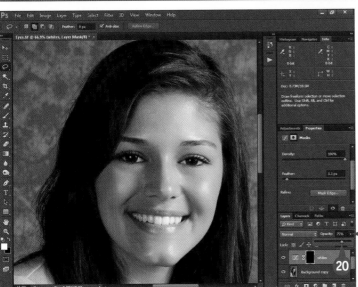

⑱ Press and hold Alt+spacebar (Option+spacebar) and click in the image to zoom out.

⑲ Click the Opacity drop-down menu.

Note: The whites layer should still be selected.

⑳ Click and drag the Opacity slider to lower the opacity of the whites adjustment if necessary.

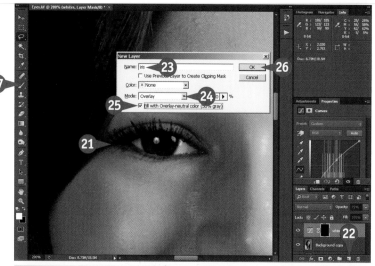

㉑ Press Ctrl+spacebar (⌘+spacebar) and click repeatedly to zoom in to one eye.

㉒ Press Alt (Option) and click the New Layer button.

The New Layer dialog box appears.

㉓ Type **iris** in the Name text entry box.

㉔ Select Overlay from the Mode drop-down list.

㉕ Select Fill with Overlay-Neutral Color (50% Gray) (☐ changes to ☑).

㉖ Click OK.

㉗ Click the Brush tool.

㉘ Select a small brush with 0% Hardness in the Brush Preset drop-down menu.

㉙ Set Opacity to 25% or less in the Options bar.

㉚ Press D to select the default foreground and background colors.

㉛ Press X to change the foreground color to white.

㉜ Paint the iris of the eye to brighten it.

㉝ Press X to change the foreground color to black.

㉞ Press the left bracket key to create a very small brush.

㉟ Paint the outer edge of the iris.

㊱ Paint the inner edge of the iris.

Note: This increases the apparent contrast of the eye.

㊲ Press the spacebar to activate the Hand tool and drag the image to the other eye.

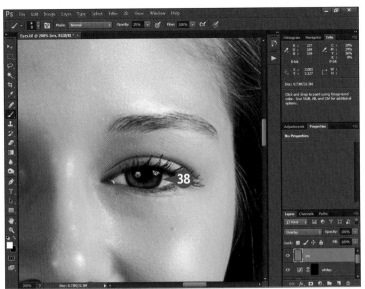

38 Repeat steps 30 to 36 in the iris of the other eye.

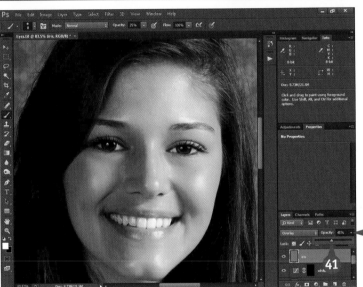

39 Press and hold Alt+spacebar (Option+spacebar) and click in the image to zoom out.

40 Click the Opacity drop-down menu.

Note: The iris layer should still be selected.

41 Click and drag the Opacity slider to 0% and then drag it to the right until the brightness of the iris looks right.

42 Save the image as a layered PSD file.

TIPS

Did You Know?

You can toggle between the Add to Selection and Subtract from Selection options when you are using the Lasso tool. Press Alt (Option) to toggle between them.

Important!

When you use any option with the Lasso tool, you must end at the same place you started. With the add and subtract options, you may need to make a circle around the area you want to add or subtract to complete the action.

More Options!

You can have a whites and iris layer for each eye. This gives you the greatest flexibility to adjust the opacity of the whites and the iris brightness of each eye.

ENHANCE A BORING SKY by adding clouds

Photoshop provides many options that you can use to enhance a dull or boring sky, including using the Graduated Filter in Camera Raw, as described in task #26. Most of these options only work well when there is very little foreground intruding into the sky. When you have a photo where there is a lot of foreground covering the sky, your options are far more limited. But you can still remove a boring sky and add a more dramatic one from another photo using the Magic Wand tool and a layer mask.

When you use the Magic Wand tool, you are selecting pixels based on their color and luminance. How close in color and luminance pixels are to the ones you choose is determined by the Tolerance setting in the Options bar. A low Tolerance setting means that Photoshop selects pixels only if they are very similar to the selected pixels. Often you need to try different tolerance settings, or add to and subtract from the selection, before it is just right. Once you have a selection, the rest is easy.

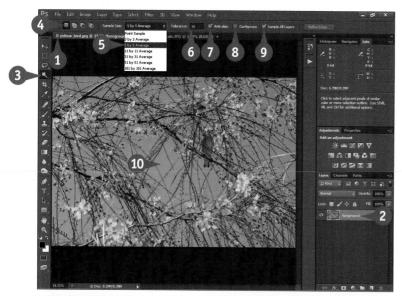

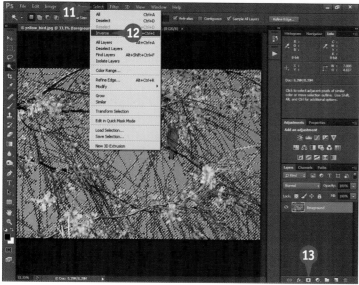

① With the foreground and background images open, select the foreground image.

② Double-click the image name, type **foreground** in the text entry box, and press Enter (Return).

③ Click the Magic Wand tool.

④ Click the New selection button.

⑤ Select 5 by 5 Average from the Sample Size drop-down menu.

⑥ Leave the Tolerance at the default 30 to start.

⑦ Leave Anti-alias selected.

⑧ Leave Contiguous deselected.

⑨ Select Sample All Layers (☐ changes to ☑).

⑩ Click in a sky area of the image.

Marching ants appear around areas of sky.

Note: You have selected the sky to save, not the rest of the image.

⑪ Click Select.

⑫ Click Inverse.

Note: The marching ants seem to be in the same place, but they are now selecting the parts of the image that are not sky.

⑬ Click the Add a Layer Mask button.

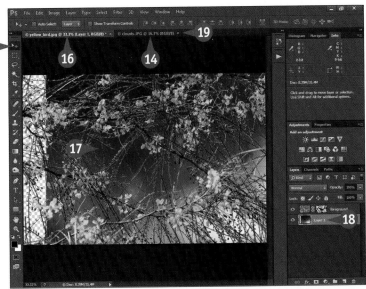

The sky is replaced with a checkerboard.

14 Click the tab of the background image.

The background image appears.

15 Click the Move tool.

16 Drag the background image onto the tab of the foreground image.

The foreground image appears.

17 Drag the background image onto the foreground image.

Note: Do not release the mouse during this process.

18 Drag Layer 1 below the foreground layer in the Layers panel.

19 Close the background image.

20 Click and drag the background image to position it.

21 Save the composite image as a layered PSD file.

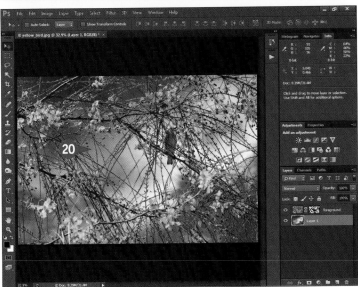

TIPS

Did You Know?

The images you use do not need to be the same size, but should be the same color space and bit depth. You can scale an active image before you position it to make it larger or smaller. Select Edit ➪ Transform ➪ Scale. Drag the corner handles to change the size of the image. Press Alt+spacebar (Option+spacebar) and drag in the image to zoom out if you cannot see the corner handles of the larger image.

More Options!

You can make an adjustment using any of the options in the Adjustments panel if the tone or color of either image does not look right. Click the layer in the Layers panel you want to adjust. Click the desired adjustment in the Adjustments panel. Make the adjustment.

One of the most common problems when capturing images is blurring caused by failing to hold the camera steady. Lens and camera manufacturers address this problem with vibration reduction systems built in to their equipment. However, there are many cameras without these systems, and even those cameras and lenses with vibration reduction sometimes produce blurred images. You can minimize and sometime eliminate blurring resulting from camera shake with the new Shake Reduction filter in Photoshop CC.

The Shake Reduction filter is found in the Filter ➪ Sharpen menu. It opens in a new dialog box with a default shake reduction applied. The dialog box contains a scalable preview, settings sliders, and a Detail preview. The Detail preview can show an area of the image at magnifications of 0.5x, 1x, 2x, and 4x. The Detail preview shows a 100 percent view of part of the image area that Photoshop is using to estimate the blur reduction amount needed.

The process of eliminating shake reduction blur can cause halos in high-contrast areas. The sliders control the amount of blur reduction, and you can also use them to minimize the halos.

1 With an image open, click Filter.

2 Click Sharpen.

3 Click Shake Reduction.

The Shake Reduction dialog box appears.

4 Click the Advanced disclosure triangle.

Ⓐ A square opens in the preview to show the area that Photoshop used to estimate the blur.

5 Click and drag the central pin to move the selected area.

6 Click the handles to enlarge or shrink the selected area.

7 Select Preview to toggle before and after views (☐ changes to ☑).

Ⓑ The Detail preview shows a 100 percent view within the square.

#41

DIFFICULTY LEVEL

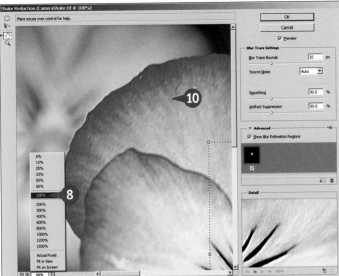

8. Select 100% in the zoom level menu.

9. Click the Hand tool.

10. Drag through the image to find halo artifacts.

11. Click and drag the Artifact Suppression slider to minimize halos.

12. Click OK.

The image redraws in Photoshop with the blur minimized.

TIPS

Important!

Allow time for Photoshop to run the filter and update the preview. Wait for the progress sliders to complete before clicking Preview to view before and after views. And allow time for the preview to redraw when you toggle Preview.

More Options!

You can increase or decrease the amount of blur reduction with the Blur Trace Bounds slider. Dragging it to the right increases apparent sharpness, but also increases artifacts. Dragging the slider to the left minimizes artifacts, but less blur reduction is applied.

Important!

Do not drag the Blur Estimation Region square over an area that is very much out of focus. Photoshop tries to sharpen it at the expense of the rest of the image.

Adjust Photos with Layers, Selections, and Masks

The power of Photoshop lies in your ability to use layers, selections, and masks to create unique documents that become new images. New layers lie on top of your original image, which Photoshop calls your *Background* layer.

There are many types of layers other than background layers. A *layer* can start out empty, or *transparent*. A layer can contain text, adjustments to your image, and your selections and masks. Every layer is independent of every other layer, allowing you to transform and adjust each without affecting any other. You can combine layers in complex ways with blending modes, copy and paste them, and flatten them to a single file when you are done.

By making a *selection*, you can modify an isolated region of an image without affecting any part of the image outside the selection. You can make selections with geometric shapes, automated controls based on image information, and manually. You can make adjustments to selections, copy and paste them, and create a new layer from a selection.

You can also turn a selection into a mask. A *mask* is a grayscale copy of a selection. The white areas of the mask are the areas you selected and can adjust. The black areas are unselected areas and protect the image information below them from adjustments. Gray areas represent partially selected areas. You can paint directly onto masks to revise them and adjust the edge of a mask to precisely outline an object.

Make a selection with the QUICK SELECTION TOOL

You can use the Quick Selection tool to quickly select an area in an image. The tool works best when the area is much lighter or much darker than the surrounding pixels.

You use a brush to brush on the selection, or you can simply click in the image to select values similar to those in the area where you click. After you make your initial selection, the tool changes to the Add to Selection tool. Using this tool, you can select additional areas of the

image. If you or Photoshop selects an area you do not want, you can press Alt (Option) to switch to the Subtract from Selection tool and paint that area away.

Once you select an area you can move it to its own layer, mask it with a layer mask, adjust it using the Adjustments panel tools, delete it, copy and paste it, or invert the selection to select everything else in the image. Use the steps in task #43 to improve the edges of the selection.

① With an image open, click the Quick Selection tool.

② Click the New Selection button.

③ Click the Brush Picker button.

④ Click and drag the Size slider to adjust the brush size.

⑤ Leave the Hardness slider set to 100%.

⑥ Select Sample All Layers (☐ changes to ☑).

⑦ Select Auto-Enhance (☐ changes to ☑).

⑧ Click and drag inside the area of the image you want to select.

Ⓐ Marching ants appear around your selection.

Ⓑ After you make your first selection, the Quick Selection tool changes to the Add to Selection option.

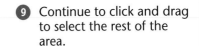

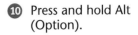

9 Continue to click and drag to select the rest of the area.

Note: Change the brush size, zoom in or out, and pan through the image as needed.

10 Press and hold Alt (Option).

C The Quick Selection tool temporarily changes to the Subtract from Selection option.

11 Click and drag in areas you want to remove from the selection.

12 Press Ctrl+J (⌘+J) to put the selection on a new layer.

The selection appears on a new layer with a checkerboard background above the Background layer.

13 Click the Background layer eye icon to toggle the visibility of the layer to see the selection better.

Note: The selection outline is seldom perfect using the Quick Selection tool. See task #43.

14 Save the image as a layered PSD file.

TIPS

Did You Know?
The Quick Selection tool "learns" as you paint in the image. As you toggle between Add to Selection and Subtract from Selection, you teach Photoshop to more precisely choose the areas to include in or remove from the selection.

More Options!
You can change the brush size by clicking the left bracket key to decrease the brush size, and clicking the right bracket key to increase brush size.

Did You Know?
You can hide the marching ants temporarily so that you can see the edge of the selection. Toggle Ctrl+H (⌘+H) to hide and view the marching ants.

IMPROVE THE EDGES OF A SELECTION with Refine Edge

The selection tools in Photoshop make it possible to move an area of one image to another image, but there is usually something of the original image along the edges that also travels along. You can eliminate or at least minimize that problem using the tools in the Refine Edge panel.

The Refine Edge button is available in the Options bar whenever a selection tool is active. Clicking it opens the Refine Edge floating panel, which you can position anywhere on the monitor where it does not block your view of the image. Dragging it to a second monitor is ideal.

You can use the View drop-down menu in the Refine Edge panel to preview your image against different backgrounds. Toggle through the views and choose the background that gives you the clearest definition of the selection edges. Then use the other options in the panel to clean up the edges and remove any contamination remaining from the original image.

1 Open an image and make a selection with any of the selection tools.

A Marching ants appear around your selection.

2 Click the Refine Edge button in the Options bar.

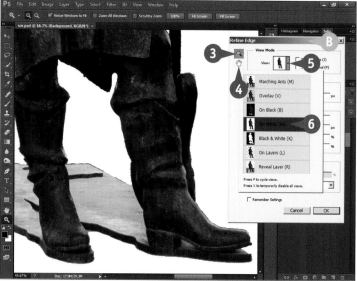

B The Refine Edge floating panel appears. You can click and drag it off of the image.

3 Click the Zoom tool in the panel and click and drag in the image to enlarge an area.

4 Click the Hand tool and click and drag in the image to navigate in the image.

Note: The edges of the selection are ragged.

5 Click the View drop-down menu.

The View menu appears.

6 Click the view that you feel best shows the edges.

Note: This example uses the On White view.

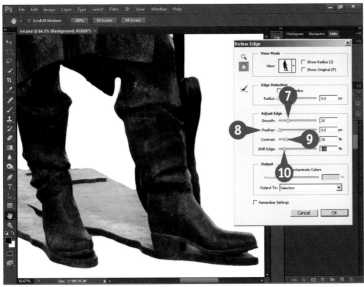

#43

DIFFICULTY LEVEL

7 Click and drag the Smooth slider to eliminate jagged edges.

8 Click and drag the Feather slider to create a softer transition.

9 Click and drag the Contrast slider to increase edge contrast.

10 Click and drag the Shift Edge slider to the left to remove the last bits of the original image from the selection.

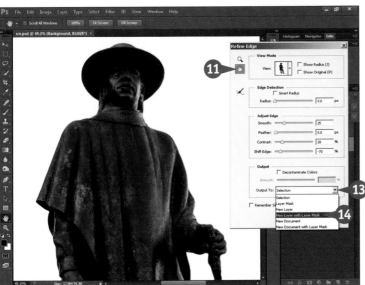

11 Click the Hand tool and pan around the image to see the adjusted edge in other areas.

12 Press P to toggle between your original edge and the refined edge.

13 Click the Output To drop-down menu.

The Output To menu appears.

14 Select New Layer with Layer Mask to save your refined selection.

15 Click OK.

Your refined selection is saved to a new layer with a layer mask.

Note: If you saved your selection to a layer before using Refine Edge you can delete that layer.

TIPS

More Options!

You can bring back the marching ants around your selection when the selection is on a layer with a transparent background. Deselect the other layers. Select the layer with your selection. Click the Magic Wand tool () and select the checkerboard background. Press Shift+Ctrl+I (Shift+⌘+I) to invert the selection. The marching ants surround your selection.

Did You Know?

You can cycle through the Refine Edge View options with a keyboard shortcut rather than opening the View drop-down menu. Press F to cycle through the view options. Press X at any time to temporarily disable all view modes. Press X again to return to your previous view mode.

Camera Raw provides tools to make global adjustments to your images, and the ability to make a few local adjustments. But using the selection tools in Photoshop enables you to make far more precise local pixel-level adjustments with the aid of a layer mask.

You can turn any selection into a layer mask by clicking the Layer Mask button at the bottom of the Layers panel. However, when you have an active selection and click an adjustment icon, Photoshop knows you want to target the adjustment to the selection, and automatically creates an adjustment layer with a layer mask. This is true even when you make a selection on the Background layer, which is locked to many of the tools in Photoshop.

The automatic layer mask is no different from any other mask created in Photoshop. You can use Refine Edge to adjust the edge, open the Masks panel for further refinements, and paint on the mask to add or subtract from it.

1. With an image open on the Background layer, zoom in to the area you want to select.

2. Click the Quick Selection tool.

3. Create a brush in the Brush Picker.

4. Click and drag in the image to make an initial selection.

5. Use Add to Selection and Subtract from Selection to refine the selection area.

6. Click the Hue/Saturation adjustment button in the Adjustments panel.

A. Photoshop automatically creates a Hue/Saturation adjustment layer in the Layers panel with a layer mask displaying your selection.

The Properties panel opens.

7. Click and drag the Hue slider to change the color of the selection.

8. Click and drag the Saturation slider to adjust the saturation of the selection to the rest of the image.

9. Click the Masks button.

The Masks panel opens.

10 Click and drag the Feather slider to soften the edge of the mask.

11 Click the Zoom tool.

12 Click the Fit Screen button.

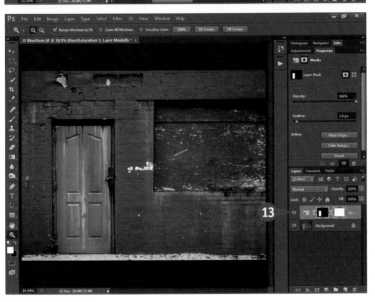

The image shrinks to fit in the screen.

13 Click the adjustment layer eye icon to see before and after views of the adjustment.

14 Save the image as a layered PSD file.

TIPS

More Options!

You can refine the edges of the selection in two ways if needed. After making your selection, click the Refine Edge button and proceed as in task #43. Or in the Masks panel of the Properties tab, click the Mask Edge button to open the Refine Mask panel. The options in the Refine Mask panel are identical to those in the Refine Edge panel.

Did You Know?

You can add an adjustment layer to the selection in an image by clicking Layer ⇨ New Adjustment Layer and selecting the type of layer to add. Photoshop creates a new adjustment layer with a layer mask of your selection.

Did You Know?

You can zoom out to the Fit Screen view with a keyboard shortcut. Press Ctrl+0 (⌘+0) any time the image is zoomed in to zoom it back out to fit in your screen.

SELECT AREAS OF SIMILAR COLOR
with the Magic Wand tool

If the areas you want to adjust are similar in color and brightness, you can use the Magic Wand tool to let Photoshop automatically select them. The advantage of the Magic Wand tool over other selection tools that you use directly on the image is that it can select areas that are not connected to one another. As long as the image tones are within the tolerance range you set, the Magic Wand tool can select them wherever they may lie in the image.

Setting the tolerance of the Magic Wand tool is critical for you to use it successfully. Where the tones you want to select are within a narrow range, set a high Tolerance value for the first pass. For areas that were not selected in the first pass, use a lower Tolerance value for subsequent passes. A Sample Size of 5 by 5 Average works well in nearly all cases.

As with the other selection tools, you can add to and subtract from the Magic Wand selection.

1. With an image open, click the Magic Wand tool.

2. Click the New Selection button.

3. Select 5 by 5 Average in the Select Size drop-down menu.

4. Type a value in the Tolerance text entry box based on image information.

   Note: The background of this image is uniformly close in tonal value, so a setting of 50 is acceptable. The default setting of 30 is suitable for most images.

5. Click in the image.

Marching ants appear where Photoshop has selected pixels.

6. Click the Add to Selection button.

7. Type a lower value in the Tolerance text entry box.

8. Click in an area of the image that was not selected in the first pass.

9 Repeat steps 7 and 8 until all of the areas are surrounded by marching ants.

Ⓐ You can click the Subtract from Selection button and click areas that should not be selected.

10 Click the Adjustments tab.

11 Click the Gradient Map adjustment.

The Properties panel opens.

12 Click the Gradient Picker drop-down menu.

13 Select a prebuilt gradient to fill the selection.

The gradient fills the background.

14 Save the image as a layered PSD file.

Important!

When the original image includes a subject with hair, or without a distinct sharp edge, you must refine the mask before making the adjustment. See task #47.

Did You Know?

You can temporarily disable the adjustment layer in the Properties panel. Click the eye icon next to the trash can in the Properties panel.

More Options!

You can limit the Magic Wand selection to only those pixels that are in one continuous area, even though there are similar pixels in other areas of the image. In the Magic Wand Options bar, select Contiguous (☐ changes to ☑). Only adjoining pixels are selected.

Photoshop provides an array of tools to adjust skin, from removing colorcasts to correcting exposure. With only a few people in a photo, you can use the Quick Selection tool used in task #35. But when there are multiple people that need the same adjustment, the selection process is no longer quick using this technique. However, you can automatically detect the skin tone of multiple people quickly by using the Skin Tones option of the Color Range tool.

You can further refine the automatic detection by selecting the Detect Faces check box, which is only available when

you select the Skin Tones option from the drop-down menu in the Color Range floating panel. Several preview options are available in the panel. Cycle through them to find the preview that shows the selected faces most clearly to you.

Having Photoshop make the initial face detection saves time, but there is still other work that you need to do to refine the selection so that only faces are selected. When you have the faces selected, you can apply the adjustments that the faces need.

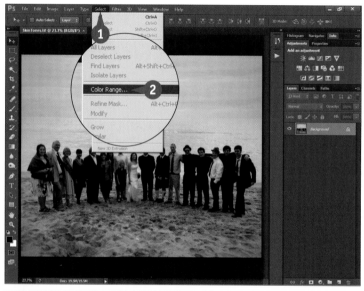

① With an image open, click Select.

② Click Color Range.

Ⓐ The Color Range floating panel appears. You can drag it as far off of the image as possible.

③ Click the Select drop-down menu and select Skin Tones.

④ Click the Selection Preview drop-down menu and select White Matte.

The image changes to show the white matte view.

5 Select Detect Faces
(☐ changes to ☑).

The image shows the skin tones in color and everything else in grayscale.

6 Click and drag the Fuzziness slider all the way to the left.

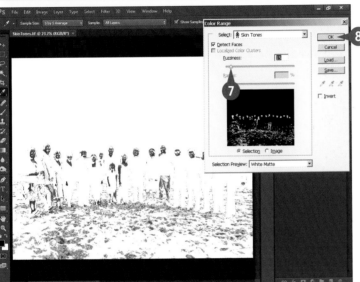

The image changes to completely white.

7 Click and drag the Fuzziness slider to the right.

Skin tones begin to appear in color.

8 Click OK when most of the skin tones are selected.

TIPS

Did You Know?

You can adjust the Fuzziness slider using the keyboard. Click and drag the slider all the way to the right. With 0 highlighted, press the up arrow key to increase the fuzziness by one increment. Press Shift+up arrow to increase the fuzziness by increments of ten.

Try This!

Cycle through the other Selection Preview options if you cannot clearly see the selected skin tones with the White Matte preview. **None** shows the original image. **Grayscale** shows the selected areas as white, unselected areas as black, and partially selected areas as tones of gray. This is the same view shown in the Color Range panel preview. **Black Matte** shows the skin tones in color and the rest of the image black. **White Matte** shows the skin tomes in color with the rest of the image white. **Quick Mask** adds a red overlay on the unselected areas.

Making selections with any of the automated tools in Photoshop generally requires some touch-up to the selection. You can use any of the selection tools to do this, but the easiest way is usually to touch up the mask Photoshop creates from the selection. Once you have a mask, you can zoom in and paint on the mask with black to eliminate areas or paint on the mask with white to add areas.

All of the options in the Adjustments panel that you would apply to skin tones automatically create a layer mask when you select them. To lighten the skin tones, a simple Levels adjustment is usually sufficient. With the skin tones adjusted, you can invert the mask and adjust the background color, contrast, or any other adjustment option without affecting the skin tones.

Marching ants appear around the selected areas.

⑨ Click the Adjustments tab to open the Adjustments panel.

⑩ Click the Levels adjustment button.

The marching ants disappear.

Photoshop creates a new Levels adjustment layer with a layer mask of the selection in the Layers panel.

The Levels panel appears in the Properties tab.

⑪ Alt+click (Option+click) the layer mask thumbnail in the adjustment layer of the Layers panel.

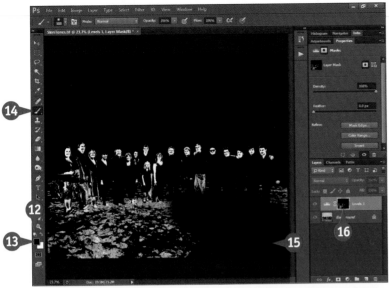

The image shows the layer mask in grayscale.

⑫ Click the default colors icon.

⑬ Press X to make black the foreground color.

⑭ Click the Brush tool.

⑮ Paint with black over areas that are not skin tones.

⑯ Alt+click (Option+click) the layer mask thumbnail in the adjustment layer of the Layers panel.

The image returns to the normal view.

⑰ Click the Levels button in the Properties panel.

⑱ Click and drag the slider to the left to lighten the skin tones.

The adjustment is applied only to the skin tones that are unprotected by the layer mask.

⑲ Save the image as a layered PSD file.

TIPS

Important!

Be careful when you paint black on the mask. If you make a mistake, painting on the mask with white does not easily correct errors. When you paint black on the mask, zoom in as needed. Change the brush size with the left and right bracket keys. Paint small areas at a time. If you make a mistake, use Ctrl+Z (⌘+Z) to remove the last stroke.

Try This!

You can adjust levels in the image background. Press Ctrl+J (⌘+J) to duplicate the Levels adjustment and mask. Click the Masks button (▣) in the Properties panel. Click the Invert button. Click the adjustment icon of the new layer and adjust levels in the image background without adjusting levels of the skin tones.

Most of the selections you make in Photoshop are in areas with definite edges, and the Quick Selection, Lasso, Magic Wand, and Color Range tools work very well, with only minor adjustment needed. But there are times when you need to mask areas such as hair where some of the background shows through. You can do this by making a rough selection with the most appropriate selection tool and then using some of the more sophisticated options in Refine Edge.

The Refine Edge button is available in the Options bar of every selection tool once you make a selection. You can

use it to refine the edge of a selection as shown in preceding tasks. But you can also use it to refine the selection itself.

You can paint over a problem area in the selection and it seems like nothing is happening. Then the selection redraws with the refinement added. You can see the selection and the refinements you make to it using the various view options in the panel.

① With an image open, click the Quick Selection tool.

Note: Select a different selection tool if it works better for your image.

② Click the New Selection button.

③ Click the Brush Picker button.

④ Click and drag the Size slider to adjust the brush size.

⑤ Leave the Hardness slider set to 100%.

⑥ Select Sample All Layers (☐ changes to ☑).

⑦ Select Auto-Enhance (☐ changes to ☑).

⑧ Click and drag inside the area of the image you want to select.

Ⓐ Marching ants appear around your selection.

Ⓑ After you make your first selection, the Quick Selection tool changes to the Add to Selection option.

9 Continue to click and drag to select the rest of the area.

Note: Change the brush size, zoom in or out, and pan through the image as needed.

C The initial selections select too close to the edge.

10 Press and hold Alt (Option).

D The Quick Selection tool temporarily changes to the Subtract from Selection option.

11 Click and drag around the edges of the selection to move the selection away from the edge.

12 Click the Lasso tool.

13 Click the Add to Selection button.

14 Click and drag in the image to increase the selection until it is just inside any area with flyaway hair.

Note: Zoom in and out and pan through the image as needed.

15 Click the Refine Edge button.

A The Refine Edge floating panel appears. You can click and drag it off of the image.

16 Click the View drop-down menu.

17 Click Overlay.

A red overlay appears over the unselected areas.

18 Click in the Refine Mask panel to close the View drop-down menu.

19 Select Smart Radius (☐ changes to ☑) in the Edge Detection section.

20 Click and drag the Radius slider to the right until the red overlay is close to the flyaway hairs.

Note: It is okay if the red overlay is outside of the subject in some areas and inside in other areas.

21 Click the Zoom tool in the Refine Edge panel.

22 Zoom in.

23 Click the Refine Radius brush.

24 Press the right bracket key to enlarge the brush or the left bracket key to make the brush smaller.

25 Click and drag the Refine Radius brush in areas with flyaway hairs.

26 Select Decontaminate Colors (☐ changes to ☑).

27 Select New Layer with Layer Mask from the Output To drop-down menu.

28 Click OK.

B Photoshop calculates the mask and adds a new layer with the layer mask in the Layers panel.

29 Save the image as a layered PSD file.

Important!

It is always best to output the image to a new layer with a layer mask. No matter how carefully you work, there will still be a need to do some manual cleanup of the mask after it is output.

Did You Know?

If you select the Zoom tool or the Hand tool in the Refine Edge panel, you can press E to return to the Refine Radius brush.

Try This!

If you are masking the background to place the foreground on a different background, place the new background on a layer below the original image. When the image opens after you output it, it opens with the new background behind it.

ADD LAYERS AS SMART OBJECTS for flexibility

A Smart Object is a special type of layer in Photoshop. *Smart Objects* preserve the original content of a raster or vector image, enabling you to perform nondestructive editing to the layer. You can create a Smart Object layer, apply adjustments, and return to it at a later time to undo or revise the adjustments without altering the image quality. Smart Objects add a high degree of flexibility because the changes you make to them never affect the underlying pixel information.

You can use Smart Objects to scale, rotate, skew, or warp a layer without losing or altering the original image

information. You can apply filters to Smart Objects and edit them at any time, or remove them without altering pixel data. And you can add vector information, such as an Illustrator file, to a Smart Object and work with it without rasterizing it as shown in task #55.

You can open an image as a Smart Object, place an image as a Smart Object into a file open in Photoshop, convert one or more layers to a Smart Object, and open a RAW file as a Smart Object.

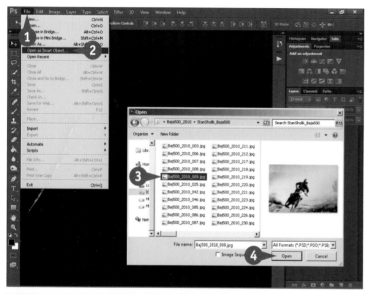

Open an Image as a Smart Object

1. Click File.

2. Click Open as Smart Object.

   The Open dialog box appears.

3. Navigate to the image and select it.

4. Click Open.

   The image opens as a Smart Object.

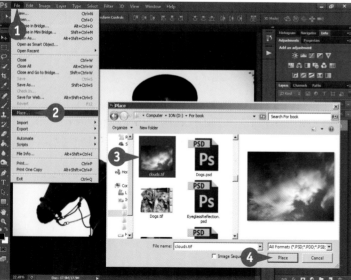

Place an Image as a Smart Object into a File Open in Photoshop

1. With an image open in Photoshop, click File.

2. Click Place.

   The Place dialog box appears.

3. Navigate to the new image and select it.

4. Click Place.

   The image opens as a Smart Object layer.

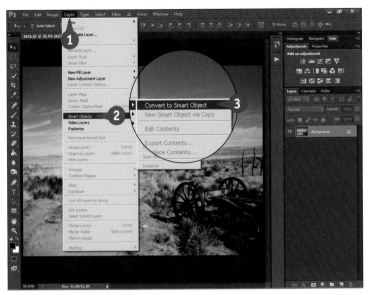

Convert an Image Layer to a Smart Object

#48

DIFFICULTY LEVEL

① With an image open, click Layer.

② Click Smart Objects.

③ Click Convert to Smart Object.

The layer is converted to a Smart Object layer and renamed layer 0.

Convert a Camera Raw Image to a Smart Object

① In Photoshop, click File ⇨ Open and double-click a RAW file.

The image opens in Camera Raw.

② Press Shift and click Open Image.

The RAW file opens as a Smart Object in Photoshop.

TIPS

Did You Know?
You can make edits in Photoshop to a RAW file opened as a Smart Object and return to Camera Raw to make additional changes without ever altering the original RAW file.

Important!
You can open or place a JPEG file as a Smart Object. However, it is best to use a TIFF or PSD file, which you can resave without data loss. Saving a JPEG file requires that you flatten the layers and recompress the file, creating data loss.

Did You Know?
You cannot perform editing operations directly to a Smart Object that would change pixel information. You cannot paint, dodge, burn, or clone directly on a Smart Object layer.

SELECT A COMPLEX BACKGROUND
with the Color Range command

The Magic Wand is a handy tool for selecting simple, evenly toned backgrounds. But when the foreground intrudes into the background, or when the background tone varies widely, the Magic Wand is less helpful. The Tolerance control of the Magic Wand is not very selective, and the marching ants make it difficult to evaluate the selection. In these situations, you can still make an automated selection using the Color Range command.

Using the Sampled Colors option, you can select the color range of the background. Using the Fuzziness slider, you

can fine-tune the selection. There are several preview options that allow you to judge the accuracy of your selection. You can add and subtract from the selection as you work.

Because you are selecting the background, you must invert the Color Range selection when you are finished. Photoshop applies your selection to the image. You can convert the selection to a mask and clean up any areas that were in the same color range as your selection.

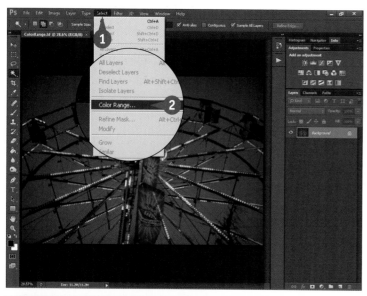

① With an image open, click Select.

② Click Color Range.

Ⓐ The Color Range floating panel appears. You can click and drag it off of the image.

③ Select Sampled Colors from the Select drop-down menu.

④ Select Image (○ changes to ⦿).

⑤ Click the Eyedropper tool.

⑥ Select None from the Selection Preview drop-down menu.

⑦ Press Shift and click and drag through the background in the preview.

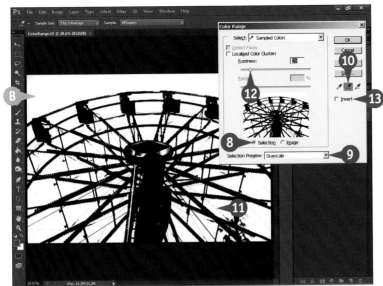

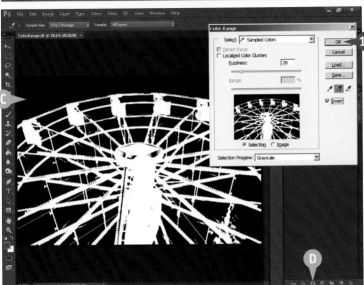

8 Select Selection (○ changes to ◉).

9 Select Grayscale from the Selection Preview drop-down menu.

Ⓑ The preview changes to a grayscale image. The sampled colors are shown as white and unselected colors are black.

10 Click the Add to Selection eyedropper.

11 Click any areas of the background that are gray to select them.

12 Click and drag the Fuzziness slider all the way to the left and then slowly back to the right until only the background is white.

13 Select Invert (☐ changes to ☑).

Ⓒ The grayscale image inverts tonal values.

14 Click OK.

Photoshop loads Color Range as a selection.

Ⓓ You can click the Add a Mask button at the bottom of the Layers panel to convert the selection to a Layer mask.

TIPS

More Options!
You can clean up the layer mask to fine-tune the selection before you add a new background. Alt+click (Option+click) the layer mask to view it in the preview. Press B for the Brush tool. Press D for the default colors. Paint with white in any black or gray areas that do not belong in the selection.

Try This!
Open a new image that you want for the background. Press V for the Move tool. Click in the image and drag it to the tab of the image you just masked. When the masked image appears, drag the background image to the masked image and release the mouse. In the Layers panel, drag the Background image layer below the masked image layer. The masked image appears in the foreground masked into the background.

ADD A TEXTURE using Blending Modes

Blending Modes are an essential part of Photoshop. They are available in the Options bar for many tools, but are most commonly used from the Layers panel. Blending Modes are powerful tools for making corrections. But more importantly, you can use Blending Modes to create a new image that combines elements of other images in an artistic way that could not be achieved without blending.

To use Blending Modes creatively, you must have two or more images on layers in the same document. The image you want as the base must be below the image you want to blend into it in the Layers panel.

With the image layer selected that you are blending into the background, you cycle through the Blending Modes to find the one that creates the look you want. If the look is too strong, you can adjust the opacity of the top layer to decrease the blending effect.

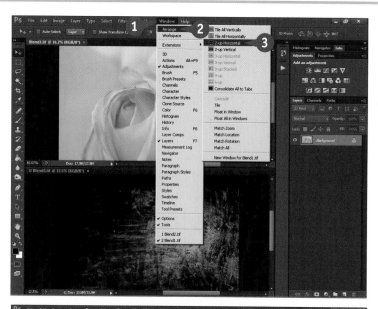

1 With two images open, click Window.

2 Click Arrange.

3 Click 2-up Horizontal.

Note: Alternatively, click 2-up Vertical for vertical images.

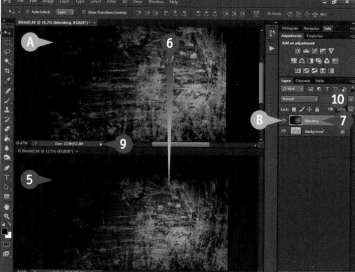

The image windows rearrange.

4 Click the Move tool.

5 Click the blending image.

6 Press and hold Shift, and click and drag the blending image onto the background image.

Note: Holding Shift centers the blending image on the background image.

A The blending image appears over the background image.

B A new layer appears.

7 Double-click the name of the new layer, and type **blending** in the text entry box.

8 Press Enter (Return).

9 Close the original blending image.

10 Click the Blending Modes drop-down menu.

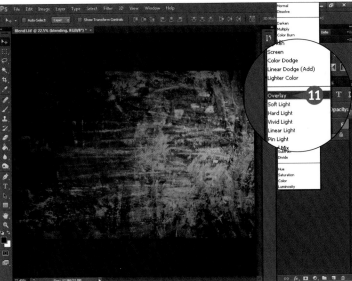

The Blending Modes menu appears.

⑪ Click Overlay.

The blended image appears.

⑫ Click the Opacity drop-down menu.

⑬ Click and drag the slider until the opacity appears correct.

⑭ Save the image as a layered PSD file.

TIPS

Did You Know?

The Blending Mode menu is arranged in five groups below the Normal group. The groups are roughly based on the function of the Blending Modes in the group. The five modes in the top group darken images when blending. The five in the next group lighten images. The next group of seven adds contrast. This group contains the two Blending Modes most often used by photographers, Overlay and Soft Light. The next group of four is useful for creative effects, and the last group affects color.

Did You Know!

You can cycle through the Blending Modes in the Layers panel with a keyboard shortcut. This eliminates the need to open the Blending Modes menu to visualize the effects. Press V to select the Move tool. Press Shift and the plus key to cycle forward through the modes. Press Shift and the minus key to cycle backward.

Once you are familiar with the selection tools and masking options in Photoshop, you can composite images together easily. As you did in order to blend images in task #50, you open the background image and the image to composite into it. Then, rather than using Blending Modes, you make a selection in the image to composite into the background and create a layer mask.

As with all automatic selections and subsequent masks, you need to adjust the mask to remove any pixels left on the edges from the original image. You also need to soften the edges so that the foreground image does not look pasted onto the background.

Once you have composited the images, you can copy the layer mask to an adjustment layer and adjust the image to blend its tonality better with the Background layer. With a keyboard shortcut, you can toggle the layer mask on and off. Layer masks are powerful tools for image composition and image adjustments.

① With two images open, click Window.

② Click Arrange.

③ Click 2-up Horizontal.

④ Click the Move tool.

⑤ Click the image that composites into the background.

⑥ Press and hold Shift, and click and drag the blending image onto the background image.

Note: Holding Shift centers the image on the background image.

Ⓐ The composing image appears over the background image.

Ⓑ A new layer appears.

⑦ Double-click the name of the new layer, and type **foreground** in the text entry box.

⑧ Press Enter (Return).

⑨ Close the original composing image.

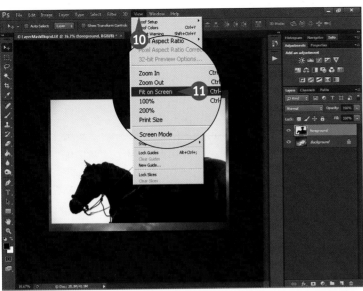

The foreground and background images appear as one layered document.

⑩ Click View.

⑪ Click Fit on Screen.

⑫ Click the foreground layer in the Layers panel.

⑬ Click the Magic Wand tool.

⑭ Click the New Selection button.

⑮ Select 5 by 5 Average from the Sample Size drop-down menu.

⑯ Type **50** in the Tolerance text entry box.

⑰ Select Anti-alias (■ changes to ☑).

⑱ Deselect Contiguous (☑ changes to ■).

⑲ Deselect Sample All Layers (☑ changes to ■).

⑳ Click in the largest area of even tone.

Marching ants appear.

Note: Continue until all of the area that you want to save or remove is selected.

㉑ Click the Add a Mask button if the marching ants surround the area you want to compose into the background.

Note: If the marching ants surround the area you want to delete, press Alt (Option) and click the Layer Mask button.

㉒ Click the Zoom tool.

㉓ Click in the preview to look for halos around your selection.

24 Click the Properties tab.

25 Click Mask Edge.

Ⓐ The Refine Mask floating panel appears. You can click and drag it off of the image.

26 Click the View drop-down menu.

27 Select On Layers in the View drop-down menu.

28 Click in the Refine Mask panel to close the View drop-down menu.

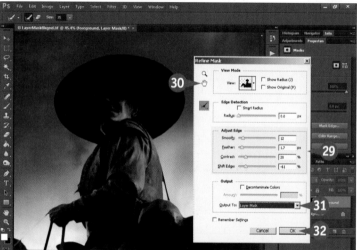

29 Click and drag the sliders in the Adjust Edge subpanel until the halos disappear.

30 Click the Hand tool and pan through the image to ensure that all of the halos are gone.

31 Select Layer Mask in the Output To drop-down menu.

32 Click OK.

33 Click Fit Screen in the Zoom tool Options bar.

34 Click the foreground image Layer thumbnail.

35 Click the Adjustments tab.

36 Click the Curves button to adjust the tonality of the foreground image.

B The Curves Adjustments panel appears.

C A Curves adjustment layer appears in the Layers panel with a Reveal All layer mask.

37 Press Alt (Option) and click and drag the foreground layer mask to the layer mask in the adjustment layer.

The Replace Layer Mask dialog box appears.

38 Click Yes.

The foreground layer mask is copied to the Curves adjustment layer mask.

39 Click the Curves icon in the Curves adjustment layer.

40 Click and drag the curve in the Curve panel until the tonality of the foreground image looks right.

41 Click the Crop tool.

42 Select Delete Cropped Pixels (■ changes to ☑) in the Options bar.

43 Drag the crop handles.

44 Press Enter (Return) to commit the crop.

45 Save the image as a layered PSD file.

TIPS

Did You Know?
If you need to decontaminate colors in the Refine Edge panel, you cannot output the refined mask to the existing layer mask. Photoshop creates a new layer with a new layer mask.

More Options!
You can double-click a layer mask to access the Masks panel of the Properties tab.

Did You Know?
You can drag a layer mask to another layer without leaving it in the original layer. Click the layer mask thumbnail in the Layers panel and drag it to the new layer without holding Alt (Option).

Dodge and burn are traditional photographic techniques used in wet darkrooms to hold back or add exposure to selected areas of photographic paper exposed under an enlarger. Photoshop includes Dodge and Burn tools in the Toolbox. But these tools destructively change pixels. There are two alternative techniques you can use to dodge and burn that work nondestructively.

With both methods, you dodge and burn on a new layer without changing pixels in the original image. When you save the image with layers as a PSD file, the dodge and burn layer is saved. You can open the PSD file later and reedit the dodge and burn layer without changing image information.

One method uses the Overlay blend mode. The other uses the Soft Light blend mode. With either method, you paint at a low opacity with white or black on the new layer to burn or dodge. Use the method that suits you or the image better.

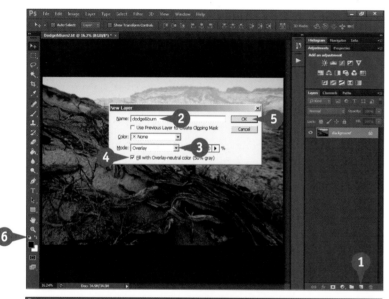

Dodge and Burn with the Overlay Blend Mode

1. With an image open, press Alt (Option) and click the New Layer button.

2. In the New Layer dialog box, type **dodge&burn** in the Name text entry box.

3. Click the Mode drop-down menu and select Overlay from the menu.

4. Select Fill with Overlay-Neutral Color (50% Gray) (☐ changes to ☑).

5. Click OK.

6. Click the Default Colors icon to set the colors to black and white.

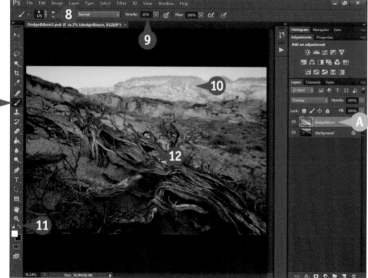

Ⓐ A new layer filled with gray appears in the Layers panel. The preview is unchanged.

7. Click the Brush tool.

8. Click the Brush Preset drop-down menu and select a large brush with 0% Hardness.

9. Set the Opacity to 15%.

10. Click and drag to paint with black in light areas to darken them.

11. Click the Switch Colors icon to swap foreground and background colors.

12. Click and drag to paint with white in dark areas to lighten them.

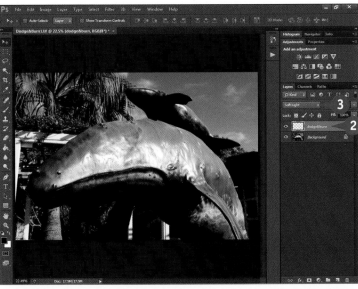

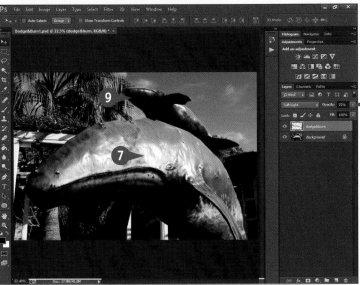

Dodge and Burn with the Soft Light Blend Mode

1. With an image open, click the New Layer button in the Layers panel.

   A new empty layer appears.

2. Double-click the default name and type **dodge&burn** in the text entry box.

3. Select Soft Light from the Blend Mode drop-down menu.

4. Click the Default Colors icon to set the colors to black and white.

5. Repeat steps 7 and 8 in the subsection "Dodge and Burn with the Overlay Blend Mode."

6. Set the Opacity to 15%.

7. Click and drag to paint with black in light areas to darken them.

8. Click the Switch Colors icon to swap foreground and background colors.

9. Click and drag to paint with white in dark areas to lighten them.

TIPS

Try This!

Set your brush at a very low opacity and just larger than the area you are adjusting when dodging and burning. Click and drag quickly multiple times over the area to build up or remove density slowly. Using a large soft brush and low opacity prevents streaks of tonal difference.

Did You Know?

You can press X to toggle the foreground and background colors.

Try This!

Paint the dodge and burn corrections on separate layers for more control. You can do this with either method. You can adjust the opacity of each layer to fine-tune the dodge correction separately from the burn correction.

Photoshop contains a number of prebuilt nondestructive effects that can be applied to many types of layers. These effects are called *layer styles*. One of the most often used layer styles is the drop shadow. You can apply a drop shadow to a type layer. And if you add another type layer later, you do not need to remember the settings of the original type layer or even open the Layer Style dialog box. To apply the same layer style to other layers, you can simply drag and drop it. The layers can be type layers or any other layer that can be modified with a layer style.

You apply type with the Type tool. While Photoshop is not a page layout program, the type options are extensive. Adding type to photographs is valuable when creating title slides for multimedia shows, web pages, and print projects. Applying a consistent drop shadow to the type ensures a professional look.

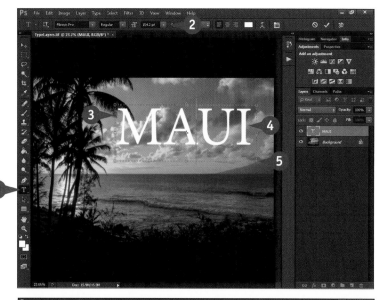

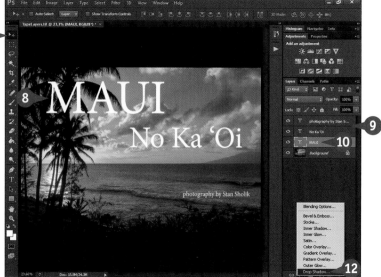

① With an image open, click the Type tool.

② Select the font family, style, size, and color from the Options bar.

③ Click and drag a text box in the image.

④ Type in the text block.

⑤ Press and hold Ctrl (⌘) and drag a transformation handle to enlarge the text. After you begin dragging, press and hold Shift.

   Note: *Before you press Shift, the type distorts. Shift constrains it to its proper proportions.*

⑥ Press Ctrl+Enter (⌘+Return) when the type looks right.

⑦ Click the Move tool.

⑧ Click and drag the type to a new position.

⑨ Repeat steps 1 to 8 with additional type layers.

⑩ Click the layer containing the largest size type.

⑪ Click the Effects button (*fx*) at the bottom of the Layers panel.

⑫ Select Drop Shadow from the pop-up list.

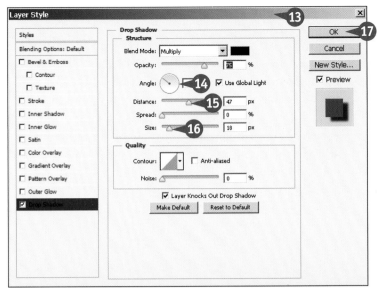

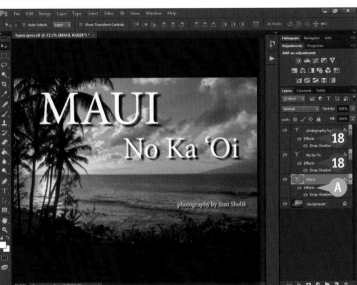

The Layer Style dialog box appears with Drop Shadow selected.

⑬ Click and drag the Layer Style dialog box so you can see the type in the type layer you selected.

⑭ Rotate the Angle of Light Source to select the direction the light is coming from.

⑮ Click and drag the Distance slider to set the shadow offset.

⑯ Click and drag the Size slider to soften the shadow.

⑰ Click OK.

Ⓐ The drop shadow appears with the text layer you selected in step 10.

⑱ Press and hold Alt (Option), and click and drag the word Effects to the other text layers.

The drop shadow appears with each text layer.

⑲ Save the file as a layered PSD.

TIPS

Try This!

You can create a drop shadow without using the sliders in the Layer Style dialog box. Click a type layer to make it active. Click the Effects button (𝑓𝑥) and open the Drop Shadow effect in the Layer Style dialog box. Click and drag the Layer Style dialog box so you can see the type. Click in the preview and drag a shadow the direction and distance that looks right and release the mouse. Click and drag the Size slider to soften the shadow.

Did You Know?

You can make any effect your default. As your default, the settings are always available when you select the effect. Click Make Default in the Layer Style dialog box for the effect.

Try This!

You can add multiple effects to a layer. After you create a drop shadow effect, add a stroke outline to type that is difficult to read where it blends into the photo below. Click the Stroke effect and set the options.

Chapter 6

Modify Photos with Transform, Straighten, Crop, and Resize

Modifying your images to fit your project is an essential part of the photographic and design process. You may need to use a still photo as part of an HD video project, or transform a vertical image into a square as part of a collage, or even into a landscape for a multimedia presentation. And to preserve the quality of the original image, you want to destroy as few pixels as possible when you perform these modifications.

Very often you need to crop and resize your images. But when you crop an image for one project, you may still want the uncropped version for another. You can do this using the Crop tool without saving a copy of the original file.

There are also times when a small modification makes a big difference. Straightening a curved or tilted horizon, or correcting the extreme perspective caused by using a wide-angle lens, can improve an image dramatically.

And you can creatively use the same tools that perform these modifications to modify your images or create new ones. You can incorporate an illustration or another photo into an image and distort it to the shape of the underlying image.

Photoshop provides the tools you need to perform these tasks. Many of them require destructive changes to image information, so performing them properly, or on a Smart Object, is essential to maintaining image quality.

DIFFICULTY LEVEL

Often you find that the proportion of one image does not match the proportion of your project. You may want to change the aspect ratio of a digital capture to fit an 8 × 10 print without cropping and sizing it. Or you may need to incorporate a still image into a high-definition video where the proportions are very different from a digital SLR camera image. If you simply scale the image to fit the new proportions, all of the content in the image, including the subject, also scales. This results in the subject becoming proportionally distorted. You can modify the proportions

of your image without distorting the proportions of the subject by using Content-Aware Scale.

Content-Aware Scale changes the proportion of your image without distorting the subject. It accomplishes this by compressing or expanding areas in the image where there is no important subject information. In many instances, Content-Aware Scale automatically senses the subject and performs the scaling. With other subjects, you must select the subject first to protect it before scaling.

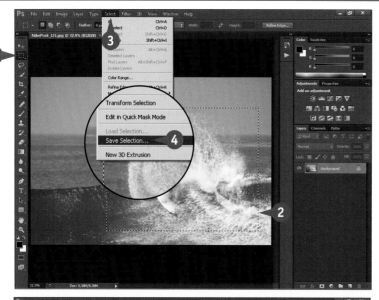

1. With an image open, click the Rectangular Marquee tool.

2. Click and draw a selection around the area in the image you want to preserve.

3. Click Select.

4. Click Save Selection.

   The Save Selection dialog box appears.

5. Click OK.

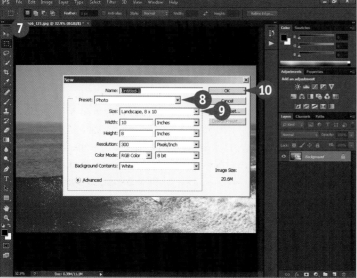

6. Press Ctrl+D (⌘+D) to deselect the rectangular marquee marching ants.

7. Click File ➪ New.

   The New dialog box opens.

8. Select Photo from the Preset drop-down menu.

9. Select Landscape, 8 x 10 from the Size drop-down menu.

10. Click OK.

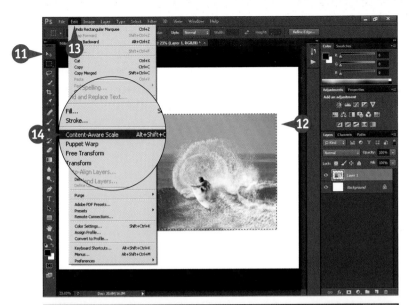

11 Click the Move tool.

12 Click and drag your original image onto the new image tab and then drag to the blank document before releasing the mouse.

The original image opens in the blank document.

13 Click Edit.

14 Click Content-Aware Scale.

Transform handles appear around the original image.

15 Select Alpha 1 from the Protect drop-down menu in the Options bar.

Note: This loads a mask protecting your subject selection.

16 Click and drag the transform handles to fill the background.

17 Click the Commit Transform button to save the result.

18 Close the original image.

19 Save the new image as a layered PSD file.

Did You Know?

You have the best result using Content-Aware Scale for extending or compressing the background when there is a lot of low-detail information surrounding the subject. Fine details can look blocky when they are scaled.

Try This!

Click Protect Skin Tones (🧍) in the Content-Aware Scale Options bar when there are people in the photo. Photoshop identifies the location of the people and automatically protects them from scaling without your having to select them. Often this works even if the face of the subject is not seen.

Did You Know?

You do not need a very precise selection when using Content-Aware Scale. Often the Rectangular Marquee or Lasso tools work fine. The Quick Selection tool is also an excellent choice for a more precise selection.

You can combine illustrations with images to create new images, including realistic-looking images that exist only virtually on your computer. The advantage of using illustrations is that they are *vector* based, that is, they exist only mathematically, without any underlying pixel information. Only when you display them on your screen do they take on their virtual form. Because they only exist mathematically, they can be twisted, bent, extruded, and scaled repeatedly without harming any pixel information. You are only manipulating the math.

Vector objects are ideal candidates for Smart Objects (see task #48). You place them in Photoshop as a Smart Object layer and you can continually modify them nondestructively. However, in order to use all of the transformation tools, you must save the Smart Object within a Smart Object, placing one Smart Object inside another.

When you finish transforming, you can blend the layer in complex ways with the underlying layer so that it looks less like a drawing pasted on a photo, and more like the photo of a subject that incorporates an illustration.

① With an image open, click File.

② Click Place.

③ Navigate to the vector-based illustration and click Place.

Ⓐ The file opens as a Smart Object on a new layer with transform handles.

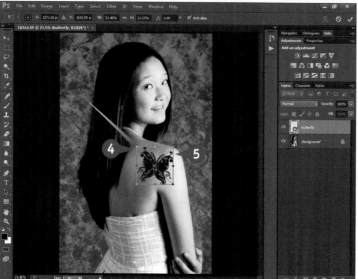

④ Press Shift, click and drag one of the corner transform handles to roughly scale the vector file, and then release the mouse.

⑤ Click and drag the scaled file to the approximate position you want it.

⑥ Press Enter (Return).

Note: *Because the vector file is a Smart Object, you can save each transformation without harming the object, and return to it later.*

⑦ Click the Zoom tool and zoom in to the vector file.

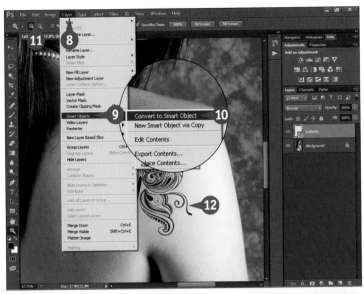

The image zooms in.

8 Click Layer.

9 Click Smart Objects.

10 Click Convert to Smart Object.

Note: You can now use all of the transform tools.

11 Click Edit ⇨ Free Transform.

12 Click and drag the vector file to its final position, press Shift and drag a corner handle to scale it, and click and drag the double-headed arrow outside a corner to rotate it.

13 Click the Warp button.

14 Click the Warp drop-down menu in the Options bar.

15 Click Custom from the drop-down menu.

Note: Click each of the options in the drop-down menu to see if one gives a good starting point.

The overlay changes to a grid.

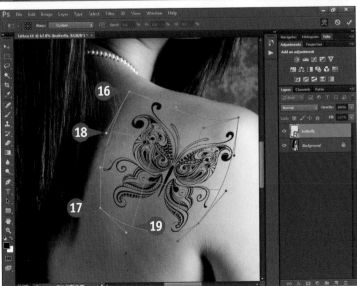

16 Click and drag a corner handle.

Control handles appear at the end of lever arms.

17 Click and drag the corner handles to warp the vector file to the background image.

18 Click and drag the corner lever handles to shape the corners.

19 Click and drag the points where the horizontal and vertical lines meet on the sides to warp the vector file better to the background image.

Note: Press Enter (Return) to see your progress without the overlay.

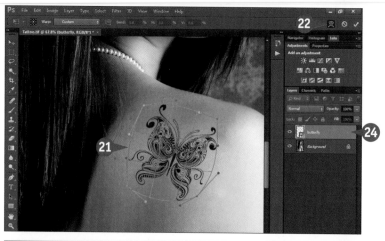

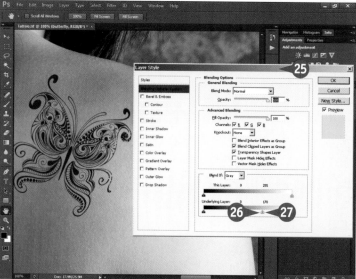

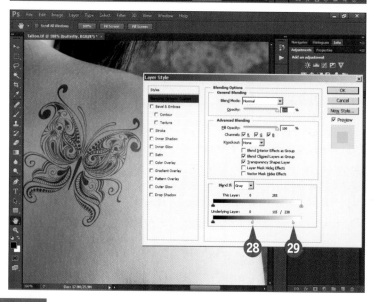

20 Press Ctrl+T (⌘+T) to return to the Free Transform tool.

21 Repeat step 12 to make further changes to the size and rotation angle of the vector file.

22 Click the Warp tool to make additional changes to the shape of the vector file.

23 Press Enter (Return) when the transformation looks correct.

24 Double-click in the gray area of the vector mask layer of the Layers panel.

The Layer Style dialog box appears.

25 Click and drag the Layer Style dialog box to see the vector file and the background image.

26 Click and drag the triangle below the right edge of the Underlying Layer slider to the left to reveal some of the upper tones of the skin through the vector layer.

27 Alt (Option)+click the triangle to split it in two.

28 Drag the left half of the triangle to the left to reveal some skin texture in the darker tones.

29 Drag the right half of the triangle to the right to restore more of the tattoo.

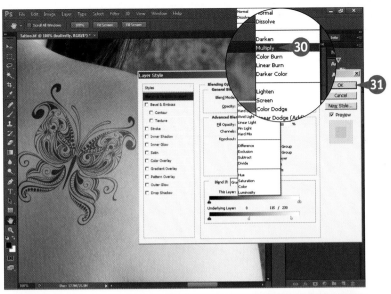

30 Click the Blend Mode drop-down menu and select Multiply from the menu.

31 Click OK.

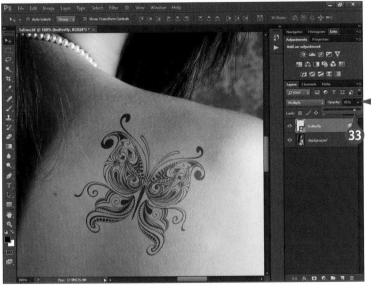

32 Click the Opacity drop-down menu for the tattoo layer.

33 Click and drag the slider until the blending looks correct.

34 Save the file as a layered PSD file.

TIPS

More Options!

You can transform the image when you are using the Warp tool by clicking and dragging the image itself rather than clicking and dragging the transform handles. The handles allow somewhat finer control.

Did You Know?

You can return to the tattoo Smart Object at any time and edit the transformations and the blending. If you created the artwork or have software that can edit it, you can edit the contents of a Smart Object layer by clicking Layer ⇨ Smart Objects ⇨ Edit Contents. Click OK in the warning dialog box that appears. Edit the original file and press Ctrl+S (⌘+S). The Smart Object updates.

Important!

If you click Layer ⇨ Flatten Image, the image flattens to a background layer without a warning box. The Smart Object vector layer becomes rasterized and is no longer editable.

When you find a tilted horizon in one of your images, you can level it in Photoshop using two different methods. But you still need to know where Photoshop has hidden the tools.

Both methods use tools that you can access through the Crop tool in the Toolbox. One method uses the Crop tool itself. You rotate the image to align it with the grid overlay that appears automatically. The other method uses the Straighten tool in the Options bar of the Crop tool. After clicking it, you click and drag in the image, and Photoshop straightens the horizon.

The cost of either method over getting it right in the camera is the need to crop the portion of the image that is rotated.

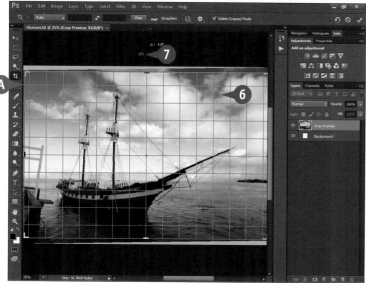

Level the Horizon Using the Crop Tool

1 With an image open, click the Crop tool.

2 Select Delete Cropped Pixels in the Options bar (☐ changes to ☑).

3 Press and hold Ctrl+spacebar (⌘+spacebar) to activate the Zoom tool.

4 Click in the preview to enlarge the horizon.

Note: Leave some of the border around the preview visible.

5 Move the cursor outside the image into the surrounding border.

The cursor changes to a double-headed arrow.

6 Press and hold the mouse button.

A A grid overlay appears on the preview.

7 Drag to the left to rotate the image counterclockwise or drag to the right to rotate the image clockwise until the horizon aligns with the grid.

Photoshop straightens the horizon and indicates the needed crop.

8 Press Enter (Return) to commit the crop.

Level the Horizon Using the Straighten Tool

#56

DIFFICULTY LEVEL

● ◖ ◖ ◖

① With an image open, click the Crop tool.

② Select Delete Cropped Pixels in the Options bar (☐ changes to ☑).

③ Press and hold Ctrl+spacebar (⌘+spacebar) to activate the Zoom tool.

④ Click in the preview to enlarge the horizon.

⑤ Click the Straighten button in the Options bar.

⑥ Click the horizon at one end of the preview and drag a line to the horizon on the other end before releasing the mouse button.

Photoshop straightens the horizon and indicates the needed crop.

⑦ Press Enter (Return) to commit the crop.

TIPS

Did You Know?
You can use the Straighten tool to correct a vertical line such as a telephone pole. Click the Straighten tool. Click a point on the edge of the pole, and drag a line down the side. Photoshop corrects the pole to vertical and indicates the crop that is needed.

Did You Know?
You can see the number of degrees of rotation that are needed to correct the horizon tilt. Both methods display the rotation angle as you work.

More Options!
You do not need to delete the pixels that are outside the crop when the horizon is straightened. Deselect Delete Cropped Pixels (☑ changes to ☐) in the Options bar. When you open the image later and click the Crop tool (🔲), the pixels outside your crop reappear under a gray mask.

After you spend your time optimizing an image, you may want to make a large print for display. You know that you need a larger size than your original capture permits, and you want to preserve as much of the original image detail as possible. You can do this using the Image Size command.

Photoshop offers a number of resizing options in the form of *scaling algorithms* to resample your image. These algorithms add new pixels or subtract pixels when you resample to a smaller size, and smooth the transitions between pixels. But before you resample, it is important to set your final resolution. This is the step that preserves the maximum amount of detail.

Photoshop engineers continually adjust the scaling algorithms with little fanfare. Photoshop CC offers a new, resizable Image Size dialog box with preview, and a new Preserve Details algorithm for enlargement. You can make test prints using each of the algorithms and decide for yourself which produces the best result on your equipment.

1 With your final saved and adjusted PSD image open, click Image.

2 Click Image Size.

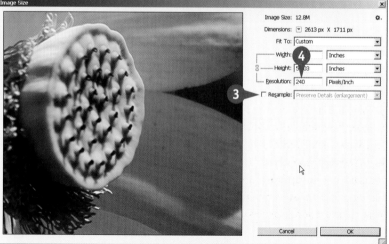

The Image Size dialog box appears.

3 Deselect Resample (☑ changes to ☐).

4 Type the image resolution you need in the Resolution text entry box.

*Note: For commercial printing, type **300**; for Epson printers, type **240** or **360**; for Canon printers, type **300**; for your photo lab, do what it recommends.*

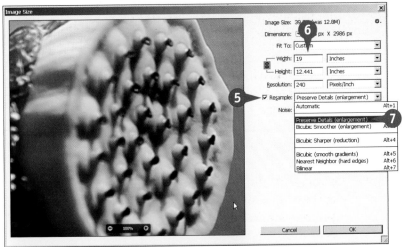

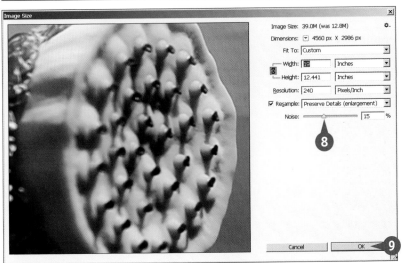

⑤ Select Resample (☐ changes to ☑).

⑥ Type the image width or height in the appropriate text entry box.

Note: Leave the lock between the Width and Height text entry box locked to preserve image proportions.

⑦ Select Preserve Details (enlargement) from the Resample drop-down menu.

⑧ Click and drag the Noise slider as you watch the 100% preview. Low settings improve sharpness slightly with some images.

⑨ Click OK.

Your image resizes ready for printing.

⑩ Flatten and save the resampled image as a new image with the image size as part of the name.

TIPS

Did You Know?

You can drag the corner of the new Image Size dialog box to enlarge the preview. You can move your cursor into the preview window of the dialog box and view the image from 800% to the full image.

More Options!

You can save an Image Size preset that you use repeatedly for resizing. Select your options in the Image Size dialog box and click the Fit To drop-down menu. Select Save Preset and give it a descriptive name in the dialog box that opens. Select Load Preset from the Fit To drop-down menu the next time you need it, or incorporate it as part of an Action. Creating an Action is described in task #7.

Did You Know?

You can open the Image Size dialog box with a keyboard command. Press Alt+Ctrl+I (Option+⌘+I).

For some images, such as when you are leveling the horizon in task #56, there is little need to save the uncropped area. But for other images, you can crop nondestructively, saving the uncropped area. This allows you to crop the image for the size you need for a specific project, but still have the original uncropped version available for a different crop in a different project, all without making an additional copy of the image.

In Photoshop CC, there are additional prebuilt crop options, including popular print and video ratios,

additional width by height by resolution presets, and the ability to save a custom crop preset. The width, height, and resolution text entry boxes are still available but have been incorporated into the Options bar rather than a floating panel.

It is easy to switch a horizontal to a vertical crop by clicking the opposing arrows icon in the Options bar. But most valuable of all is the ability to crop your image without cropping the original.

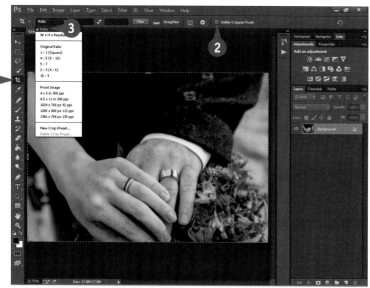

Crop the Image with an Unconstrained Crop

1 With an image open, click the Crop tool.

Crop handles appear in the corners and sides of the image.

2 Deselect Delete Cropped Pixels (☑ changes to ☐).

3 Select Ratio from the Crop Presets drop-down menu.

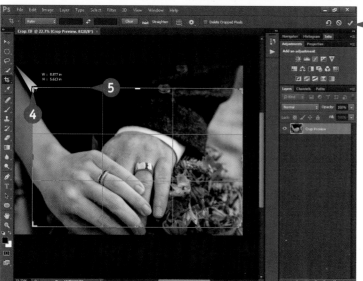

4 Click and drag the crop handles to crop the image with an unconstrained crop.

A Rule of Thirds overlay appears on the image, along with the print dimensions of the image at the existing resolution.

5 Click and drag the image to position it in the crop.

6 Click the Commit Crop button.

Crop the Image with a Prebuilt Crop

1 Repeat steps 1 and 2 in the subsection "Crop the Image with an Unconstrained Crop."

2 Select a prebuilt crop from the Crop Presets drop-down menu.

3 Click the Swap Height and Width button if needed.

4 Repeat steps 4 to 6 in the subsection "Crop the Image with an Unconstrained Crop."

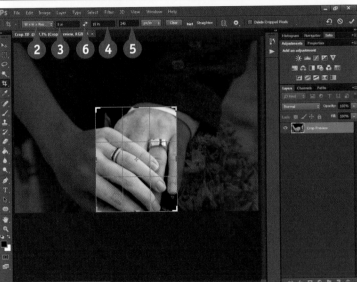

Crop the Image with Custom Height, Width, and Resolution Settings

1 Repeat steps 1 and 2 in the subsection "Crop the Image with an Unconstrained Crop."

2 Select W x H x Resolution from the Crop Presets drop-down menu.

3 Type **8** in the Width number entry box.

4 Type **10** in the Height number entry box.

5 Type **240** in the Resolution number entry box.

6 Click the Swap Height and Width button if needed.

7 Repeat steps 4 to 6 in the subsection "Crop the Image with an Unconstrained Crop."

TIPS

Did You Know?

You can save your custom width by height by resolution crop. Click the Crop Presets drop-down menu. Click New Crop Preset. Accept the descriptive name that Photoshop suggests or type your own. The new preset appears in the Crop Presets drop-down menu.

More Options!

You can set the Crop options so that you drag the crop frame rather than the image to position the crop. Click the gear button (⚙) in the Options bar. Select Use Classic Mode (▣ changes to ☑). Optionally, press P.

More Options!

You can select a custom color and opacity for the mask outside of the crop area. Click the gear button (⚙) in the Options bar. The Crop options menu appears. Enable Crop Shield is selected by default. Click the Color drop-down menu and select Custom. The Color Picker dialog box appears. Select a color. Click OK. Click Opacity. Click and drag the slider to a new position. Click the gear button (⚙) to close the options menu.

Correcting lens aberrations in Camera Raw using the techniques of task #23 removes problems inherent in the design and production of lenses that have been profiled, such as chromatic aberration and vignetting. It does not remove barrel or pincushion distortion. These distortions cause the lines at the edges of images captured with wide-angle and fisheye lenses to curve inward or outward. You can correct this curvature with the Adaptive Wide Angle filter.

The filter reads the metadata embedded in the capture file and determines the camera model, the lens make and model, and the focal length used if it is a zoom lens. It makes an initial automatic correction if this information is available.

You can then select the type of correction to apply from the Correction drop-down menu. You use the Constraint tool to draw along edges you want to straighten. The lines you draw curve to match the perspective distortion. When you release the mouse, Photoshop straightens the line.

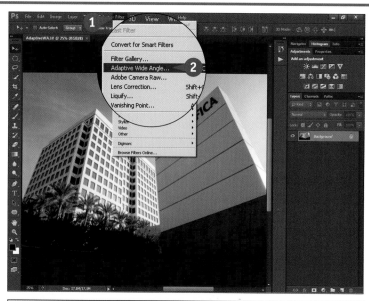

① With a photo taken with a wide-angle lens open, click Filter.

② Click Adaptive Wide Angle.

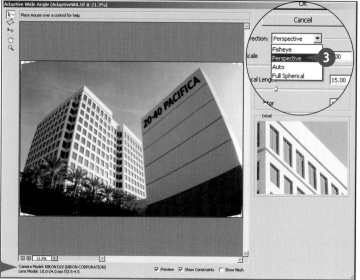

The Adaptive Wide Angle dialog box appears.

Ⓐ If Adaptive Wide Angle recognizes your lens it applies an automatic correction and notes the lens make below the preview.

③ Click the Correction drop-down menu and click Perspective.

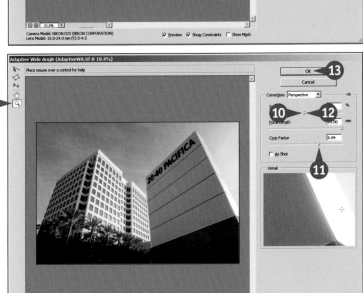

4 Click and drag the Scale slider until you can see the edges of the image.

5 Click the Constrain tool.

6 Click and drag along a line in the subject close to the edge of the image.

The line straightens and the image adjusts.

7 Repeat step 6 with other horizontal and vertical lines.

The image adjusts with each constraint line.

8 Click the Zoom tool.

9 Click and drag a zoom box outside the preview window.

The preview zooms to nearly fill the window.

10 Click and drag the Scale slider to the left to view the entire image.

11 Click and drag the Crop Factor slider until the image is rectangular.

12 Click and drag the Scale slider until you cannot see the checkerboard background.

13 Click OK.

Photoshop applies the Adaptive Wide Angle correction and the image opens on a layer.

TIPS

Try This!
Rather than remove the checkerboard background using the Adaptive Wide Angle filter, click OK without using the Scale and Crop Factor sliders. Crop the image in Photoshop, or use Content-Aware Fill to add information into those areas.

Did You Know?
You can delete a constraint line. Click one of the endpoints and press Backspace (Delete).

Try This!
Each constraint line has a circle as well as endpoints associated with it. The circle is an angle constraint. It has two anchor points. Click and drag an anchor point to adjust the angle of the line.

DIETING with Liquify

You can slim a full-length photo of your subject using the Liquify filter in ways similar to those you used to slim a portrait subject in task #33.

The Liquify tool includes the Forward Warp tool, the Reconstruct tool, the Pucker and Bloat tools, and the Push Left tool in the Basic mode. The Advanced mode includes a Twirl tool, Masking tools, and additional tool options.

The Liquify tool is a brush with a cross hair in the center. If you do not see a cross hair, press Shift. The Liquify brush is at full strength at the edge of the cross hair and at zero strength at the outer circle. Use the Reconstruct tool to remove the effect of other tools. The Pucker tool pushes the area under the brush in and the Bloat tool pulls it out. The Push Left tool at low brush pressure acts like the Warp tool, but along a line. Using these tools you can save your subject years of dieting and gym visits.

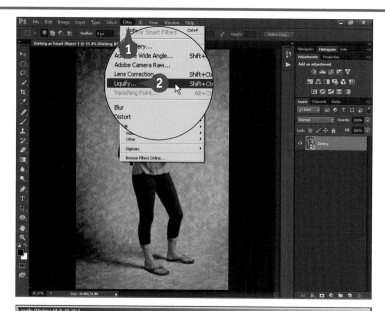

1. With a full-length portrait open as a Smart Object, click Filter.

2. Click Liquify.

The Liquify dialog box opens.

3. Select Advanced Mode (☐ changes to ☑).

4. Click the Zoom tool.

5. Click and drag in the preview to enlarge the area to work on.

6. Click the Warp tool.

7. Press the right bracket key to create a larger brush.

8. Click and push toward the subject to slim an area.

   Note: The Liquify brush is the cross hair in the center. The effect of the brush diminishes from the cross hair to the outer circle, where it is zero.

9. Repeat steps 7 and 8 where needed on the right leg of the subject.

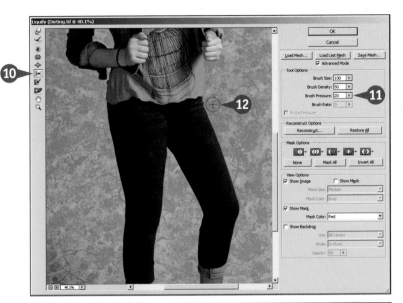

#60

DIFFICULTY LEVEL

⑩ Click the Push Left tool.

⑪ Type **20** into the Brush Pressure text entry box.

⑫ Using a much smaller brush, click just outside the left knee of the subject, press Shift, and click outside the left hip.

The outer edge of the pant leg moves to the left.

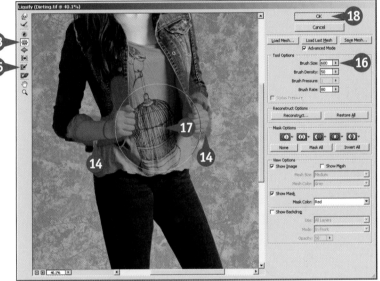

⑬ Click the Free Mask tool.

⑭ Paint a mask over the subject's hands, arms and jacket to protect those areas.

The masked areas appear with a red overlay.

⑮ Click the Pucker tool.

⑯ Click and drag the Brush Size slider to create a large enough brush to cover the area to adjust.

⑰ Click and hold the mouse button until the area looks correct.

The area shrinks inward toward the center.

Note: The longer you hold the mouse button, the greater the effect.

⑱ Click OK.

Photoshop applies the Liquify filter to the Smart Object layer.

TIPS

Important!

The task of slimming a full-length photo can be considerably more difficult than slimming a portrait. Unless the photo is shot against a white or evenly toned seamless background, you must be careful not to cause strange distortions in the background. Also, you must be aware of fabric patterns in clothing so as not to distort them so much they become misaligned or smeared.

Remove It!

You can remove your adjustments several ways. Paint over an area that you have warped with the Reconstruct tool ( ) until it is returned to the original form. Click the Reconstruct button to fade the reconstructions. Click the Restore All button to restore the image to its original form before you began using the Liquify tools.

More Options!

You can use the Push Left tool ( ) to push pixels to the right. Shift+click when you drag a line down to push pixels right in a straight line. To push pixels left, but not in a straight line as you drag up, press Alt (Option) as you drag. To push pixels right, but not in a straight line as you drag down, press Alt (Option) as you drag.

Puppet Warp is a powerful transform tool. You can use it to reposition arms, legs, and hair; make a smile larger, reposition flowers on a stem, and totally distort any part of an image while protecting other parts. You can also use Puppet Warp to slightly tilt the head of a subject to create a more dynamic portrait.

Puppet Warp places a mesh over the subject. You place anchor pins around the area that you want to move to anchor those places. Then you place a pin and drag it to perform the transformation. There are controls to hide the

mesh, showing only the adjustment pins. This gives a clearer view of the adjustment. You can also increase the number of intersections in the mesh and expand or contrast it from the image or mask border.

Puppet Warp is best applied to a Smart Object so that the transformation you apply is nondestructive. When you use Puppet Warp, you invariably leave holes at some point in the background you need to fill before you save the new image.

1 With an image open as a Smart Object, click Edit.

2 Click Puppet Warp.

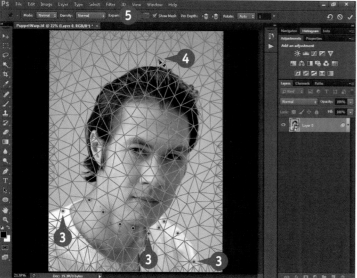

The Puppet Warp mesh appears over the image.

3 Click to add anchor pins to protect an area of the image.

Anchor pins in this image protect the neck, shirt, and below.

4 Click to add a pin outside the hair.

5 Deselect Show Mesh (☑ changes to ■).

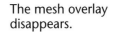

The mesh overlay disappears.

6 Click the pin outside the hair and drag left to straighten the head, or right to give the head more tilt.

Checkerboards appear where there is no longer background.

7 Click the Commit Puppet Warp button.

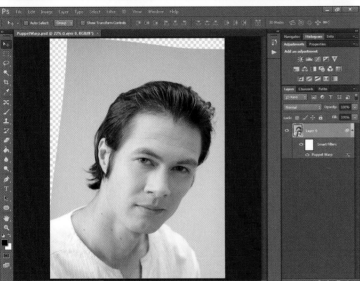

Photoshop performs the transformation.

8 Save the image as a PSD file.

Note: This saves the transformation as a Smart Object so you can return and edit it later.

TIPS

Try This!
You can fill the checkerboard areas and save the portrait as a TIFF or JPEG. With the PSD file open, click Layer. Click Flatten Image. Photoshop makes the transformation permanent. The checkerboard areas fill with white. Click the Magic Wand (). Click in the white areas. Marching ants appear. Click Edit ➪ Fill. Click OK. The white areas fill with background. Press Ctrl+D (⌘+D) to deselect the marching ants. Click File ➪ Save As. Save the new image as a TIFF or JPEG.

Did You Know?
You can increase the number of mesh points in the Puppet Warp tool. Click the Density drop-down menu in the Options bar and select More Points. More points increase precision, but require additional processing time.

Transformation tools have many uses in correcting and adjusting images. But you can use them to create images that never existed in reality. You can merge an illustration into a photo, or merge two unrelated photos together. The transform tools are ideal for this. Used in combination, you can scale, rotate, skew, distort, adjust perspective, and warp one image into another. With other tools in Photoshop, you can clean up the edges of the merged

photos and adjust them to look like the final photo actually did exist.

Each transform is destructive, so when merging two images it is best to merge them as Smart Objects. And when making transformations you can make them successively before finalizing the image. Scale, rotate, adjust perspective, skew, and readjust until the image is transformed correctly before committing the transformation. This ensures the highest image quality and the most believable result.

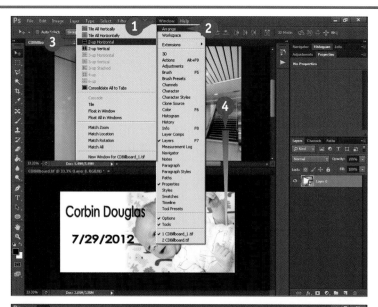

① With the two images to merge open as Smart Objects, click Window.

② Click Arrange.

③ Click 2-up Horizontal.

The image windows rearrange.

④ Click and drag the foreground image into the background image.

The foreground image appears as a new layer.

⑤ Close the original foreground image.

⑥ Click Edit.

⑦ Click Free Transform.

Transform handles appear on the foreground image.

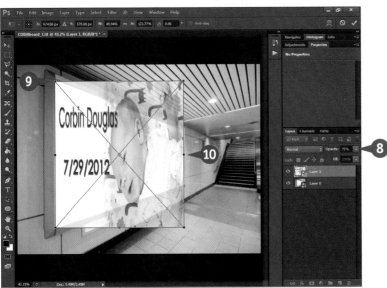

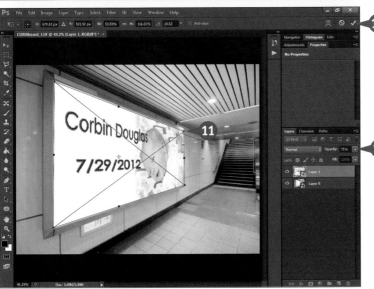

#62

DIFFICULTY LEVEL

8 Adjust the Opacity slider to 75% to see the background image more easily.

9 Click and drag the height at one end to the height needed.

10 Click and drag the width at the other end to the width needed.

The foreground image is the correct height at one end and the correct width at the other.

11 Press Shift+Ctrl (Shift+⌘) and drag corner handles to skew the image to fit.

12 Click the Commit Transform button to accept the transformation.

13 Adjust the Opacity slider to make the final image look like a backlit sign.

14 Save the image as a layered PSD file.

TIPS

Did You Know?

You can use keyboard shortcuts in Free Transform so that you never need to click the Edit menu to change transforms. To distort free, press Ctrl (⌘) and drag a transform handle. To skew, press Shift+Ctrl (Shift+⌘) and drag a transform handle. To apply perspective, press Ctrl+Alt+Shift (⌘+Option+Shift) and drag a corner handle. To undo the last handle adjustment, click Edit ➪ Undo.

Did You Know?

When you drag one image onto another and select Free Transform, you may not be able to see the transform handles if the foreground image is larger than the background image. You can force the images to resize by pressing Ctrl+0 (⌘+0). Note that this shortcut is a zero, not an O.

Create Stunning Black-and-White Photos

Many photographers work only in color. After all, we see in color, cameras capture in color by default, and Photoshop and other imaging software provide a wide range of tools for working in color. But there is a growing interest in black-and-white photography. The latest inkjet printers are capable of creating incredibly rich black-and-white prints, more accurately called grayscale or monochrome prints. To take full advantage of these printers, you must first create a stunning black-and-white photo with your computer.

Photoshop includes a full set of tools you can use to convert your color images to black and white. You can leave a bit of color in them for an interesting effect, or convert them fully to monochrome or more complex *quadtone* images. You can also create a simulated infrared look, which is as close as you can come to this beautiful classic technique without access to a wet darkroom. You can also simulate other classic looks such as sepia toning, split toning, and colorizing.

Whenever you make the conversion to black and white, you must be careful not to discard the color information in the original file or it is lost forever. By applying the conversion and adjustments on a separate layer, a duplicate layer, or on a Smart Object layer, you can preserve the underlying color information while making nondestructive changes to the image.

DIFFICULTY LEVEL

The first and most important step in working with a black-and-white image is converting your color image to monochrome. You can convert your color image to black and white in a number of ways in Photoshop. One of the easiest and most visual techniques is using a black-and-white adjustment layer.

Clicking the Black & White button in the Adjustments panel opens the Black & White Adjustments panel. The Black & White panel includes sliders for reds, greens, and blues, plus sliders for yellows, cyans, and magentas. You can click and drag these sliders to increase or decrease the intensity of each color. But a better technique is to use the Targeted Adjustment tool in the Properties panel to drag in the image to adjust the amount of a targeted color. You can even begin with a preset adjustment before you start making further changes.

Open the histogram before you make custom adjustments and click the warning triangle to periodically update the histogram. Be careful not to clip highlights or shadows by dragging a color too much. And if you become lost, there is a Reset button you can click to start over. Finish your conversion with a contrast adjustment using a Curves adjustment layer.

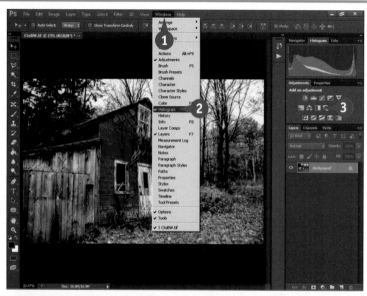

1. With an image open, click Window.

2. Click Histogram.

   The Histogram panel opens. You can drag it to the right panel.

3. Click the Black & White button in the Adjustments panel.

   The Black & White Adjustments panel appears. The image changes to a default grayscale conversion.

4. Click the Preset drop-down menu.

5. Click a preset appropriate to the image if it looks closer to the result you want than the default.

6. Click the warning triangle in the histogram to update the curve.

The image updates using the preset conversion.

7 Click the Targeted Adjustment tool in the Properties panel.

8 Click and drag the Targeted Adjustment tool in the image to the right to lighten the tone under the tool.

9 Click and drag the Targeted Adjustment tool in the image to the left to darken the tone under the tool.

10 Click the warning triangle in the histogram to update the curve.

11 Adjust the sliders if the histogram extends into the highlights.

12 Repeat steps 8 to 11 until the image looks correct.

13 Click the Adjustments tab and then click the Curves tool (⬚).

14 Click and drag an S curve to add contrast.

15 Save the image as a layered PSD file.

TIPS

Remove It!

You can reset the black-and-white adjustments in the Black & White Adjustments panel. Click the Reset button (⬚). The sliders return to zero and the Preset adjustment returns to Default.

Did You Know?

You can see the areas where tones are clipping in the Curves panel. Press Alt (Option) and click the white triangle (⬚) at the bottom right of the histogram to see clipped highlights. Press Alt (Option) and click the black triangle (⬚) at the bottom left of the histogram to see clipped shadows.

Important!

Converting a color image to grayscale with this method is not the same as changing the mode to grayscale by clicking Image ➪ Mode ➪ Grayscale, which has the effect of reducing saturation to zero and discarding color information. When you use an adjustment layer, you selectively map colors to gray values. And because you do this on an adjustment layer, the original color information is not destroyed.

ADD A SPOT OF COLOR to a black-and-white photo with a layer mask

You can add a spot of color from the original color image to a black-and-white conversion of the image using a layer mask. This is an effective technique to draw the viewer's eyes to what you want him to concentrate on in the image.

You can do this by combining the use of tools and techniques covered in previous chapters. Make a selection of the areas you want to remain in color in a copy of your original image and then invert the selection to protect those areas. Make a layer mask (task #44) to protect those

areas. Use the technique in task #63 to convert the image to black and white and then drag the mask from the Background copy layer to the grayscale layer to complete the task. You may need to soften the edges a bit on this final mask for a smooth blending of the effect.

Doing this on layers gives you control of the effect if you decide to adjust the grayscale image later. You also have control over the masked areas so that you can add or delete areas later.

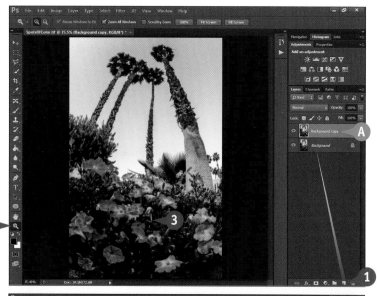

① With your image open, click and drag the Background layer to the New Layer icon.

Ⓐ Photoshop creates a Background copy layer.

② Click the Zoom tool.

③ Click and drag in the preview to zoom in to the area to select.

The preview zooms in.

④ Click the Quick Selection tool.

⑤ Select the areas you want to remain in color.

Marching ants appear around the selected areas.

⑥ Press Ctrl+Shift+I (⌘+Shift+I) to invert the selection.

⑦ Click the Layer Mask button.

B A layer mask appears in the Background copy layer in the Layers panel.

8 Repeat the steps in task #63 to convert the Background copy layer to black and white and adjust the contrast.

C Black & White and Curves layers are created.

9 Press Alt (Option) and click and drag the Background copy layer mask onto the Black & White layer mask.

10 Click Yes in the dialog box to replace the Black & White layer mask with the Background copy layer mask.

D The areas of color are revealed.

11 Feather the Black & White layer mask.

12 Refine the edge as needed.

13 Save the image as a layered PSD file.

More Options!

You can also press Alt (Option) and drag the Background copy layer mask onto the Curves layer mask. This removes the Curves adjustment from the areas of color. Try it to see if you like the look of the color areas with less contrast. If not, press Ctrl+Z (⌘+Z) to undo the layer mask change.

Try This!

Create an image with the opposite effect. You can create a color image with areas of black and white. You can apply special effects to these areas, colorize them, or tone them in various ways using techniques in the tasks that follow in this chapter. Proceed as in this task, but do not invert the selection in step 6. The black-and-white conversion and curves adjustments affect the areas you select, not the inverse.

Simulate an INFRARED LOOK

Monochrome infrared film produces grainy, high-contrast images, often with a soft glow surrounding the highlights. Because the film is primarily sensitive to infrared radiation, and you must use a filter on your lens to block other wavelengths of light, photographers use infrared film to create abstract high-contrast images with dark skies and glowing, grainy highlights unlike any seen by the unaided eye. You can simulate this effect in Photoshop.

In order to have maximum control over the infrared conversion, you do the conversion on an adjustment layer.

To create the glow and graininess, you must use a filter from the Filter Gallery. The filter is destructive unless you use it as a Smart Filter; that is, a filter used on a Smart Object. But you cannot make the pixel-level adjustment needed by the infrared conversion to a Smart Object. The process then involves two operations: one to apply the infrared conversion, and the other to supply the glow and graininess. Together, the final result simulates the look of infrared film, but only to those who have never shot with, processed, and printed the real thing.

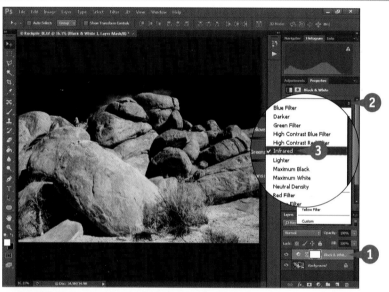

① With an image open, repeat steps 1 to 3 in task #63.

The image opens with the Default black-and-white conversion.

② Click the Preset drop-down menu.

③ Click Infrared.

Photoshop applies the default infrared adjustment.

The preview image adjusts.

④ Click the warning icon in the histogram to update the histogram.

⑤ Click and drag the Reds slider to the right to make the reds brighter.

Note: Click the histogram warning icon after each drag to be sure that no highlight pixels are clipping.

⑥ Click and drag the Blues and Cyans sliders to the left to make those colors darker.

Note: Click the histogram warning icon after each drag. It is okay to clip shadow pixels in the areas containing little necessary image information.

⑦ Click the Background layer in the Layers panel.

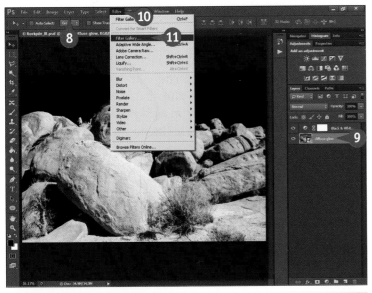

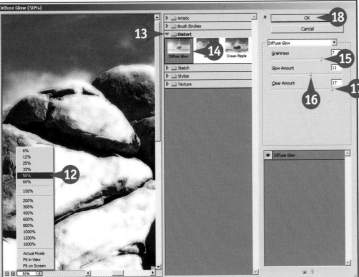

8 Click Layer ⇨ Smart Objects ⇨ Convert to Smart Object.

The Background image converts to a Smart Object.

9 Rename the Smart Object **diffuse glow** and press Enter (Return).

10 Click Filter.

11 Click Filter Gallery.

The Filter Gallery appears. The image opens in color. The infrared conversion cannot be seen until you return to the main Photoshop preview.

12 Click the zoom level menu and click 50%.

13 Click the Distort disclosure triangle.

14 Click Diffuse Glow.

15 Click and drag the Graininess slider to the right to add more grain.

16 Click and drag the Glow Amount slider to the right to add more glow.

17 Click and drag the Clear Amount slider to the right to show more background through the glow.

18 Click OK.

Photoshop returns you to the main window. The image appears in grayscale with the infrared conversion applied to the Smart Object.

#65

DIFFICULTY LEVEL

TIPS

Try This!

Click the Black & White adjustment layer in the Layers panel to make it active. Lower the opacity of the layer. Some of the underlying color shows through for a glowing, partially desaturated look.

Did You Know?

You can turn a layer into a Smart Object without using the Layer drop-down menu. Right-click the layer you want to convert to a Smart Object in the Layers panel. Click Convert to Smart Object from the menu that appears.

More Options!

You can return to both the infrared conversion and the Diffuse Glow filter to fine-tune the result. To edit the diffuse glow, double-click the diffuse glow layer in the Layers panel. To edit the infrared conversion, click the Layer thumbnail icon of the Black & White adjustment layer.

Chapter 7: Create Stunning Black-and-White Photos   163

Sepia toning in the traditional darkroom applied a stronger tone to the shadows than to the highlights in order to warm and stabilize them. You can achieve this same look, with much more control than a darkroom technician ever had, by applying a sepia gradient map to a black-and-white image.

The first step is to create a grayscale image that is appropriate to the subject. The Gradient Map adjustment converts your image to grayscale, but in order to adjust the blending mode, you need a grayscale image, not your

color image, below it. A landscape image should have a much higher contrast than a portrait for sepia toning. Both need enough contrast to have dark areas to show the sepia tone. The next step is to apply a gradient map to the grayscale image. There are nine prebuilt sepia toning options in the Gradient Map panel, but they are hidden.

Once you are happy with the sepia tone in the Gradient Editor, you can adjust the blending mode and opacity in the Layers panel to finalize your image.

1 With an image open, repeat steps 1 to 12 in task #63 to create a grayscale image.

2 Click the Gradient Map button in the Adjustments panel.

3 Click the default gradient in the Properties panel.

The Gradient Editor dialog box opens.

A You can drag the Gradient Editor away from the preview.

4 Click the Preset gear icon.

The Presets menu appears.

5 Click Text Only.

The Presets menu closes.

6 Click the Preset gear icon again.

7 Click Photographic Toning.

8 Click OK in the next dialog box to replace the current gradients with the photographic toning gradients.

9 Scroll down to the sepia presets.

10 Click each one to see the preset on your image.

11 Click the sepia preset that you prefer.

Note: This image uses Sepia 3.

12 Click and drag the gradient stops under the gradient to adjust the sepia toning.

13 Click OK.

14 Click the Blending Modes drop-down menu.

15 Try some different blending modes on your image, such as Color, Overlay, Soft Light, or Normal.

Note: Color looks best for this image.

16 Adjust the opacity of the Gradient Map layer if needed.

17 Save the image as a layered PSD file.

TIPS

Try This!

Add a vignette to the image to make it look like it was taken with an older lens. Add additional sepia into the highlights by moving the stops in the Gradient Editor to make the image look more faded and lower in contrast due to aging.

More Options!

You can tone with the look of traditional darkroom toning techniques other than sepia. The Photographic Toning list offers options for platinum, selenium, gold, blue, cyanotype, copper, and others. There are also combinations of these toning options, with one tone added to the highlights and another to the shadows.

Did You Know?

You can create a custom gradient and save it for future use. Even if it is not exactly right for the next image, it gives a much closer starting point. Create the gradient in the Gradient Editor and click Save. Give the gradient a descriptive name in the File Name text entry box in the next dialog box and click Save.

Sepia and similar toning looks, such as selenium and gold, add the same color into the highlights and shadows. You can use the Gradient Map adjustment to add one toning hue into the highlights and a different hue into the shadows.

The technique is similar to that used in task #66, but the result can be far more interesting. Adding a warm tone into the highlights brings them forward, while adding a cooler tone into the shadows causes them to recede, adding depth to the image, but in a subtle way. Many of

the prebuilt split toning options in the gradient map are designed to produce this effect. They are a good starting point for experimentation.

With a prebuilt split toning loaded, you can adjust the stops below the gradient map to control the amount of each tone, and the mix where one tone changes to the other based on the grayscale values of the image. When you return to the Photoshop workspace, you can adjust the opacity of the layer, or use a Curves adjustment to complete the split toning.

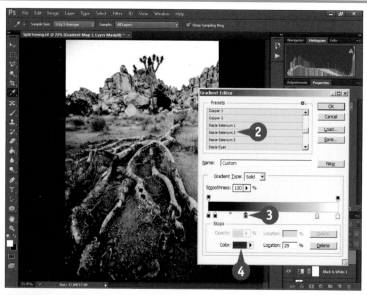

① With an image open, repeat steps 1 to 8 of task #66.

② Click Sepia-Selenium 2.

   Note: Click other combinations from the list to examine other looks. Sepia-Selenium 2 is a good combination to start for this image.

③ Click the shadow stop loaded with the selenium color.

④ Click inside the Color box.

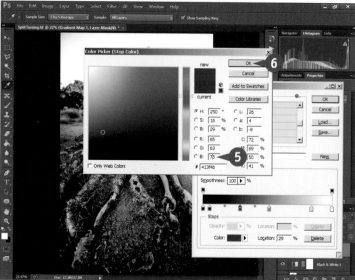

The Color Picker appears.

⑤ Type **75** in the text entry box for B (blue).

   The Color Picker displays the new color and the shadows change to that color.

⑥ Click OK.

7 Click and drag the shadow stop with the new color to the left.

The new shadow color affects less of the darker midtones.

8 Click and drag the darker sepia stop to the left.

Lighter sepia fills the upper midtones.

9 Click OK.

10 Adjust the Opacity slider to 90%.

The saturation decreases slightly.

11 Leave the Blending Mode set to Normal.

12 Save the image as a layered PSD file.

TIPS

Did You Know?

You can toggle the visibility of the active adjustment layer in the Properties panel. Click the eye icon (◉) at the bottom of the Properties panel.

More Options!

You can try viewing different blending modes for the Gradient Map adjustment without clicking through each of them in the Layers panel menu. With the Move tool (▶⊹) selected, press and hold Shift and press the plus key to cycle through the blending modes.

Try This!

Select Reverse in the Gradient Map Properties panel (☐ changes to ☑). Cycle through the blending modes. Some results are wild, but Color works well with this image.

CREATE A GRUNGY BLACK-AND-WHITE PORTRAIT in Camera Raw

Portrait styles come and go. The grunge look is popular now, especially with high school seniors. You can create this look in Camera Raw without resorting to High Dynamic Range, known as HDR, processing that is more commonly used to create the effect. The effect with Camera Raw is not nearly as strong, but it is much faster and easier.

The technique works best with a RAW format file, but you can often obtain a satisfactory result with a TIFF or JPEG

file. You begin with a color image in Camera Raw and drag sliders to produce the grunge effect. You can stop at that point if you want a color image, but portraits look grungier in black and white. Adding grain and a vignette in Camera Raw strengthens the effect.

Select or shoot a contrasty portrait to take full advantage of this technique. Select an appropriate subject, also. Young men appreciate the result far more than anyone else.

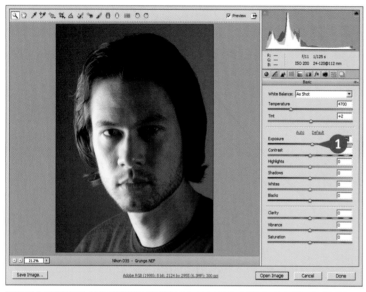

① With a RAW file format image open in the Basic panel of Camera Raw, do not make any corrections to improve the image other than a small exposure correction if needed.

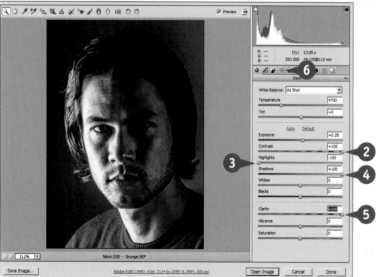

② Click and drag the Contrast slider to 100%.

③ Click and drag the Highlights slider to –100%

④ Click and drag the Shadows slider to 100%.

⑤ Click and drag the Clarity slider to 100%.

The color image takes on a grungy, high-contrast look.

⑥ Click the HSL/Grayscale button.

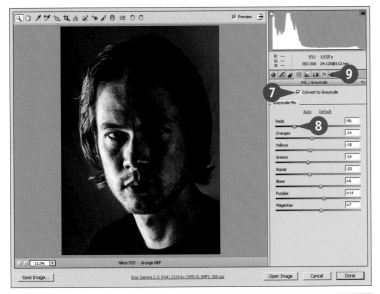

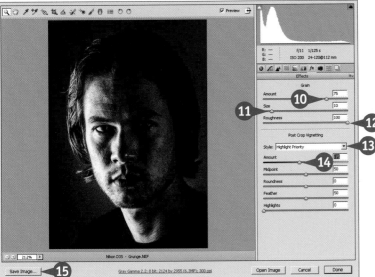

7 Select Convert to Grayscale (☐ changes to ☑).

8 Click and drag the sliders until the effect looks correct.

Note: For this image, dragging the Reds slider to the left darkened the sweater to draw more attention to the face.

9 Click the Effects button.

The Effects panel appears.

10 Click and drag the Grain Amount slider to 75% to increase the amount of grain.

11 Click and drag the Size slider to make the grain small and sharp.

12 Click and drag the Roughness slider to 100%.

13 Select Highlight Priority from the Post Crop Vignetting Style drop-down menu.

14 Click and drag the vignetting Amount slider to the left to create a dark vignette.

Adjust the other sliders as needed.

15 Click Save Image.

16 Save as a PSD file in the Save Options dialog box.

TIPS

Try This!

Open the original color image and the grungy black-and-white image in Photoshop. Press Shift and drag the black-and-white image on the color image. Adjust the opacity of the black-and-white image to let some of the underlying color show through.

Did You Know?

You can see the grain adjustment most accurately in the Effects preview when you view the image at 100%. Click the zoom level menu at the bottom left of the Camera Raw panel and select 100%.

Try This!

After you save the grayscale image, remain in Camera Raw and create a variation using split toning. Click the Split Toning button (▤). Click and drag the Saturation slider in the Highlights and Shadows subpanels to 50. Drag the Hue sliders to select a color for the highlights and the shadows. Adjust the Saturation sliders until the effect looks correct.

COLORIZE a black-and-white photo

It is very difficult and time consuming to hand color or *colorize* a traditional black-and-white print. Photoshop has made it much easier. Once you have a grayscale image to work from, you can add color to colorize any photo.

Traditional hand-tinted photos use dyes to paint over a print, with the print showing through the dye. The colors are muted and tend toward the pastel. You can achieve a similar effect by not picking saturated colors to paint with, and by adding each color on a separate layer. You can

then reduce the opacity of each layer to desaturate it and show more of the underlying grayscale image.

You can paint directly on separate layers, but if the image lends itself to easily creating selections of the areas to colorize, this is a faster, more accurate technique. Once you make a selection, colorizing it with a fill layer set to the proper blending mode leaves all of the brush work to Photoshop.

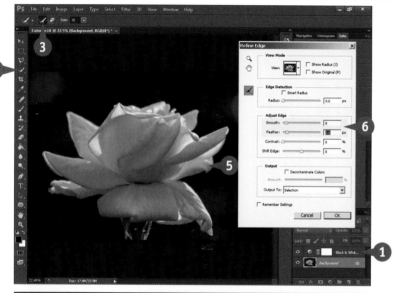

1. With an image open, repeat steps 1 to 12 in task #63 to create a grayscale image.

2. Click the Quick Selection tool.

3. Click the New Selection button.

4. Press the left or right bracket key to select the correct brush size.

5. Click in the image and paint a selection.

   Marching ants appear.

6. Click the Refine Edge button in the Options bar and smooth and feather the selection edge in the Refine Edge floating panel.

   Note: See task #43 for more about Refine Edges.

7. Click Layer.

8. Click New Fill Layer.

9. Click Solid Color.

   The New Layer dialog box opens.

10. Click the Mode drop-down menu and click Color.

11. Click OK.

   The New Layer dialog box closes.

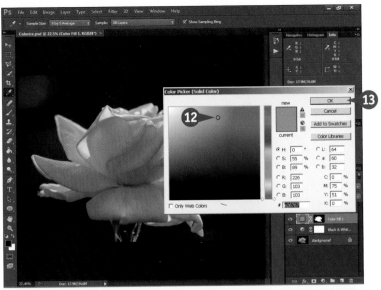

The Color Picker opens.

⑫ Select a color.

⑬ Click OK.

The color fills the selection.

⑭ Repeat steps 2 to 13 for each color you want to add.

⑮ Click and drag the Opacity slider for each layer to desaturate and mute the color.

⑯ Save the image as a layered PSD file.

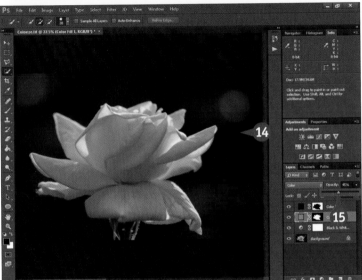

TIPS

Try This!

Use a blending mode other than Color in the Mode drop-down menu of the New Layer dialog box. Your colorizing need not look like traditional colorizing. Try Overlay for a strong color effect, or Soft Light for a less contrasty effect. You can always dial back the effect using the Opacity slider for the layer in the Layers panel.

Try This!

Colorize just a part of your image. Rather than using the color in the original image for spots of color, as described in task #64, colorize parts of your image. Use the technique in this task to colorize precise areas of the image. Or paint in color using a brush set to paint in Color, Soft Light, or Overlay blending mode. Paint each color on a separate layer and adjust the opacity later. And do not worry — it is okay to paint outside the lines.

USE QUADTONING for the richest black-and-white look

Just as you used split toning to add tone and depth to the highlights and shadows in task #67, you can use quadtoning to increase the sense of depth and dimension. And you can do this easily in Photoshop using a quadtoning preset if you know where to find one.

The four tones can be four shades of gray, or a mixture of grays and colors. You can use the same technique in this task to create duotones with two colors and tritones with three colors. There are more than 100 presets available.

The presets require a grayscale image, so the first step is to do a conversion of your color image to grayscale either in Camera Raw, or by using a Black & White adjustment layer and converting the result to grayscale. When you do this, the Duotone option is no longer grayed out in the Image menu. When you convert the result back to RGB and print the image on a high-quality inkjet printer, the image has a depth and range of tones that is outstanding.

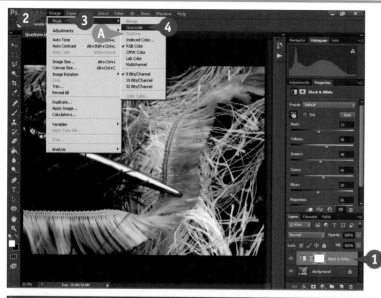

1. With an image open, repeat steps 1 to 12 in task #63 to create a grayscale image.

2. Click Image.

3. Click Mode.

4. Click Grayscale.

A. Duotone is grayed out for an RGB image.

5. Click OK in the next dialog box to change modes.

6. Click OK in the next dialog box to discard color information.

7. Click Image ⇨ Mode again.

   Note: Duotone is no longer grayed out.

8. Click Duotone.

   The Duotone Options dialog box appears.

9. Click the Preset drop-down menu and click Default.

   The Preset toning drop-down menu appears.

   Note: There seems to be no logic to the list. Duotones are mixed with tritones and quadtones are mixed in also.

10. Scroll through the list.

11. Click Bl CG10 CG4 WmG3.

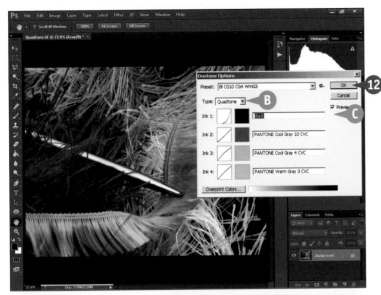

The preview redraws using the four gray tones in the preset.

B The Type is shown as Quadtone.

C The tone curves and color of each gray are shown on a separate line.

12 Click OK.

The Duotone Options dialog box closes.

13 Click Image.

14 Click Mode.

15 Click RGB Color to save the quadtone image for output on an inkjet printer.

16 Save the image with a different name than the name of the original.

TIPS

Important!

This task is very destructive. Your original color image is destroyed in the process of converting the image to grayscale in Photoshop. Immediately after you open the original image, save it under a new name and then proceed with the task.

More Options!

You can create your own duotone, tritone, or quadtone mix. Click the color squares for an ink in the Duotone Options dialog box. For black, the Color Picker opens. For other colors, the Color Libraries dialog box appears. Choose a color from one of the libraries for that tone curve. Click the gear button (✿.) in the Duotone Options dialog box and save your custom preset.

Create Unique Images with Filters and Special Effects

You can use the tools in Photoshop to create new and unique images that were difficult or impossible to create with earlier processes using film or traditional darkroom techniques. Many of these tools are located in the Filters menu, but others are available throughout the program. No filter or special effect can turn an uninteresting photo into a great one, but it can turn a good photo into one that is unique and visually captivating.

Some special effects, such as adding a vignette, 3-D lighting, subtle toning, or an Instagram look serve to simply enhance an existing image. But you can also completely change the mood of a photo by applying photo effects borrowed from the film industry. These include overlaying a photo filter, desaturating a portrait photo, or applying a day-for-night look to your photo.

You can also create unique images by merging a series of exposures of a subject into a High Dynamic Range photo, or merging a series of overlapping images into a panorama. Photoshop tools allow you to both increase and decrease the depth of field in an image, or create a miniature effect outside of the camera. You can even add a reflection where none existed in the original image, and turn an image into a simulated oil painting.

Add a CUSTOM VIGNETTE

Camera lenses, especially wide- angle lenses, naturally darken the edges of an image capture, and you can remove this vignetting automatically or manually in Camera Raw or Photoshop if you want the sky or background to be evenly toned. But you can also add a vignette to draw the eye of the viewer into your photo. Using Camera Raw or Photoshop, you can add a post-crop vignette, but if you want to apply the same vignette to another photo, you must re-create it each time.

Using a vector shape in Photoshop and converting it to a mask, you can create a custom, nondestructive vignette that you can drag and drop onto other images. The vignette remains editable in both the original and subsequent images. It can be dark like a lens vignette, or light like an antique photo, where light was held back when the print was made. Although this vignette does not have the versatility of refitting itself to the image like a post-crop vignette when you crop the image, the added versatility in other ways makes it a valuable technique to learn.

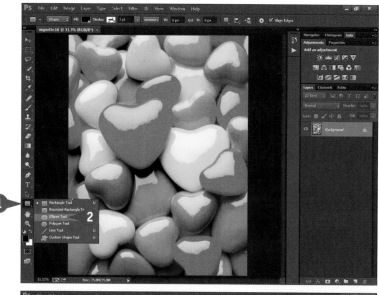

① With an image open, click the Rectangle tool.

② Click the Ellipse tool.

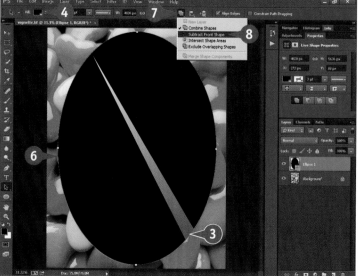

③ Click and drag an ellipse in the image.

④ Click the Fill button and select black from the swatches.

Note: *For a light vignette, select white. For a color vignette, choose a color.*

⑤ Click the Path Selection tool.

⑥ Click the path to select it.

⑦ Click Path Operations.

⑧ Click Subtract Front Shape.

Saddletowne Library
Self Checkout

04:54 PM   2015/10/19

---

1. Photoshop CC : top 100 simplified tips & tricks
39065141226280   Due: 11/9/2015,23:59

Total 1 item(s).

To check your card and renew items
go to www.calgarypubliclibrary.com
or call 262-2928

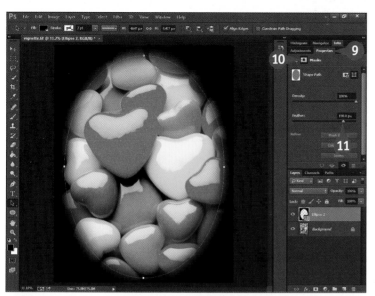

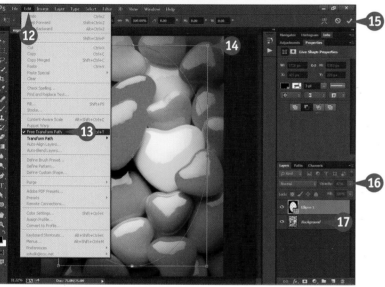

The shape inverts to cover the outer portion of the image.

⑨ Click the Properties tab.

⑩ Click the Masks button to open the Properties panel.

⑪ Click and drag the Feather slider until the vignette edge looks right.

⑫ Click Edit.

⑬ Click Free Transform Path.

⑭ Click and drag the path handles to resize or reshape the vignette if needed.

⑮ Click Commit Transform.

⑯ Click and drag the Opacity slider for the Ellipse layer until the vignette looks correct.

⑰ Click the Background layer to see the final image.

⑱ Save the image as a layered PSD file.

TIPS

Did You Know?

You can adjust the path symmetrically. Press and hold Alt (Option) as you drag the handles of the shape when you are in the Free Transform Path (step 14). Both sides of the path move symmetrically around the center point.

Try This!

Drag and drop the vignette on another image. With the image with the vignette applied open, open another image. Tile them horizontally or vertically. Click the Move tool (⊹) and drag the vignette from the original image to the new image. Click Edit ⇨ Free Transform to fit the vignette to the new image. Change the feather as needed. The vignette is a vector file so it can be scaled and transformed at will because it is resolution independent.

More Options!

Using the method described in this task, you can change the dark vignette to a light or color vignette easily. Click the Ellipse layer. Click the Fill button in the Options bar. Select white from the swatches or select a color.

Photographic filters are used on the lens by film photographers and some digital photographers to correct the color temperature of the light or, more often, to adjust the overall color balance of the image to suggest a mood or feeling. You can do the same with a Photo Filter adjustment layer in Photoshop.

There are 20 prebuilt filters, but access is available to the Color Picker and the full spectrum of colors. By adjusting the Density slider to a high value, you can select colors in the Color Picker and preview them on the image. After

you select the color, you can adjust the density of the color overlay by moving the Density slider to the left.

Because you are working on an adjustment layer, Photoshop automatically creates a mask when you select the adjustment. You can paint black on the mask to eliminate the color from areas. You can also adjust the overall opacity of the layer, which functions like the Density slider, but saves you from reentering the Adjustments panel.

① With an image open, click the Adjustments tab.

② Click the Photo Filter button.

The Photo Filter panel opens.

Photoshop creates a new adjustment layer and layer mask.

③ Select Preserve Luminosity if it is not already selected (■ changes to ☑).

④ Click and drag the Density slider to 100%.

⑤ Click the custom filter color box.

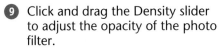

The Color Picker opens.

Ⓐ You can click and drag the Color Picker off the image.

⑥ Slowly click, drag, and release the slider on the spectrum at different places. When you release the mouse, the color is applied to the image.

⑦ Click in the main color box to choose the final color.

⑧ Click OK.

⑨ Click and drag the Density slider to adjust the opacity of the photo filter.

⑩ Click the layer mask.

⑪ Press D to select the default foreground and background colors.

⑫ Click the Brush tool.

⑬ Select a large, soft brush.

⑭ Paint black onto the image to restore any areas to their original color.

⑮ Save the image as a layered PSD file.

TIPS

More Options!

You can create a stronger filter opacity that works well with some sunsets and other strongly backlit, silhouetted scenes. Deselect the Preserve Luminosity slider (☑ changes to ⬛), and decrease the Density slider or the layer Opacity slider.

Important!

Photo Filter is also found in the Image ➪ Adjustments menu. However, this option to select the Photo Filter is destructive. The changes are applied to the active layer and if that is your Background layer, the pixels are changed. Select Photo Filter as described in this task or choose Layer ➪ New Adjustment Layer to work nondestructively.

Try This!

To change the contrast of the Photo Filter adjustment layer, try different blending modes. Click the Blending Mode drop-down menu for the Photo Filter adjustment layer and try Overlay for high contrast or Soft Light for lower contrast.

Hollywood sets the trends in our visual world, and now the look in movie posters, films, and celebrity portraits is desaturated skin tones. You can create these distinctive portraits easily in Photoshop by combining color and black-and-white layers in one composite image.

You first need to create some duplicate layers and then desaturate the portrait, but not completely. You do this by selecting Image ➪ Adjustments ➪ Desaturate, or by pressing Shift+Ctrl+U (Shift+⌘+U) and lowering the opacity.

Finally, you use the color in the top layer to blend with the layers below in Soft Light mode, or in Overlay mode if you want more contrast. Graphic artists in the film industry often tone the black-and-white layer to further remove the skin tones from reality, but still create a believable result. You can bring back some or all of the original image with a layer mask for an even more distinctive image.

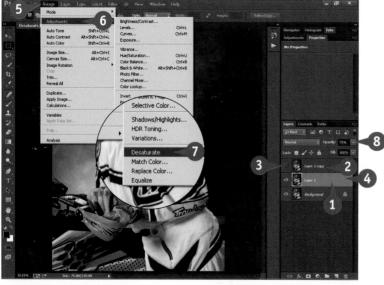

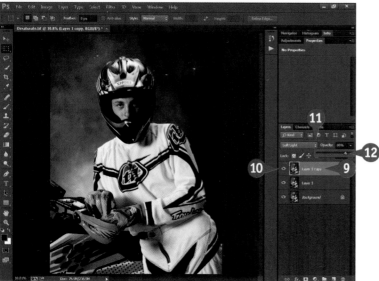

① With an image open, Press Ctrl+J (⌘+J) to duplicate the Background layer.

② Press Ctrl+J (⌘+J) to duplicate Layer 1.

③ Click the layer visibility button for Layer 1 copy to hide the layer (👁 changes to ▣).

④ Click Layer 1 to make it active.

⑤ Click Image.

⑥ Click Adjustments.

⑦ Click Desaturate.

⑧ Click and drag the Opacity slider of Layer 1 to the left until some color shows through.

⑨ Click Layer 1 copy to make it active.

⑩ Click the layer visibility button for Layer 1 copy to show the layer (▣ changes to 👁).

⑪ Click the Blend Mode drop-down menu and click Soft Light.

⑫ Click and drag the Opacity slider until the skin looks correct.

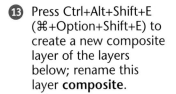

#73

DIFFICULTY LEVEL

⬤ ⬤ ⬤ ◡

13 Press Ctrl+Alt+Shift+E (⌘+Option+Shift+E) to create a new composite layer of the layers below; rename this layer **composite**.

Note: This type of composite layer creates a flattened copy of the layers below it.

14 Click the Add Layer Mask button to add a layer mask to this layer.

15 Click the layer visibility button for Layer 1 copy to hide the layer (⬤ changes to ■).

16 Click the layer visibility button for Layer 1 to hide the layer (⬤ changes to ■).

17 Click the Brush tool.

18 Select a large, soft brush.

19 Click and drag the Opacity slider in the Options bar to 50%.

20 Press D to select the default foreground and background colors.

21 Paint black in the image with the layer mask selected to bring back some of the color from the Background layer.

22 Save the image as a layered PSD file.

TIPS

Did You Know?

You can use a keyboard shortcut other than Ctrl+J (⌘+J) to duplicate a layer. Press and hold Alt (Option) as you drag a layer into a blank area in the Layers panel. When you release the mouse, Photoshop creates a duplicate of the layer.

More Options!

You can have more control over the layer that desaturates the image by using the Hue/Saturation adjustment for Layer 1. Click the Adjustment tab. Click the Hue/Saturation button (▦). Drag the Saturation slider to 0%.

Did You Know?

When you create a composite layer using Ctrl+Alt+Shift+E (⌘+Option+Shift+E), you can no longer change the image by adjusting the opacity or blend mode of the layers beneath the composite layer. If you decide you need to adjust these lower layers, you must delete the composite layer, make the adjustments, and create a new composite layer.

You can create a look that mimics the Instagram app with a combination of adjustment layers and filters. The best part about it is that you really cannot go wrong once you know which controls to adjust.

The typical Instagram look is square, so you start with a square crop. Then you add adjustments to give the vintage look common to many Instagram digital filters. These adjustments include adding a simple vignette, adding noise to simulate film grain, lowering contrast, increasing saturation or vibrance or both, and adjusting

individual color curves. You can even add a white or black border.

There are no rules for creating an Instagram look, only general guidelines. You can be as creative as you like within the general framework. It is good to perform as many filter steps as possible after converting the image to a Smart Object. You can then revisit the image and make changes in the future to convert it to a different Instagram look.

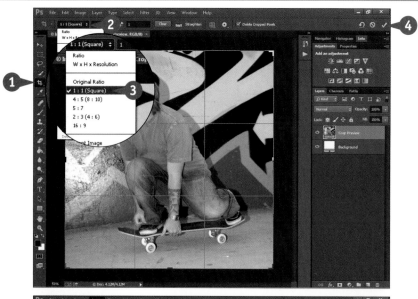

① With an image open, click the Crop tool.

② Click the Crop presets drop-down menu in the Options bar.

③ Click 1:1 (Square).

④ Click Commit Crop.

⑤ Click Layer.

⑥ Click Smart Objects.

⑦ Click Convert to Smart Object.

8 Click Filter ⇨ Noise ⇨ Add Noise.

The Add Noise dialog box appears.

9 Type **20** in the Amount text entry box.

10 Select Uniform (○ changes to ⊙).

11 Select Monochromatic (☐ changes to ☑).

12 Click OK.

Noise is added to the image and the Smart Object layer is updated with the Noise Smart Filter.

13 Click Filter ⇨ Blur ⇨ Field Blur.

The Blur Tools panel opens.

14 Click and drag the Blur slider to 3 px.

15 Click OK.

Blur is added to the image and the Smart Object layer is updated with the Blur Smart Filter.

16 Click the Adjustments tab.

17 Click the Brightness/Contrast button (🔅) in the Adjustments panel.

The Properties panel opens.

18 Deselect Use Legacy if selected (☑ changes to ☐).

19 Click and drag Contrast to –50.

20 Click the Adjustments tab.

21 Click the Vibrance button (▼).

The Properties panel opens.

22 Click and drag the Vibrance slider to 100.

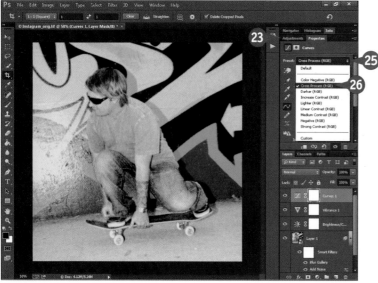

23 Click the Adjustments tab.

24 Click the Curves button (▦).

The Properties panel appears.

25 Click the Presets drop-down menu.

26 Click Cross Process (RGB).

27 Click the Adjustments tab.

28 Click the Color Balance button (⬙).

The Properties panel appears.

29 Select Shadows in the Tone drop-down menu.

30 Click and drag the Cyan/Red slider to the right to 50.

31 Click and drag the Yellow/Blue slider to the right to 50.

32 Repeat steps 29 to 31 by selecting Midtones and Highlights from the Tone drop-down menu and adjusting the sliders until the image looks correct.

33 Press Ctrl+Alt+Shift+E (⌘+Option+Shift+E) to create a new composite layer of the layers below.

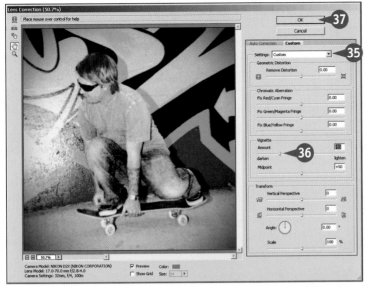

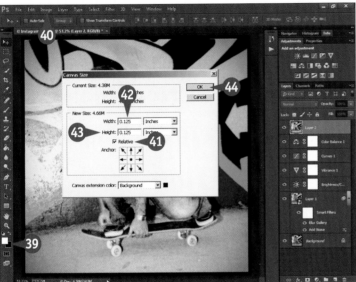

A new composite layer appears in the Layer panel.

34 Click Filter ⇨ Lens Correction.

The Lens Correction dialog box appears.

35 Click Custom from the Settings drop-down menu.

36 Click and drag the Vignette Amount slider to –50.

37 Click OK.

38 Press D to set the default foreground and background colors.

39 Press X to change the background color to black.

40 Click Image ⇨ Canvas Size.

The Canvas Size dialog box appears.

41 Select Relative (☐ changes to ☑).

42 Type **0.125** in the Width text entry box.

43 Type **0.125** in the Height text entry box.

44 Click OK.

Photoshop adds a black border to the image.

45 Save the image as a layered PSD file.

TIPS

More Options!

You can perform fewer of the steps in this task, or add additional adjustments. In the Curves adjustment, rather than selecting Cross Process (RGB) in step 26, select Green from the drop-down menu. Click and drag the bottom left of the diagonal line up to add green to the shadows. Do the same to the blue curve to add blue to the shadows. Together they add cyan. Experiment with other settings.

Try This!

You can convert your image to black and white at any point in the Instagram process to simulate a black-and-white Instagram photo. Use the steps in task #63.

More Options!

You can protect skin tones if necessary when making the Instagram adjustments. Click the layer mask for the adjustment layer that is causing the skin areas to look strange. Paint with black on the skin areas to protect them from the adjustment.

The human visual system sees detail in bright sunlit areas and dark shadows at the same time. A digital sensor cannot. This range of brightness is called the *dynamic range* of the scene. By making multiple captures with your digital camera and processing them using the Merge to HDR command in Photoshop, you can expand the dynamic range of your digital image into a *High Dynamic Range* photo. A High Dynamic Range photo is also known as an HDR photo.

You need three to as many as nine captures to create a good HDR photo. With the camera on a tripod, capture a scene by capturing different exposures with the shutter speed at settings 1 or 2 stops apart and the aperture constant. Save the captures as RAW format files if possible to preserve as much information as possible.

Select the photos in Bridge and send them without any processing to Photoshop. Photoshop processes them and opens the image in HDR Pro. You can select options in the HDR Pro dialog box to create a realistic or stylized image from your exposures.

1 In Bridge, Ctrl+click (⌘+click) your exposures to select them.

2 Click Tools.

3 Click Photoshop.

4 Click Merge to HDR Pro.

Photoshop processes the files and the Merge to HDR Pro dialog box appears with the default image.

5 Click the Preset drop-down menu.

6 Click More Saturated from the drop-down menu.

Note: The Preset drop-down menu includes prebuilt HDR options for photorealistic and stylized conversions. There are also options for monochrome or color conversions. More Saturated is one of the color stylized conversions.

The preview image redraws with the More Saturated preset.

7 Select Edge Smoothness (☐ changes to ☑).

8 Click and drag the Gamma slider to the right to decrease overall contrast.

9 Click and drag the Exposure slider to the right to adjust overall exposure.

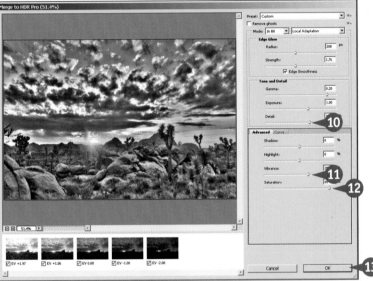

10 Click and drag the Detail slider to the right to increase local contrast.

Note: The Detail slider creates the gritty HDR look when dragged all the way to the right.

11 Click and drag the Vibrance slider to the left to decrease saturation of subtle colors.

12 Click and drag the Saturation slider to the left to reduce overall saturation.

13 Click OK.

Photoshop merges the images and opens the HDR.

14 Save the image as a 16-bit PSD.

TIPS

More Options!

You can adjust the contrast of the HDR image even though there is no Contrast slider in the Merge to HDR Pro dialog box. Click the Curve tab. Click a point in the center of the diagonal line. Click a point halfway between the center and the upper end and drag this point upward to create an S curve to add contrast.

Did You Know?

You can create a better HDR image if you use more dark images than light captures. When you are selecting images to merge in HDR Pro, choose three dark captures, the normal exposure, and one light exposure.

More Options!

You can remove movement if some elements in your HDR capture changed position in different frames. Movement can occur if a flag is moving in the wind or a person moves in the scene. Movement can also occur if you are handholding the camera and you move slightly between captures. Do not expect to remove large movements such as a car moving through the scene. To remove slight movement, select Remove Ghosts (☐ changes to ☑) in the Merge to HDR Pro dialog box.

You can use the Photomerge command in Photoshop to combine a sequence of images into a single larger image to create a panorama of a scene. The original images can be horizontal or vertical. Using a level tripod makes it easier for Photoshop to assemble the panorama and requires less cropping after the images are assembled, but you can also handhold the camera and Photoshop merges the captures together.

When you capture the images, you should overlap them by at least 25 percent. You should also use the same

manual exposure for every frame and turn off autofocus. Leave as much room as possible around the subject if you are handholding the camera so there is room to crop when the panorama is assembled.

Photomerge offers several options for merging, but the safest is Auto. With the Auto setting, Photoshop determines the best method and applies it to the captures. The Photomerge operation is completely automatic, but there is generally lots of work to do once it is complete.

1 With the folder containing the panorama captures open in Bridge, Ctrl+click (⌘+click) the thumbnails to select the images.

2 Click Tools.

3 Click Photoshop.

4 Click Photomerge.

The Photomerge dialog box appears with the images you selected in step 1 listed.

5 Make sure Auto is selected (◉).

6 Make sure Blend Images Together is selected (☑).

7 Click OK.

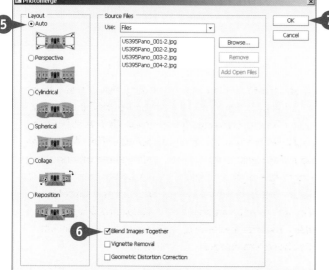

Photomerge blends the images together into a single image with each capture on a separate layer.

A Photomerge first aligns the images without blending.

B Photomerge creates layer masks for each image to blend the edges together for smooth transitions.

C A checkerboard appears behind the merged images where there was no image data.

TIPS

Did You Know?

You can choose the blending option manually if the Auto blending option does not work. Photoshop offers five Layout blending options. Perspective favors the center of the image and Distortion increases to the ends. Cylindrical favors horizontal lines and is good for keeping horizons straight. Use Spherical for fisheye lens captures. Use Collage or Reposition if you move parallel to the subject rather than pivoting the camera, or for blending together documents you scanned in sections.

Did You Know?

You can create a better horizontal panorama by holding the camera vertically. This allows more room to crop if the alignment is slightly off, and gives a wider field of view for the final panorama. If you plan on making a vertical panorama, shoot horizontal images.

Try This!

Merge RAW files. Open the files in Camera Raw. Press Ctrl+A (⌘+A) to select all files. Adjust one file and the others receive the same adjustment. Click Done. Return to Bridge and process beginning with step 1.

Once Photomerge creates the panorama, there are areas around the blended images that appear as a checkerboard. The distortion required to blend the images together causes the frame to distort and leaves areas without image data. You can crop these areas out making your panorama even narrower. Or you can fill these areas with image information to increase the panorama to fit the frame around it.

You can also perform other corrections and adjustments to the assembled panorama. You can use Free Transform or Puppet Warp to reshape the image. From the Filter menu,

you can use Adaptive Wide Angle, Lens Correction, and Liquify to remove any distortion. Adaptive Wide Angle is especially useful if there are clouds in the sky that should be straight but appear curved.

Once the image is corrected, you can select the checkerboard areas and fill them with image information using Content-Aware Fill to finalize the panorama. You may also need to use the Clone Stamp and Healing Brush tools to touch up any areas where the blending, or your original captures, was not perfect.

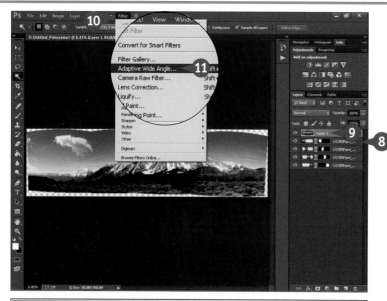

8 Click the top layer in the layers panel.

9 Press Ctrl+Alt+Shift+E (⌘+Option+Shift+E) to create a new composite layer of the layers below.

10 Click Filter.

11 Click Adaptive Wide Angle.

The Adaptive Wide Angle dialog box appears. The clouds are straighter and the image fills more of the frame.

A Panorama is selected in the Correction drop-down menu.

12 Click and drag the Scale slider to the left to add some background to fill, or to the right to crop out all of the nonimage area.

13 Click OK.

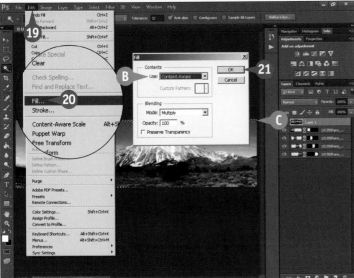

Photoshop applies the Adaptive Wide Angle filter and you return to Photoshop.

14 Click the Magic Wand tool.

15 Click New Selection.

16 Deselect Contiguous (☑ changes to ■).

17 Deselect Sample All Layers (☑ changes to ■).

18 Click a checkerboard area.

Marching ants surround the checkerboard areas.

19 Click Edit.

20 Click Fill.

B The Fill dialog box opens. Content-Aware is selected.

21 Click OK.

C The marching ants fill with image information.

22 Press Ctrl+D (⌘+D) to deselect the marching ants.

23 Save the panorama as a layered PSD file.

#76

TIPS

More Options!

You may still have some artifacts after you fill empty areas with Content-Aware Fill. Zoom to 100 percent and pan through the image by pressing and holding the spacebar and dragging through the image. For small artifacts or light lines left by Content-Aware Fill, press J to select the Spot Healing Brush tool and click and drag over the areas. If there is a large area that needs work, use the Clone Stamp tool.

More Options!

In the Photomerge dialog box, select Vignette Removal (☐ changes to ☑) if you have not removed lens vignetting in the original images in Camera Raw. If you are using a fisheye lens for your captures, select Geometric Distortion Correction (☐ changes to ☑).

The area in an image that appears to be in focus from the closest object to the farthest object is called the *depth of field* of the image. The depth of field is determined by many factors including the sensor size, focal length of the taking lens, lens-to-subject distance, lens aperture, and image viewing distance. You can increase the depth of field in an image beyond that which your camera can capture using Photoshop.

There are many times when a greater depth of field in an image is desirable. In close-up and macro photography

this is often the case. But there are other situations, such as when you want a foreground object and a distant object to both be in focus in a landscape.

To increase depth of field it is necessary to take multiple captures of the subject and vary your focus from the foreground to the distance. Photoshop blends these captures into one composite image, using the sharpest areas of each.

① With the folder containing the images open in Bridge, Ctrl+click (⌘+click) the files to select them.

② Click File.

③ Click Open With.

④ Click Adobe Photoshop CC (default).

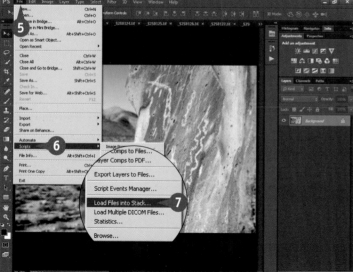

The images open in tabs.

⑤ Click File.

⑥ Click Scripts.

⑦ Click Load Files into Stack.

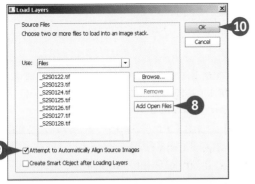

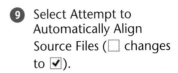

The Load Layers dialog box appears.

8 Click Add Open Files.

The images are added to the Source Files list.

9 Select Attempt to Automatically Align Source Files (☐ changes to ☑).

10 Click OK.

The images align and open as a single document with each image on a separate layer.

A The bottom layer is selected.

11 Shift+click the top layer to select all layers.

TIPS

Did You Know?

You can open the images from Photoshop to start the process. Click File ➪ Scripts ➪ Load Files into Stacks. The Load Layers dialog box opens. Browse to the image files. Ctrl+click (⌘+click) to select them. Click Open. Continue beginning with step 9.

Try This!

Correct your RAW files before blending them. If your original images are RAW format files, the Open with Adobe Photoshop CC command opens the files in Camera Raw. Shift+click to select the files. Adjust one file and the same adjustments are copied to the others. Click Save to save the images as TIFF or JPEG files. Repeat step 1 and choose these files rather than the RAW files.

When you are capturing images to increase depth of field, you should mount your camera on a tripod and use manual exposure when you capture images to blend them to increase depth of field. Set the lens aperture for a middle value between wide open and stopped down where the lens delivers the sharpest image.

Focus manually, first on the closest point, and then a little farther into the scene. Continue to change your focus and make additional captures until the farthest point is in

focus. As you change focus, you can see the size relationship of elements in the captures change as you change focus. Photoshop takes care of this as it aligns the images, but leave room around the captures to crop later. More captures are better than fewer.

If you prefer not to crop the final image, you can use the Content-Aware Fill command to fill any empty areas around the perimeter.

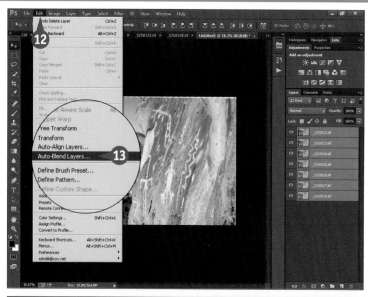

⑫ Click Edit.

⑬ Click Auto-Blend Layers.

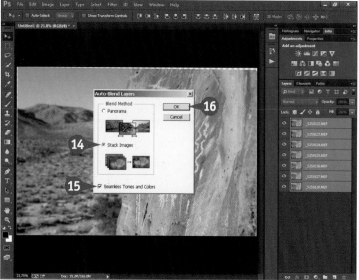

The Auto-Blend Layers dialog box appears.

⑭ Select Stack Images (○ changes to ◉).

⑮ Select Seamless Tones and Colors (☐ changes to ☑).

⑯ Click OK.

Photoshop blends the images based on in-focus areas of each image and creates layer masks.

The depth of field is increased.

17 Click the Zoom tool.

18 Click in the image to see the near and far objects in focus.

19 Press and hold Alt (Option) and click in the image to zoom out to the full image.

20 Click the Crop tool to crop out the checkerboard areas.

Alternatively, repeat steps 14 to 23 of task #76 to Content-Aware Fill the checkerboard areas.

21 Close the source images.

22 Save the blended image.

#77

TIPS

Try This!

You can leave just a little bit of the foreground or background out of focus to add a touch of reality to the blend. Images that are sharp everywhere from foreground to background, especially close-up and macro images, look strange. Leave some insignificant area out of focus when you capture the images, and leave it in the final image.

More Options!

You can check to see that the Load Layers command properly aligned the layers. Toggle the layer visibility icon of each layer when the Load Layers stacking is finished. The preview image should never move. If it does, select all of the layers and click Edit ➪ Auto-Align Layers to align them.

More Options!

You can flatten the image before you save it. There is no need to save the original files and layer masks, which only create a very large file. Click Layer ➪ Flatten Image before you save the file.

You can decrease depth of field as well as increase it. By decreasing the depth of field you draw attention to the subject by throwing other parts of the image out of focus. Photoshop has several options for applying blur. Iris Blur is one of the most interesting.

Iris Blur is found in the Filter menu. It is a destructive filter, but there are several ways to apply it so as not to destroy image information. One is to convert the original image to a Smart Object before you use the filter. Applied as a Smart Filter, the effect is nondestructive and you can return to the image and change the blur effect later.

The subject should be on its own plane in the image and separate from the background to be most effective. You can apply more than one Iris Blur to an image. It is often more effective to apply the softening to several small areas than to try and control one blur to meet your needs.

1 With an image open, right-click the Background layer.

2 Click Convert to Smart Object.

The thumbnail changes to a Smart Object thumbnail.

3 Click Filter.

4 Click Blur.

5 Click Iris Blur.

The Blur Tools panel opens.

The Iris Blur filter opens with an oval in the center of the image.

6 Click and drag the center pin of the oval over the area that you want sharp.

7 Click and drag the large white dots to the edge of the area that you want sharp.

8 Click and drag the solid oval-shaped line to the edge of the area where you want full blur.

Note: The area between the white dots and the solid oval gradually transitions from sharp to blur.

9 Position your cursor over the small white circles on the oval. When it changes to a curved arrow, click and drag to rotate the oval and change the shape.

10 Click and drag the Blur slider to set the blur for this pin.

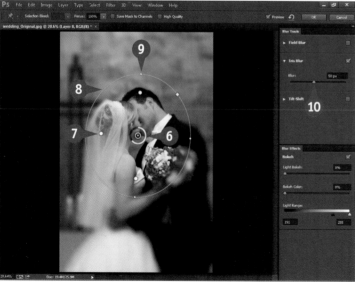

Note: *Alternatively, click and drag inside the gray part of the ring around the pin. As you drag, the gray part turns white and the blur increases. The amount of blur is shown in a box above the ring.*

⑪ Click another area of the image.

Another oval and pin appear.

⑫ Repeat steps 6 to 10 to set the blur for this pin.

⑬ Repeat steps 11 and 12 as needed for other areas.

⑭ Toggle Preview to view the image before and after blur.

⑮ Click OK.

The Blur Tools panel closes.

⑯ Save the image as a PSD file.

TIPS

Did You Know?

You can use keyboard shortcuts to hide and show different views for Iris Blur. Press and hold H to hide the pins and overlays. Press P to toggle the before and after preview. Press and hold M to view the mask that Photoshop makes for the blur. These same keyboard shortcuts work for many of the blur and other filters.

Did You Know?

You cannot use the Opacity slider or a blend mode from the Layers panel on a Smart Object layer if the effect looks too strong when you close the Blur Tools panel. However, if you immediately click Edit ➪ Fade Blur Gallery, you can both adjust the opacity and change the blend mode.

More Options!

You can have control over opacity of the Iris Blur filter in the future. Instead of applying Iris Blur to a Smart Object, apply it to a copy of the Background layer. You lose the flexibility of returning to the filter to adjust it in the future, but you gain the ability to adjust opacity or the blend mode.

Creating a reflection of an object so that it appears to be standing on a shiny, white surface is an everyday task for professional retouchers. It can be a complex task, but you can create a reflection just like the professionals because the basic steps are the same.

The subject might be a model, a car, or fine jewelry. Creating the reflection often requires removing the subject from the background on which it was shot, placing it on white, and then creating the reflection. But with the right image, you can create a reflection quickly.

The task is easier if there is already enough space below the subject for the reflection. If not, you can extend the canvas using Image ➪ Canvas Size. Place the Anchor in the center top and extend the canvas by 10 percent. You can always crop later. Fill the extended area with white like the rest of the background, or use Content-Aware Fill command if you can. Now you are ready to select the subject and create the reflection.

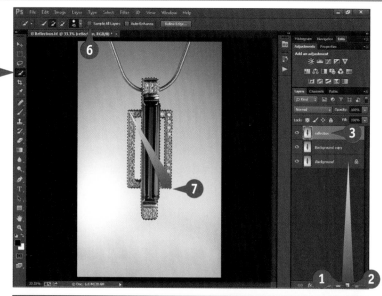

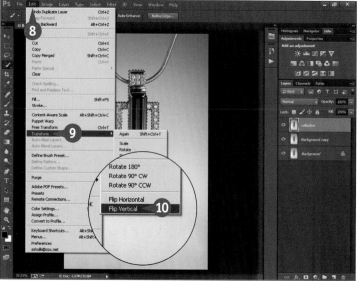

① With an image open, drag the Background layer to the New Layer icon to create a copy of the Background layer.

② Drag the Background layer to the New Layer icon again.

③ Double-click the layer name and rename it **reflection**.

④ Press Enter (Return).

⑤ Click the Quick Selection tool.

⑥ Deselect Sample All Layers (☑ changes to ☐).

⑦ Click and drag to select the subject.

Marching ants appear around the subject.

⑧ Click Edit.

⑨ Click Transform.

⑩ Click Flip Vertical.

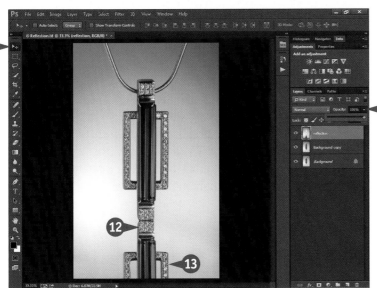

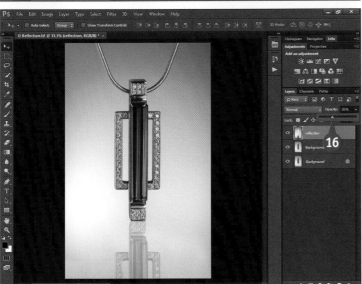

Photoshop flips the selection and lays it over the original.

⑪ Click the Move tool.

⑫ Click the flipped image.

⑬ Press Shift and drag it down to line with the bottom of the original.

⑭ Press Ctrl+D (⌘+D) to deselect the image.

⑮ Click the Opacity drop-down menu for the reflection layer.

⑯ Click and drag the Opacity slider to less than 40%.

⑰ Save the image as a layered PSD file.

79

DIFFICULTY LEVEL

 TIPS

Try This!
You can make the reflection fade out as it goes further from the original. With the reflection layer active, click the Layer Mask button (▣) in the Layers panel. Press D to set the default colors to black for the foreground and white for the background. Click the Gradient tool (▦). With the layer mask selected, click and drag from the bottom of the preview to the place where the original and reflection meet. Release and drag again and again until you are happy with the fade.

More Options!
You can use other transform tools if the original image is more complex. You may need to use the Distort, Warp, or Puppet Warp tools to make the reflection touch the original.

Try This!
Make a black reflective layer. Click the New Layer button (⬚) to create a new layer filled with transparency. Use the Rectangular Marquee tool (▦) to make a selection from the bottom of the preview to above the bottom of the original. Fill the layer with black. Click and drag the reflective layer below the original layer and the reflection layer in the layers panel.

Chapter 8: Create Unique Images with Filters and Special Effects   199

You can quickly turn your photo into a simulated oil painting with Photoshop's Oil Paint filter. You can simply click the filter in the filter menu, accept the default settings, click OK and you are done. But the six controls that are available are worth a little time to explore in order to paint your masterpiece.

There are four brush controls: Stylization, Cleanliness, Scale, and Bristle Detail. Stylization controls the style of the brush from short, hard strokes at the left to longer, smoother strokes at the right. Cleanliness controls the

amount of detail that remains in the painting, from detailed and realistic on the left to more impressionistic on the right. The size of the brush is controlled by the Scale slider. For a small brush move the slider to the left and for a large brush, move it to the right. The Bristle Detail slider makes the strokes sharp when it is to the left and soft when it is to the right.

The two Lighting sliders control the angle and contrast of light that might fall on the painting. Their effect depends on your selections for the brush controls.

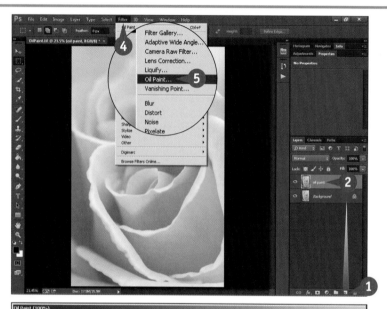

1 With an image open, click and drag the Background layer to the New Layer button.

2 Double-click the layer name and rename it **oil paint**.

3 Press Enter (Return).

4 Click Filter.

5 Click Oil Paint.

The Oil Paint dialog box appears.

6 Click the zoom level menu.

7 Click 100%.

8 Adjust the sliders until the oil painting looks correct.

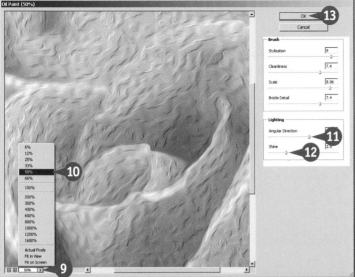

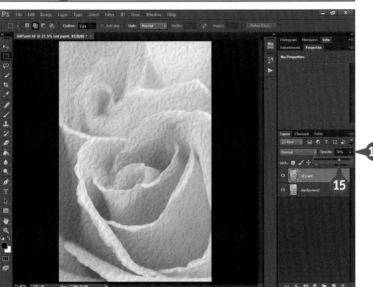

⑨ Click the zoom level menu.

⑩ Click 50% to see more of the painting.

⑪ Click and drag the Angular Direction slider from 0 degrees on the left to 360 degrees on the right.

Note: *Zero, 180, and 360 degrees generally show more pronounced brush strokes while 90 and 270 degrees make the strokes look flatter.*

⑫ Click and drag the Shine slider until it looks right.

⑬ Click OK.

Photoshop applies the filter.

⑭ Click the Opacity drop-down menu for the oil paint layer.

⑮ Click and drag the Opacity slider to reduce the oil paint if it looks too strong.

⑯ Save the image as a layered PSD file.

 TIPS

Important!
Simple graphic images generally work better than images with a lot of fine detail when applying the painting filters in Photoshop.

Try This!
You can add a canvas texture in Photoshop by clicking Filter ➪ Filter Gallery ➪ Texture ➪ Texturizer and selecting Canvas from the Texture drop-down menu. However, the canvas texture does not print well. You are better off printing the image on one of the many canvas inkjet products available. The less expensive ones are textured papers, but there are true canvas surfaces available that you can stretch and mount to stretcher bars. From a distance the result is indistinguishable from an actual oil painting.

More Options!
Try other blend modes before you save your image. In the Normal blend mode, brush strokes are obvious with a digital look at 100 percent. Try Overlay to soften them but add some contrast, or Soft Light for a subtle effect. Try Lighten to bring out the highlights on the strokes and lower the contrast.

Create a MINIATURE EFFECT

You can create a miniature or scale model effect using the Tilt-Shift filter. Many digital cameras include this effect for you to use when capturing images, but you have far more control when you apply it in Photoshop.

The most difficult part about creating the miniature effect is finding an appropriate original image. With the wrong original, the effect looks really dumb. Ideally, you have a photo taken from a high vantage point looking down at a steep angle. The higher the vantage point and the steeper the angle the better. A photo from the top of the Eiffel

Tower looking down without showing the base of the tower would work great.

The controls for the Tilt-Shift filter are identical to those for the Field Blur and Iris Blur filters, all of which are grouped together at the top of the Blur filter menu and called Gallery Effect filters. You can apply them individually, or combinations of them when you open any one of the filters.

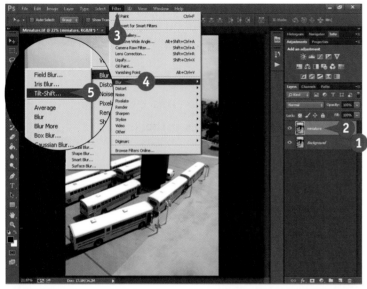

1. With an image open, press Ctrl+J (⌘+J) to create a new layer from the Background layer.

2. Double-click the layer name, rename it **miniature**, and press Enter (Return).

3. Click Filter.

4. Click Blur.

5. Click Tilt-Shift.

The Blur Tools panel opens, and the Tilt-Shift filter opens with a pin in the center of the image and lines above and below it.

6. Click and drag the pin over the center of the area that you want sharp.

7. Position your cursor over a small white circle on a solid line. When it changes to a curved arrow, click and drag to rotate the shape. Note that this was not needed for this image.

8. Click and drag the solid lines to the edge of the area that you want sharp.

9. Click and drag the dotted lines to the edge of the area where you want full blur.

Note: The area between the solid lines and the dotted lines gradually transitions from sharp to blur.

10. Click and drag the Blur slider to set the blur for this pin.

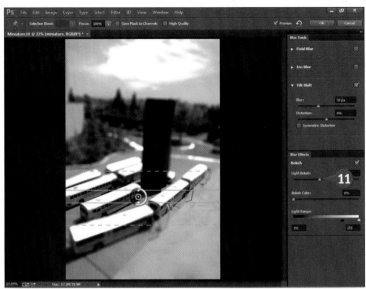

Note: The miniature effect generally looks best with a very narrow zone of full sharpness and a quick falloff to full blur.

Note: Alternatively, click and drag inside the gray part of the ring around the pin. As you drag, the gray part turns white and the blur increases. The amount of blur is shown in a box above the ring.

⓫ Click and drag the Light Bokeh slider to spread the highlights.

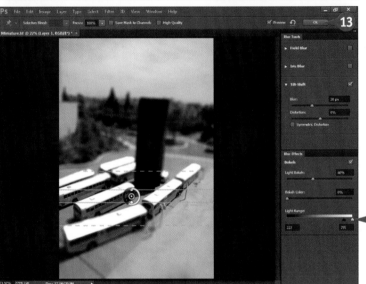
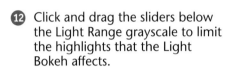

⓬ Click and drag the sliders below the Light Range grayscale to limit the highlights that the Light Bokeh affects.

⓭ Click OK.

The Blur Tools panel closes.

A progress bar appears as Photoshop renders the tilt-shift blur.

⓮ Save the image as a layered PSD file.

TIPS

More Options!

You can distort the blur in one direction or symmetrically. Click and drag the Distortion slider to the left to distort the blur toward the upper dotted line. Click and drag the slider to the right to distort it toward the lower dotted line. Select Symmetric Distortion (☐ changes to ☑) to distort the blur in both directions for something like a zoom lens effect.

More Options!

You can change the color of the Light Bokeh that you add. Click and drag the Bokeh Color slider to shift and saturate the underlying color that the Light Bokeh is affecting. A little goes a long way with the Bokeh Color slider.

Remove It!

You can remove the pins and set the sliders to their default values if you become completely lost and want to try again. Click the Reset Pins button (☒) in the Options bar. Click in the image to set a pin and repeat the steps beginning with step 6.

Photoshop has many special effects scattered throughout the program and hidden in unlikely places with unusual names. Color Lookup is one of these special effects. You can use Color Lookup to make a photo taken in daylight seem like it was taken at night or in moonlight.

Color Lookup is an adjustment, so it is found in the Adjustments panel. The button to access the Color Lookup panel is the last one in the second row and looks like a 3 × 3 chart with the top left block filled in. Even when you

click the button, the Color Lookup panel gives you no clue to the hidden gems in it.

The prebuilt color lookup tables are modeled after those used in movie and video production. Day-for-night is the traditional Hollywood name for Photoshop's NightFromDay effect. Most of the Color Lookup adjustments have no options, but there are some radio buttons in NightFromDay that vary the effect.

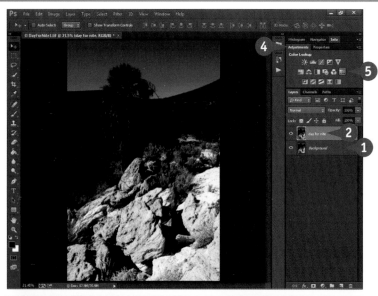

① With an image open, click Ctrl+J (⌘+J) to create a new layer.

② Double-click the layer name and rename it **day for nite**.

③ Press Enter (Return).

④ Click the Adjustments tab.

⑤ Click the Color Lookup button.

The Properties panel opens.

⑥ Click the Load 3D LUT drop-down menu.

⑦ Click NightFromDay.

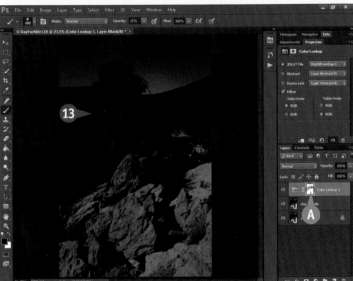

Photoshop applies the effect on an adjustment layer with a layer mask that reveals all.

8 Click the Brush tool.

9 Select a large, soft brush from the Brush Preset dialog box.

10 Click the Opacity drop-down menu in the Options bar.

11 Click and drag the Opacity slider to a low setting.

12 Press D to set the default foreground color to black.

13 Paint in the preview to remove some of the Color Lookup from the shadows to lighten them.

A The paint shows up on the layer mask as light gray.

14 Save the image as a layered PSD file.

TIPS

More Options!
Select BGR (⬜ changes to 🔘) in the Data Order subpanel to add an overall warm cast. Select RGB (🔘 changes to ⬜) in the Table Order subpanel to add a warm cast to the blues and a cooler cast to other colors.

Try This!
There are other interesting options in the Color Lookup Adjustments panel. Select the Abstract and Device Link Radio buttons to explore them after you have clicked the lookups available in the 3D LUT File menu. Do not miss Blacklight Poster in the Abstract menu.

More Options!
You can use the Color Lookup adjustments on black-and-white images. Make a black-and-white conversion of your color image using the Black & White Adjustments panel as described in task #63. Then click the Color Lookup adjustment button (▦). The NightFromDay lookup looks like a night scene from a 1950s western movie. Other options are interesting toning options for black-and-white conversions.

CREATE A DREAMLIKE LANDSCAPE
by sharpening and blurring

Some landscape images demand strong contrast and sharp details. Those require the skills of the photographer with a little help from Photoshop. Other landscapes should be just as perfectly captured, but can communicate a softer, more dreamlike feeling, perhaps what the photographer felt when capturing the image. You can create these landscapes with good photographic technique and some Photoshop filters.

Sharpening and blurring are usually thought to oppose one another and it is unusual to use them together. But this is exactly what produces the dreamlike effect. You sharpen the entire image and then blur the entire image to produce an effect; however, the final result is even more dreamlike if you soften just a portion of the image. Then the sharpening and blurring are different in different parts of the image, adding to the dreaminess and unreality.

The technique is simple, but there are no rules. You can decide how high the sharpening should be set and what areas should be blurred. Selecting the right image to start with is very important, also.

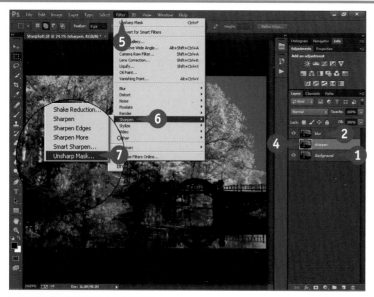

1 With an image open, press Ctrl+J (⌘+J) to duplicate the Background layer.

2 Double-click the layer name and rename it **blur**.

3 Press Enter (Return).

4 Repeat steps 1 to 3, but name this layer **sharpen**.

Note: The blur layer should be on top of the sharpen layer.

5 Click Filter.

6 Click Sharpen.

7 Click Unsharp Mask.

The Unsharp Mask dialog box appears.

8 Click and drag the Amount slider to 130%.

9 Click and drag the Radius slider to 1.5 pixels.

10 Click and drag the Threshold slider to 2 levels.

Note: You want strong sharpening, but the settings vary with different images and image sizes.

11 Click OK.

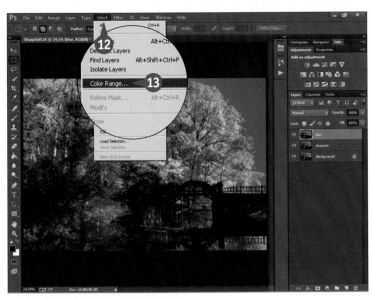

#83

DIFFICULTY LEVEL

Photoshop adds the sharpening.

⑫ Click Select.

⑬ Click Color Range.

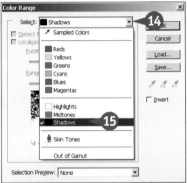

The Color Range dialog box opens.

⑭ Click the Select drop-down menu.

⑮ Click Shadows.

⑯ Select Grayscale from the Selection Preview drop-down menu.

Photoshop selects the shadows and displays the selection as a mask.

⑰ Click OK.

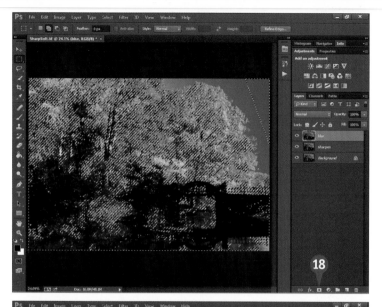

The selection appears as marching ants on the preview.

Note: *There are marching ants in the sky that you do not want.*

18 Click the Layer Mask button.

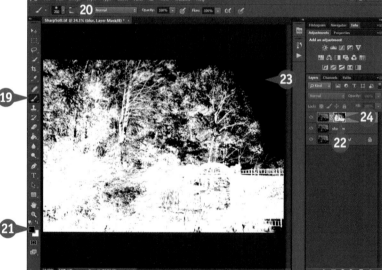

19 Click the Brush tool.

20 Select a soft, large brush in the Brush Presets dialog box.

21 Press D to select the default colors with black in the foreground.

22 Press and hold Alt (Option) and click the layer mask.

The layer mask appears in the preview.

23 Paint in the sky to add a mask where there is none.

24 Press and hold Alt (Option) and click the layer mask to return to the color view.

The color preview appears.

25 Click the image thumbnail in the blur layer.

26 Click Filter.

27 Click Blur.

28 Click Gaussian Blur.

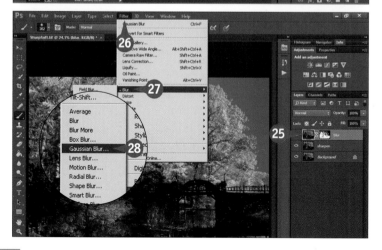

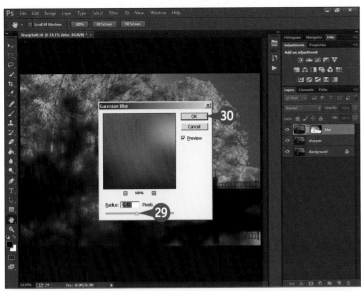

The Gaussian Blur dialog box appears.

29 Click and drag the Radius slider to 25 pixels or more.

30 Click OK.

83

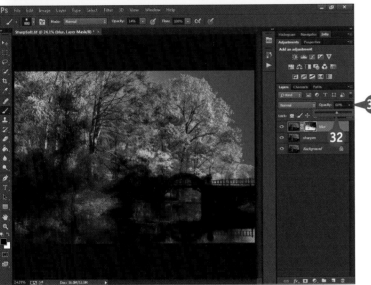

Photoshop adds the blur to the shadow areas.

31 With the blur layer still active, click the Opacity slider drop-down menu.

32 Click and drag the slider to 60%, or until the image looks correct.

The image is sharp, but the shadows are blurred.

33 Save the image as a layered PSD file.

 TIPS

More Options!

You can control the areas affected by the blur in the final image by painting in the layer mask in the blur layer. Paint with black at a very low opacity such as 15 percent to add softening to midtones and highlights. Paint with white at the same opacity to remove some of the blur from shadow areas.

Try This!

You can soften the highlights rather than the shadows. Softening the highlights makes them glow. In the Color Range dialog box, select Highlights rather than Shadows from the Select drop-down menu in step 15 and proceed with the subsequent steps as described in this task.

Try This!

Shift+click the final layer mask to disable it. Adjust the Opacity slider for the layer to see how the image looks when entirely blurred.

Chapter 9

Prepare Images for Output

Preparing your images for output is an important part of creating a professional impression. You can use Photoshop to prepare your photos for output to an inkjet printer as a straight print, and Photoshop includes the controls you need to print it with the best possible quality. You can also add a simple border and a mat surrounding the photo, or a sloppy border. Or you can make a gallery print. Gallery prints, rather than being centered on the paper, are printed off-center with a wider border at the bottom than at the top. You can add your signature to your art prints or add a watermark to a proof image.

There are many other output options for your images available in Photoshop. You can add type to your photos and distribute an announcement by e-mail or through social media channels. If you have clients who need a quick look at the images you have captured, you can create a proof sheet in Photoshop and save it for distribution. And if you have an iPad, you can create an action to convert your images for loading on any generation iPad.

Whatever means you choose for output, you need to sharpen your images. Photoshop CC includes a powerful new Smart Sharpen command you can use for this.

E-mail and social media sites are powerful ways for you to keep in contact with your friends and clients. You can create an e-mail or social media announcement by adding type to your photo. Rather than sending a plain photo like everyone else, sending a photo with type emphasizes your abilities as a visually creative person.

Working with type is one of the most powerful tools in Photoshop. Type is created as and remains a vector object until you flatten the file. Unlike photos, *vector objects* are mathematical formulae rather than pixels. They can be

scaled and transformed countless times in every imaginable way without harm or the creation of digital artifacts.

Photoshop lists the typefaces you have on your computer and shows a sample of each. It also shows common type sizes, but you can ignore these and simply click and drag type to the size you need. You can also add effects to type such as a drop shadow or outline to make your announcement stand out.

1 With an image open, click the Type tool.

2 Click the Font Family drop-down menu.

The font list appears.

3 Select a font.

4 Click the Character and Paragraph panels toggle.

The Character and Paragraph panels appear.

5 Click the bold type attribute.

6 Click the double arrow to collapse the panels.

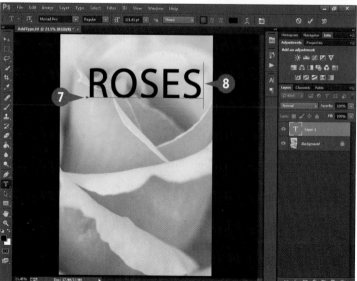

7 Click in the image.

A dot appears.

8 Type the title for your announcement.

9 Press and hold Ctrl (⌘) and drag a transformation handle to enlarge the text. After you begin dragging, press and hold Shift.

Note: Before you press Shift, the type distorts. Shift constrains it to its proper proportion.

The layer name in the Layers panel changes to the text you type.

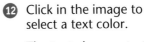

#84

DIFFICULTY LEVEL

10 Click and drag over the text to highlight it.

11 Click the text color box.

The Color Picker appears.

12 Click in the image to select a text color.

The text changes to the new color.

13 Click OK.

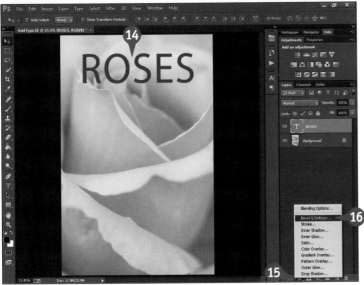

14 Click and drag the text to its final position.

15 Click the Effects button (_fx_) at the bottom of the Layers panel.

16 Click Bevel & Emboss.

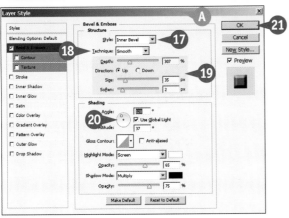

The Layer Style dialog box appears.

Ⓐ You can click and drag the dialog box away from the type.

17 Click the Style drop-down menu and select Inner Bevel.

18 Click the Technique drop-down menu and select Smooth.

19 Click and drag the sliders to set other options in the Structure subpanel.

20 Click and drag the circle within the circle in the Shading subpanel to set the angle for light.

Note: _The text updates with each change._

21 Click OK.

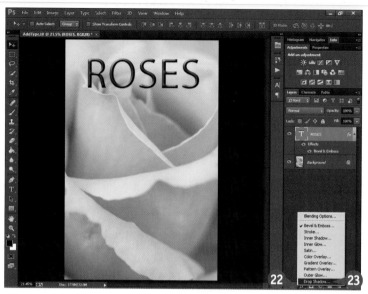

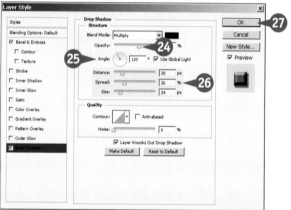

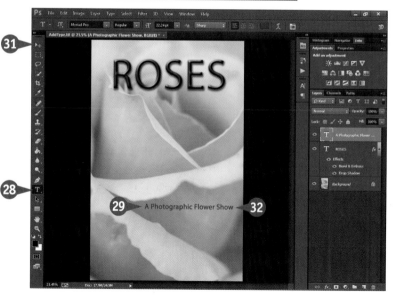

Photoshop adds the Bevel & Emboss Effect as a layer style.

22 Click the Effects button (*fx*) at the bottom of the Layers panel again.

23 Select Drop Shadow.

The Layer Style dialog box opens.

24 Click and drag the Opacity slider to the left to lighten the shadow.

25 Click and drag the Angle control to match the angle of the Bevel & Emboss you chose in step 20.

26 Click and drag the Distance, Spread, and Size sliders until the drop shadow looks correct.

Note: The image updates with each change.

27 Click OK.

Photoshop adds the Drop Shadow as a layer style.

28 Click the Type tool.

29 Add another line of text.

The text has the same color and attributes as the first line.

30 Press and hold Ctrl (⌘) and drag a transformation handle to enlarge the text. After you begin dragging, press and hold Shift.

31 Click the Move tool.

32 Click and drag the type to its final position.

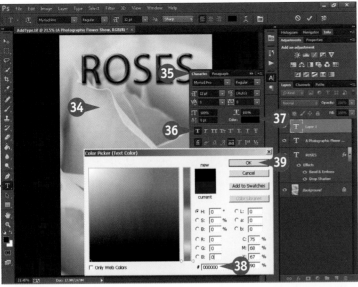

33 Click the Type tool.

34 Click in the image.

35 With the Character and Paragraph panels open, click the Character tab.

36 Click the bold type attribute to deselect it.

37 Click in the Color box.

The Color Picker appears.

38 Type **000000** in the # number entry box to select black.

39 Click OK.

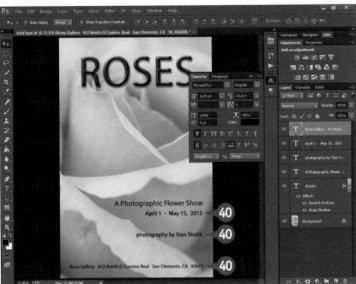

40 Add other text as needed.

The new text appears with the new attributes selected in the Character panel.

41 Save the image as a layered PSD file.

42 Resave the image as a small, lower-resolution JPEG for e-mail or social media.

TIPS

Did You Know?

You can apply the same effects to one layer that you added to another. Press and hold Ctrl (⌘) and click and drag Effects from one layer to another. Double-click the effect in the new layer to edit the attributes.

Try This!

You can change the blend mode of the effects for different looks. Double-click the Bevel & Emboss effect to open the Layer Style panel. Click Blending Options: Default. The Blending Options dialog box appears. Click Overlay or Soft Light. Lower the opacity and the type appears to be raised from the image below with the image showing through rather than the type color.

Did You Know?

You can adjust the opacity of the type without affecting the opacity of styles you applied to it. With a type layer with effects added active, click the Fill drop-down menu. Click and drag the slider. The opacity of the type changes, but the effects do not.

You can sign your artwork each time you create a piece just as a traditional painter does, or you can create and save a digital signature brush to apply your signature consistently to each piece.

You create your digital signature brush in a new document using one of Photoshop's brushes to sign the blank document. This is difficult to do with a mouse or trackpad. It is easiest to do by writing with the pen instrument on a Wacom or other graphics tablet, but it still takes a few tries

to get it right. You can also scan your signature at high resolution and save it as a custom brush preset.

Once you create a digital signature brush, you can use it on a new transparent layer in your artwork like any Photoshop brush. You can change the color by selecting a foreground color before you apply it. You can control the size and softness using the Brush Picker. You can also apply layer styles to blend it into the artwork for a signature unique to each piece of art.

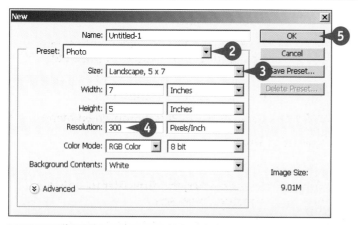

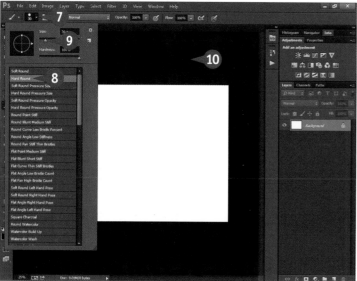

1. Click File ⇨ New.

2. In the New dialog box, select Photo from the Preset drop-down menu.

3. Select Landscape, 5 x 7 from the Size drop-down menu.

4. Type **300** in the Resolution text entry box.

   Note: This creates a large brush that you can scale down.

   Leave other settings as they are.

5. Click OK.

6. Press B to select the Brush tool.

7. Click the Brush Preset drop-down menu.

   The Brush Preset panel appears.

   Note: If the brushes appear as icons, click the gear button ( ) and select Text Only from the menu.

8. Select Hard Round.

   Note: Any brush with a hardness of 100 percent is okay.

9. Click and drag the size slider to 30 px.

10. Click in the background of the document to close the panel.

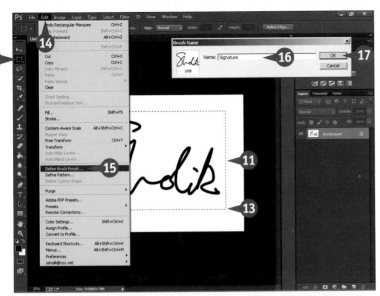

11 Click and draw in the blank document to sign your name.

12 Click the Rectangular Marquee tool.

13 Click and drag a rectangle around your signature.

14 Click Edit.

15 Click Define Brush Preset.

16 In the Brush Name dialog box, type **Signature**.

17 Click OK to save your signature as a custom brush.

18 Close the document without saving it.

19 Open an image.

20 Click the foreground color box to select a color for your signature, or press I to sample a color from the image.

21 Press B to select the Brush tool.

22 Click the Brush Preset drop-down menu.

23 Scroll down.

24 Select Signature.

25 Click and drag the Size slider to scale the signature brush size.

The signature size changes as you drag.

26 Click in the image to add your signature.

Your signature appears.

27 Click another tool to dismiss the signature brush.

TIPS

Try This!

Click the Effects button (📷). Apply a layer style such as Bevel & Emboss to your signature. Click Blending Options: Default in the Styles subpanel of the Layer Style dialog box. Try different blend modes and adjust Opacity or Fill for a unique look to your signature.

Did You Know?

You can move your signature brush to the top of the Brush preset panel. Press F5 to open the Brush window. Click Brush Presets. Click the panel menu button (▾≣). Click Preset Manager. Click and drag your signature brush to the upper-left corner. Click Done. Your signature brush is now the first brush in the Brush Presets list.

Did You Know?

You can save anything from a random set of doodles to an image as a brush preset. Select what you want to save with a marquee tool and click Edit ➪ Define Bush Preset.

To protect your images from use without your permission, you can create a transparent watermark to place over them that is difficult to remove. This can be important if you send your images to a client for approval or upload them for sale online.

You can create a simple custom watermark with type. But if you are sending commissioned photos for approval, it is more effective to use your logo and business font to increase your branding. You can add your digital signature

for a personal touch, or you can add your contact information for someone who wants to license image usage rights.

Once you add your text and logo, you can apply layer styles to them to give them some form and make them more transparent so that the underlying image shows through. You can do this by reducing the opacity of the text and logo while retaining the fill of the layer styles.

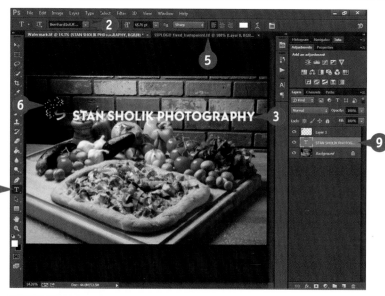

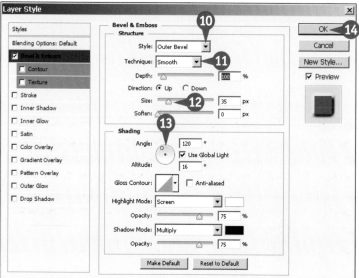

1. With an image open, click the Type tool.
2. Select the font family in the Options bar.
3. Click in the image, and add and size your type.
4. Click the Commit button (☑).
5. Open your logo file.
6. Click and drag it to the image.
7. Scale it to the needed size.
8. Click the Commit button.
9. Double-click in the gray area of the type layer to open the Layer Style dialog box.

   The Layer Style dialog box appears.

10. Select Outer Bevel from the Style drop-down menu.
11. Select Smooth from the Technique drop-down menu.
12. Click and drag the Size slider to adjust the size.
13. Click and drag the Angle control to set the light angle.
14. Click OK.

15 Rename the logo layer **logo**.

16 Press and hold Alt (Option) and click and drag the Effects from the type layer to the logo layer.

17 Press Shift and click the type layer so that both the logo and type layers are active.

18 Click the Fill drop-down menu.

19 Click and drag the slider to 5% or less.

The logo and type appear to be embossed in the image.

20 Close the logo image.

21 Save the image as a layered PSD file.

TIPS

Did You Know?

You can add a copyright symbol to your image along with your name and date. Click the Rectangle tool (▣). Click the Custom Shape tool (▨). Click the copyright symbol from the Shape drop-down menu in the Options bar. Shift+click and drag in the image to create the copyright symbol. The symbol appears in the image and on a new layer in the Layers panel.

Did You Know?

You can drag and drop the embossed type and logo layers to a new image. With two images open, click Window ⇨ Arrange to tile them horizontally or vertically. Click the embossed layers and drag them to the new image. It is easiest if the new image is roughly the same pixel dimensions as the image with the embossed layers.

Every digital image needs sharpening. You can sharpen files in several ways, but the revised Smart Sharpen in Photoshop CC offers the most options.

Sharpening produces visible digital artifacts if it is too strong. With Smart Sharpen you can sharpen the entire image, and then fade the amount of sharpening in the highlights if the sharpening creates halos and in the shadows if the sharpening emphasizes noise.

There is a large preview window in Smart Sharpen, and you should always judge the effect of sharpening by

viewing the image at 100 percent. But the best way to judge if you made the correct decisions about sharpening is to view the image after it is output. If the final output is for viewing on a monitor, then the sharpening you see is correct. If the final output is an inkjet print or a print from a photo lab, only experience will help you in making the correct settings. So sharpening should always be done on its own as the last step so that you can change it later, or for a different form of output.

1 With an image open, press Ctrl+J (⌘+J) to create a duplicate layer.

2 Set the blend mode to Luminosity.

3 Click Filter.

4 Click Sharpen.

5 Click Smart Sharpen.

The Smart Sharpen dialog box opens with the image at 100 percent and default sharpening or the last used sharpening applied.

6 Drag the image size control to make the dialog box as large as possible.

7 Click and drag the image until you see areas of highlight and shadow.

8 Select Preview (☐ changes to ☑).

9 Select Lens Blur from the Remove drop-down menu.

Note: The Remove options are names for the type of sharpening that is applied, not to indicate that something is removed. Gaussian Blur is the type used in unsharp masking.

10 Click and drag the Amount slider to 500%.

11 Click and drag the Radius slider until artifacts are visible.

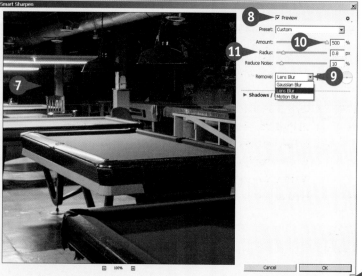

12 Click and drag the Amount slider to decrease the amount of sharpening until the artifacts are minimized.

13 Click and drag the Reduce Noise slider to lower noise overall.

Note: Lowering the noise softens the image slightly.

14 Click the Shadows/Highlights disclosure triangle.

15 Click and drag the image at 100 percent to look for halos in shadows and highlights.

16 Click and drag the Shadows sliders to reduce halos around objects in the shadows.

Note: There were no shadow highlights created in this image.

17 Click and drag the Highlights sliders to reduce halos around objects in the highlights.

18 Toggle Preview to view the image before and after sharpening.

19 Click OK.

20 Save the image as a layered PSD.

#87

DIFFICULTY LEVEL

Important!

You need to make a composite layer if you have many adjustments to the original image. Press Ctrl+Shift+Alt+E (⌘+Shift+Option+E) to create the composite layer and then duplicate the composite layer and sharpen the duplicate.

Did You Know?

You can still sharpen with the previous version of Smart Sharpen. Click the gear icon (✿) next to Preview. Select Use Legacy (☐ changes to ✔). Click More Accurate. The Reduce Noise slider grays out to indicate it is no longer available.

More Options!

You can stack sharpening layers on top of each other in the Layers panel if there are many different outputs for the image. Name each layer with *sharpen* and the output, for example, *for inkjet*. Turn one layer off before making another. When you are ready to output the image, make the appropriate sharpening layer active and turn off the visibility of the other layers.

Sloppy black borders are a popular way to add an artistic touch to your output. They are popular for portrait, landscape, and still-life photos. There are sloppy borders you can download for free and plug-in collections you can buy. You can also create your own using the brushes in Photoshop.

You begin by placing your image on a black Background layer so that you can erase the edges of the photo to black. By making a selection inside the image, you can create a layer mask. The layer mask enables you to apply a filter that roughens the area between the masked area and the edge of the underlying black layer.

Finally, painting with a spatter brush and the Eraser tool randomizes the effect. Photoshop includes an array of spatter brushes from which to choose. Each paints with a different pattern. Changing the brush size and the spatter brush while simply clicking the border of the image completes the effect.

1 With an image open, press D to set the default foreground color to black.

2 Press X to switch foreground and background colors.

3 Press Ctrl+A (⌘+A) to select the image.

4 Press Ctrl+Shift+J (⌘+Shift+J) to create a duplicate layer.

A The image is placed on its own layer above a Background layer filled with black.

5 Click the Marquee tool.

6 Click and drag a selection well inside the edge of the image.

7 Click the Layer Mask button to add a layer mask to Layer 1.

B The image has a thick black border.

8 Click the Eraser tool.

9 Click the Brush Preset picker.

10 Click the Spatter 24 pixels brush.

11 Click and drag the Size slider to create a large brush.

12 Click along the border.

The edge of the border is erased.

13 Click and click+drag around the image.

14 Change spatter brushes and brush size and paint out the edge of the border.

15 Save the image as a layered PSD file.

TIPS

Try This!

You can etch away your image to white rather than black. With the image open, press D to set the default foreground color to black. Press Ctrl+A (⌘+A) to select the image. Press Ctrl+Shift+J (⌘+Shift+J) to create a new layer filled with white below the image. Proceed with step 5.

More Options!

You can remove some of the sloppy border if you want it to be rougher or you did not like some of your border. Press X to change the foreground color to black. Press the left bracket key to select a smaller brush size. Click over some of the black and the image shows through again.

Try This!

You can make it easier to see the black border against the dark Photoshop background in the Preview panel. Right-click the dark-gray background. Click Medium Gray. The background color changes.

While inexpensive frames are readily available for displaying your prints, photos look much better with a border and mat around them when framed. You can create a simple border and mat without having to pay to have this done at a frame shop. You can even create the mat so that it brings out one of the colors in your photo.

You create the border by adding a layer style to your image. There are many choices for layer style, but a simple black stroke is effective for most images.

You create the mat with a new layer below the image layer. You can create a new transparent layer and fill it with a color, but it is quicker to choose the color first, set it as the background color, and then create the layer. You need to make this layer larger so that it surrounds the image. Using a color from the photo adds interest and draws the eye of the viewer into the photo.

① With an image open, click the Eyedropper tool.

② Click the color in the photo you want for the mat.

The color appears in the foreground color box.

③ Press X to make the foreground color the background color.

④ Press Ctrl+A (⌘+A) to select the entire image.

⑤ Press Ctrl+Shift+J (⌘+Shift+J) to create a duplicate layer.

Ⓐ The image is placed on a separate layer and a new Background layer filled with the background color is created.

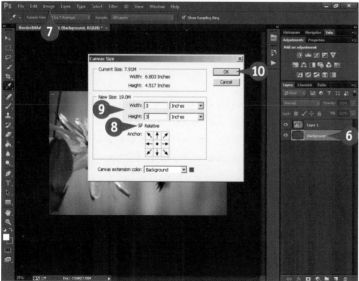

⑥ Click the Background layer.

⑦ Click Image ➪ Canvas Size.

The Canvas Size dialog box opens.

⑧ Select Relative (☐ changes to ☑).

⑨ Type **3** inches into the number entry boxes for height and width.

Note: Use a number other than 3 depending on your image size. Choose a different number for height and width to make the mat proportional to common frame dimensions.

⑩ Click OK.

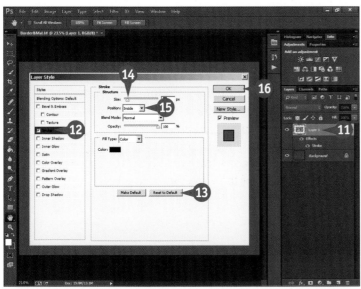

The image appears with a mat the color of the Background layer.

⑪ **Double-click** the image layer.

The Layer Style dialog box appears.

⑫ **Click** Stroke.

Note: Click the gray area, not the check box.

⑬ **Click** Reset to Default.

⑭ **Click** and drag the Size slider to 10 px.

⑮ **Click** Inside from the Position drop-down menu.

⑯ **Click** OK.

The image appears with a thin black border on the colored mat.

⑰ **Save** the image as a layered PSD file.

TIPS

More Options

You can make the stroke around your photo a color other than black. In the Layer Style dialog box for Stroke, click the Color Picker box. Select a new color, or click in the image to use a color from your photo.

More Options!

For black-and-white or toned images, a thin black stroke and a white or gray mat work best. Use a 1 or 2 px black stroke even when the image is dark on the edges. This gives the viewer a black reference. Use a white mat, or pick a gray from the Color Picker if white is too harsh. It is easiest to type the identical number into the R, G, and B number entry boxes in the Color Picker than trying to select a neutral color from the Color Picker window.

Output a photo as a GALLERY PRINT

You can add a professional finish to your photo by outputting it as a gallery print or gallery poster. Gallery prints present an image offset from the center of the background, with more space below the image than above. The space below is used for a title and subtitle. A gallery poster adds the name of the artist, the exhibit dates, and the gallery location.

You create your gallery print by clicking and dragging your image onto a new layer the size of your final print.

You center the image horizontally and then move it vertically to create roughly equal spaces left, top, and right.

Once in position, you can add a layer style to make it look as if there is a mat around the print. This gives the image a subtle three-dimensional quality. Then you can add a descriptive title and other information below the image. This is usually done in a fairly stylized font for a classic look.

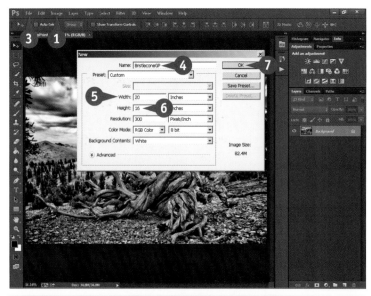

1 With an image open, click Image ➪ Image Size.

2 In the Image Size dialog box, note the length in inches of the longest side and the resolution in pixels/inch.

3 Click File ➪ New.

The New dialog box opens.

4 Type a name for the new gallery print.

5 Type a width that is 4 inches greater than the width of photo.

6 Type a height that is about 8 inches taller than the photo.

7 Click OK.

The new file appears.

8 Click the tab for the photo.

The photo appears.

9 Click the Move tool.

10 Click and drag the photo to the tab of the new layer.

11 When the new layer appears, drag the photo onto it.

12 Close the photo file.

13 Press Ctrl+R (⌘+R) to add rulers.

Rulers appear to the left and above the image.

14 Click and drag the photo until it is about 2 inches from the top of the background.

15 Press Ctrl (⌘) and click the Background layer.

Note: Both layers should be selected.

16 Click the Align Horizontal Centers button.

The photo centers horizontally.

17 Click the Background layer to make it active.

18 Click the Rectangular Marquee tool.

19 Click and drag a rectangular marquee around the photo.

Note: Use the rulers to center it around the image.

20 Press Ctrl+J (⌘+J) to put the selection on a new layer.

21 Click the Add Layer Style button (fx).

22 Click Inner Glow.

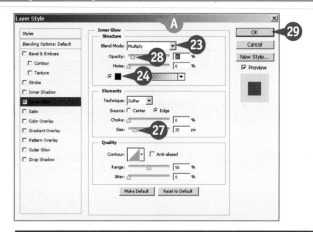

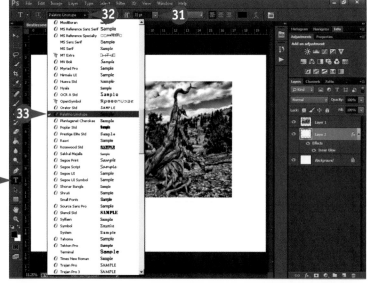

The Layer Style dialog box appears.

Ⓐ You can click and drag the Layer Style dialog box so you can see the image.

㉓ Select Multiply from the Blend Mode drop-down menu.

㉔ Click the Color Picker.

㉕ Type **0** in the # number entry box to select black.

㉖ Click OK to close the Color Picker.

The inner glow appears just inside the edges of the photo.

㉗ Click and drag the Size slider to 25 px.

㉘ Click and drag the Opacity slider to 10%.

㉙ Click OK.

㉚ Click the Type tool.

㉛ Select a large type size.

㉜ Click the Font Family drop-down menu.

㉝ Select a font.

㉞ Press Caps Lock.

㉟ Click below the photo and type the print title.

㊱ Click and drag the handles to size the type. Press and hold Shift after you begin dragging.

㊲ Click and drag the Opacity slider for the type to 75%.

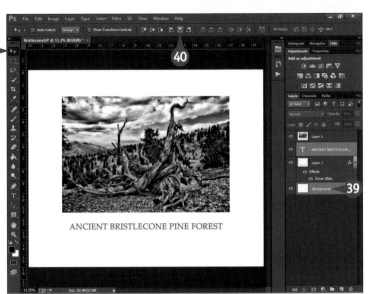

38 Click the Move tool.

39 Ctrl+click (⌘+click) the Background layer in the Layers panel so that it and the type layer are selected.

40 Click the Align Horizontal Centers button.

The type centers.

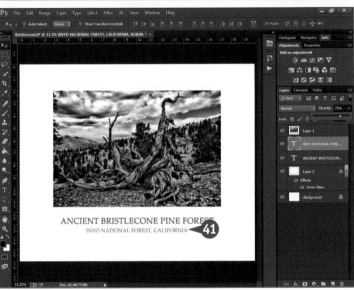

41 Repeat steps 30 to 40 to add and center other type.

42 Save the image as a layered PSD file.

TIPS

Did You Know?

You can adjust the Inner Glow layer style after you make a print if it is too dark. Inner Glow tends to print darker than it appears on the screen. To change the opacity, reopen the PSD file. Double-click the Inner Glow name in the layer. Click and drag the Opacity slider to a lower value. Make another print.

Try This!

You can make a gallery print with a black-and-white or toned photo. Open the image. Repeat steps 3 to 8 to make your new background. Double-click the foreground color box. Select black or an appropriate value of gray. Click the Paint Bucket tool (🅰). Fill the Background layer with the foreground color.

You can create high-quality prints at home on a current inkjet printer if you use the correct print settings in Photoshop. With print settings set incorrectly, the most expensive inkjet printers perform poorly. Using the correct printer profile is as important as making the correct settings. Inkjet paper manufacturers provide printer profiles for their papers for different printers. You can download profiles from the paper manufacturer websites.

Making the correct setting is a two-step process. Some of the dialog boxes look different on a Mac compared to how they look on a Windows computer, but the settings are virtually identical, especially in Photoshop itself.

When you select File ➪ Print, the Photoshop Print Settings dialog box appears. The important subpanel in this dialog box is Color Management. You must make the correct settings here to achieve a high-quality print. Most of the other important selections are made by clicking the Print Settings button. This opens the dialog box specific to your printer. The box in this task is that of an Epson Stylus Pro 3880 printer, but other printers have similar settings available and the Printer Properties dialog boxes only differ in layout.

1 With an image open, click File.

2 Click Print.

The Photoshop Print Settings dialog box appears.

3 Click the Printer drop-down menu and select your printer.

4 Click the Portrait button for vertical images or the Landscape button for horizontal images.

5 Click Print Settings.

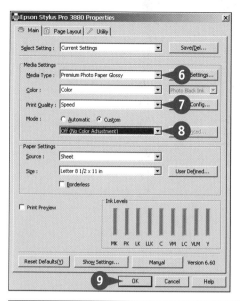

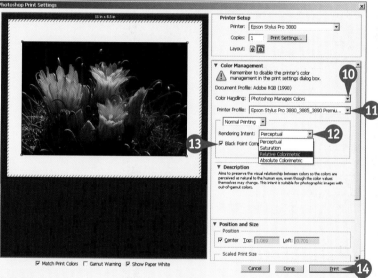

#91

DIFFICULTY LEVEL

The Printer Properties dialog box appears.

⑥ Select the correct Media Type for the inkjet paper you are using.

Note: The paper manufacturer includes this information with the paper or with the printer profile downloaded from its website.

⑦ Select Speed or High Speed for Print Quality.

⑧ Select Off (No Color Management) to disable color management by the printer.

⑨ Click OK.

⑩ Select Photoshop Manages Color from the Color Handling drop-down menu.

⑪ Select the paper profile for the paper you use in the Printer Profile drop-down menu.

⑫ Select Perceptual or Relative Colormetric for Rendering Intent.

⑬ Select Black Point Compensation (☐ changes to ☑).

⑭ Click Print.

TIPS

Important!

There is no way to know whether Perceptual or Relative Colormetric produces the best print from a photo without making one print using each Rendering Intent option. As with traditional darkroom printers, you must generally make several prints from an image before you are satisfied. Relative Colormetric delivers more accurate colors but may produce banding. Perceptual shifts colors if some are not printable with your printer, but color gradients are smoother.

Did You Know?

You can change the color behind the preview in the Photoshop Print Settings dialog box. Right-click the default Dark Gray background to open the options. You may prefer the Light Gray that gives less visual contrast when there is a wide white border around your photo.

Did You Know?

You can create your own printer profiles. Many of the same devices used to create monitor profiles to color manage your monitor can be used to create printer profiles. With your own custom profile you can match a particular box of paper to your specific printer.

Using Photoshop, you can create contact sheets of folders of your images to print and view as hard copy, or to send to clients or friends to view electronically or to print. You can save the contact sheets in any Photoshop file format, including PDF, TIFF, or JPEG. Choose the file format appropriate to your needs.

The photos in the contact sheets can be those contained in an entire folder, or in a folder and its subfolders. Although you can no longer create contact sheets in Bridge CC without downloading the separate Output module, you can still use Bridge to select specific photos to include. You can also select files from folders by filename.

In Photoshop, you have control over the layout of the contact sheets. You can set the number of photos in each row and each column, and you can add a caption to each photo. The size of the image on the contact sheet is determined by the number of photos on each page and the size of the page.

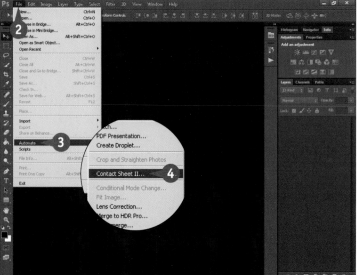

1 To choose specific photos for the contact sheet, Ctrl+click (⌘+click) them in Bridge CC.

Note: Do not close Bridge.

2 With no images open in Photoshop, click File.

3 Click Automate.

4 Click Contact Sheet II.

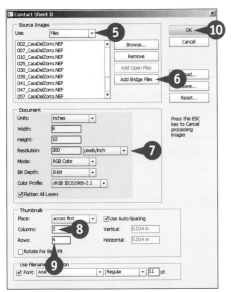

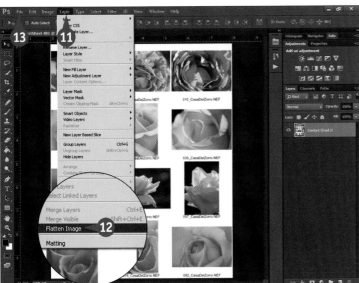

The Contact Sheet II dialog box appears.

⑤ Select Files from the Use drop-down menu.

⑥ Click Add Bridge Files.

Note: Alternatively, click Bridge from the Use drop-down menu. The number of files you selected in Bridge appears.

⑦ Type and select the appropriate options for your document in the Document subpanel.

⑧ Type the number of columns in the Column number entry box.

⑨ Type the number of rows in the Row number entry box.

⑩ Click OK.

Photoshop creates the contact sheet.

⑪ Click Layer.

⑫ Click Flatten Image.

⑬ Click File ➪ Save As.

⑭ Select a location and file format from the Save As dialog box to save your contact sheet.

TIPS

Did You Know?

You create large files when you save contact sheets as PDF. If you plan on e-mailing a set of proof sheets, save the contact sheets as resolution 8 or lower JPEGs. Current Windows and Mac operating systems have built-in viewers for JPEG files. PDF files are large and require the free Adobe Reader to view them.

More Options?

You can group your contact sheets by folders if you are printing them from a folder with subfolders. In the Source Images subpanel of the Contact Sheet II dialog box, Select Folder from the Use drop-down Select Include Subfolders (☐ changes to ☑). Select Group Images by Folder (☐ changes to ☑). The contact sheets are printed so that images in one folder do not mix with images in another folder on the same sheet.

With its good screen size, high resolution, and portability, the iPad is an excellent tool for sharing your images with others. You can create an action in Photoshop that almost instantly converts a folder of images of any type and format to the size and resolution to display on an iPad. This allows you to create custom presentations for every person with whom you want to share your images.

A Photoshop action is simply a collection of steps that you record while you apply them to a sample image. You can use actions to automate any repetitive task. For this task,

use an image that is the most complex you would save; a 16-bit, high-resolution, Pro Photo RGB, layered PSD file is ideal. An action that works on this file will work on practically any common photo file.

Photoshop includes some basic actions in the Actions panel. Rather than mix your actions with the defaults, create your own Actions folder. Then create a new action by naming it, opening a file, and begin recording. When you are finished, stop the action. Test it on a single file, or run it on a folder using the Batch command.

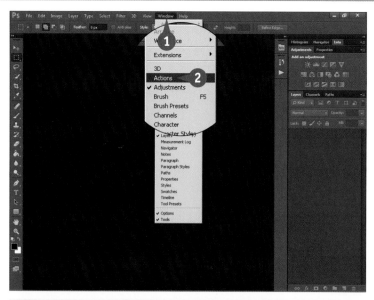

Create an Action

1 With no image open, click Window.

2 Click Actions.

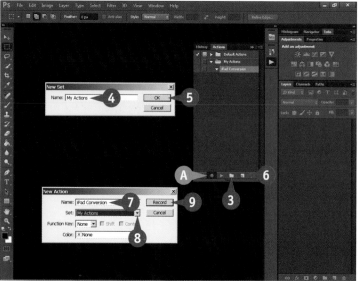

The Actions panel appears.

3 Click the Create New Set button.

The New Set dialog box appears.

4 Type **My Actions** in the Name text entry box.

5 Click OK.

6 Click the Create New Action button.

The New Action dialog box appears.

7 Type **iPad Conversion** in the Name text entry box.

8 Select My Actions from the Select drop-down menu.

9 Click the Record button.

A The Record button in the Actions panel turns red to indicate you are recording.

#93

DIFFICULTY LEVEL

⑩ Open an appropriate image file.

⑪ Click Layer.

⑫ Click Flatten Image.

Flatten Image is added to the action.

⑬ Click Image.

⑭ Click Mode.

⑮ Click 8 Bits/Channel.

Convert Mode is added to the action.

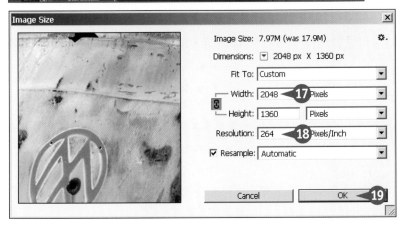

⑯ Click Image ⇨ Image Size.

The Image Size dialog box appears.

⑰ Type **2048** Pixels in the Width number entry box.

The Width entry box changes to the proportionate value.

⑱ Type **264** Pixels/Inch in the Resolution number entry box.

⑲ Click OK.

Image Size is added to the action.

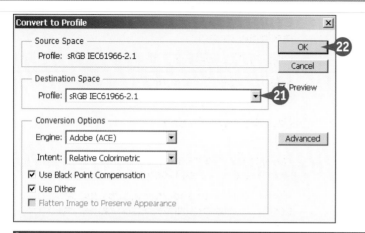

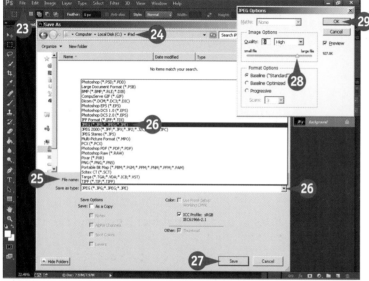

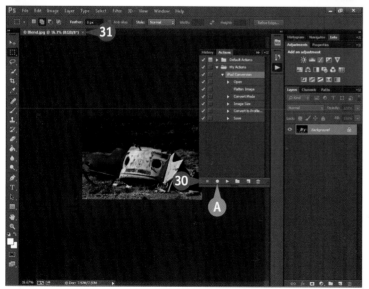

⓴ Click Edit ➪ Convert to Profile.

The Convert to Profile dialog box appears.

㉑ Select sRGB IEC61966-2.1 from the Profile drop-down menu.

㉒ Click OK.

Convert to Profile is added to the action.

㉓ Click File ➪ Save As.

The Save As dialog box appears.

㉔ Navigate to the folder where you want it saved.

㉕ Type a filename in the File Name text entry box.

㉖ Select JPEG as the Save As type.

㉗ Click Save.

The JPEG Options dialog box opens.

㉘ Click and drag the Quality sider to 9.

㉙ Click OK.

Save is added to the action.

㉚ Click the Stop Recording button.

Ⓐ The red Record button turns gray.

㉛ Close the sample image.

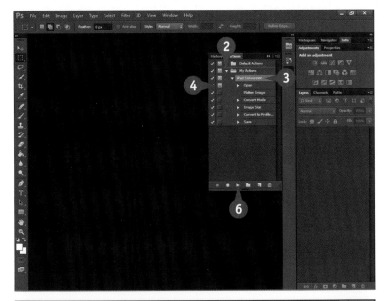

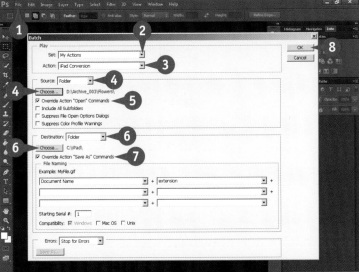

Convert a Single Image

1 With no image open, press Alt+F9 (Option+F9) to open the Actions panel.

2 Click the My Actions disclosure triangle.

3 Click iPad Conversion.

4 Select Toggle On/Off for Open (■ changes to ▨).

5 Click the Play Selection button.

6 Navigate to the image you want to convert and click Open.

Photoshop opens the image, runs the action, and saves it in the same folder you selected for the sample image.

Note: Deselect Toggle On/Off for Open (▨ changes to ■) before you run the action on a folder of images.

Convert a Folder of Images

1 Click File ➪ Automate ➪ Batch.

2 In the Batch dialog box, select My Actions.

3 Select iPad Conversion.

4 Select a source folder.

5 Select Override Action "Open" Commands (☐ changes to ☑).

6 Select a destination folder where you want to save the photos.

7 Select Override Action "Save As" Commands (☐ changes to ☑).

8 Click OK.

Photoshop opens each image, runs the action on each, and saves each one in the folder you selected.

Important!

You can use this task to convert vertical format images to the iPad, but it is not ideal. It is best to rotate your source images to horizontal before you convert. Alternatively, you could create separate actions for horizontal and vertical images if you are willing to separate them into separate folders for batch processing.

Did You Know?

You can troubleshoot an action. If you create an action and do not get the result you expect, you can run the action one step at a time to troubleshoot the problem. Press Ctrl (⌘) and double-click each step. Photoshop runs the step and pauses on the next. While the action is paused, check in Photoshop that the desired result from the step happened.

Did You Know?

You can take as long as you like to create an action. There is no time limit. Plan the steps of your action before you start recording and then record them at a comfortable, careful pace.

Chapter 10

Edit Video
in Photoshop

If you have shot some videos, but not done anything with them except download them to your computer because you do not want to buy and learn video-editing software, you probably did not realize the video capabilities within Photoshop. You can use Photoshop and many of the tools you now know to edit video clips, create a video from separate clips complete with audio and background music, and output the result in a number of formats.

In a short span of time, the world of still photography has merged with that of video. From smartphones to high-end digital single-lens reflex (dSLR) cameras, most still cameras can also capture video. From the other side, many video cameras have sufficient resolution to allow you to pull images from them as still photos. While Photoshop is not meant to replace dedicated video editing software for lengthy movies, it is more than capable of producing high-quality high-definition (HD) videos from individual video clips. This makes Photoshop ideal for everything from home video to vacation/travel videos to wedding and event videos to promotional pieces for photographers.

The best thing about editing video in Photoshop is your ability to use the same tools in video production that you use in still imaging. You can add adjustment layers, use filters to blur and sharpen, convert clips to black and white, transition them to color and back, and even add motion to still images. The same corrective and creative tools you use for still photos are available for video.

You can open video files in two ways. The goal is to end up with each clip on the same line of the Timeline. You can do this by opening one clip and then adding others, or selecting multiple files in Bridge and loading them into Photoshop layers.

You can begin by opening a single video clip with the Open command. Photoshop immediately recognizes the file as a video file, opens the Timeline, and adds the file. You can click the plus sign at the end of the clip, select another clip, and keep adding them until you have them all.

Or, you can open Bridge and select multiple files to load into Photoshop layers. Photoshop again recognizes the files as video, but places each one on a separate line in the Timeline. With this technique, once they are loaded, you must group them so they are sequential instead of stacked in the Timeline and in the Layers panel. Either way, once they are in sequential order in the Timeline, you are ready to begin editing.

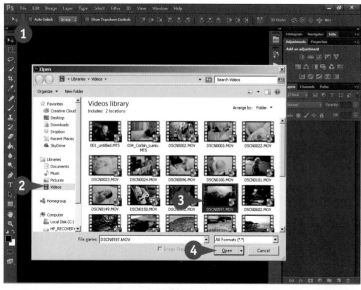

Add Video Clips One at a Time

① Click File ⇨ Open.

    The Open dialog box appears.

② Navigate to your video folder.

③ Click a video file.

④ Click Open.

Ⓐ Photoshop opens the Timeline and adds the file.

Ⓑ A preview opens.

Ⓒ Photoshop creates Video Group I in the Layers panel with the video as Layer 1.

⑤ Click the plus sign at the right of the Timeline for Video Group 1.

The Open dialog box appears.

6 Click another video file.

7 Click Open.

94

DIFFICULTY LEVEL

ⓓ Photoshop adds the video to the Timeline.

ⓔ Photoshop adds the video to the Layers panel above the layer for the first video.

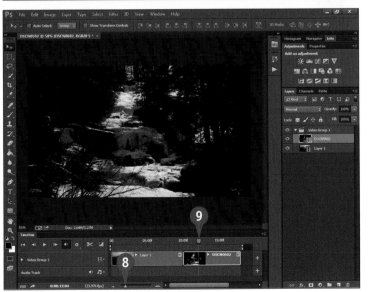

8 Click and drag the Control Timeline Magnification slider to the left to see the new video in the Timeline.

9 Click and drag the Playhead through the videos to preview them.

Note: Clicking and dragging the Playhead through a video is called "scrubbing."

Add Multiple Video Clips at One Time

1. With Bridge open, Ctrl+click (⌘+click) the video files.

2. Click Tools.

3. Click Photoshop.

4. Click Load Files into Photoshop Layers.

Ⓐ The video files open on separate layers in Photoshop.

5. Click Window.

6. Click Timeline.

   Note: If the tab for the Timeline is available at the bottom of the preview, click it.

Ⓑ The Timeline opens with the videos stacked on separate layers.

7. Ctrl+click (⌘+click) the video layers in the Timeline so that they are selected.

8. Click the filmstrip icon (▦▾) in one of the video layers in the Timeline.

9. Select New Video Group from Clips.

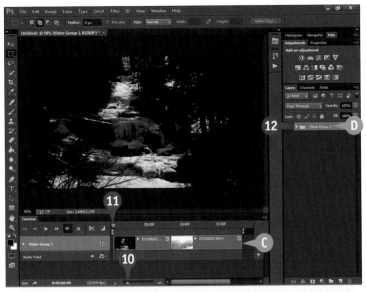

C Photoshop moves the lower layers in the Timeline up to the beginning of the top Timeline layer.

D Photoshop creates a video group in the Layers panel.

⑩ Click and drag the Control Timeline Magnification slider to the left to see the new video in the Timeline.

⑪ Scrub through the videos to preview them.

⑫ Click the video group disclosure triangle in the Layers panel.

The layers appear.

⑬ Click and drag up a lower layer in the Layers panel until a thin white line appears above the layer you want below it and then release the mouse to rearrange the order of the videos.

Alternatively, click and drag a video clip in the Timeline to position it before or after another clip.

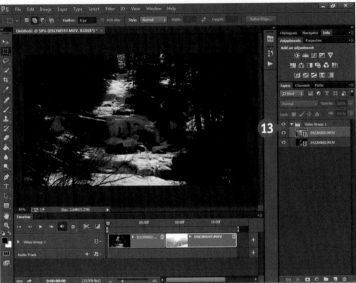

TIPS

Did You Know?

The bottom video layer in the Layers panel plays first, then the layer above it, on up to the top layer. In the Timeline, the video clips play from left to right.

Did You Know?

Timeline has its own keyboard shortcuts. Click the panel menu button (▼≣) in the Timeline. Click Enable Timeline Shortcut Keys. You can then press the spacebar to start and stop video playback, jump to the beginning of a video clip with the up arrow key, and jump to the end with the down arrow key. You can also move one frame forward with the right arrow key or ten frames by pressing Shift+right arrow, or one frame back with the left arrow key, or ten frames by pressing Shift+left arrow. Press End to go to the end of the Timeline; press Home to go to the beginning.

TRIM a video clip

When you shoot still photos, you capture a lot of images before you come up with the one you want to keep. You may even take a few after that one to try a different composition or exposure. Shooting extra frames at the beginning and end of a video is just as common. You can easily trim these sections from your video clips.

Trimming video, as with many Photoshop operations, is nondestructive. Your original file is not changed and the trimmed sections are not deleted. They simply do not become a part of this video project. They remain in the video clip and you can use them later for another project.

Trimming a video clip involves finding the place where you want the trim to begin and end. You can play through the video or scrub through it. You can also click and drag markers to trim clips. If you choose this method, Photoshop opens a preview window as you scrub through the video.

① With your video clips open in the Timeline, click the layer options arrow (▶) in a video clip to mute the audio.

Note: You can work with audio you recorded while shooting or add new audio later.

The video clip properties panel menu appears.

② Click the music notes button.

Ⓐ The audio properties panel appears.

③ Select Mute Audio (■ changes to ☑).

Audio for that clip is muted.

④ Click the Play button or press the spacebar to play the video clip.

Decide where you want to trim at the beginning and end of the clip.

⑤ Position the Playhead at the point where you want to trim the beginning of the clip.

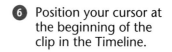

#95

DIFFICULTY LEVEL

6 Position your cursor at the beginning of the clip in the Timeline.

The cursor changes to a trim icon.

7 Click and drag in the Timeline until the trim icon snaps to the position of your Playhead marker.

The beginning of the clip is trimmed.

8 Position the cursor at the end of the video clip.

The cursor changes to a trim icon.

9 Click and drag the trim icon to the left to trim the end of the clip.

The end of the clip is trimmed.

TIPS

Did You Know?

You do not need to move the Playhead () to the positions where you want to trim video clips. You can simply click and drag the trim cursors. However, using the Playhead allows you to make more precise trims because the trim cursors snap to the Playhead marker.

Remove It!

You can bring back part or the entire clip that you trimmed. Click the beginning or end where you want to remove your trim and drag the trim cursor in the opposite direction of the one you used to trim the video. The trimmed section reappears. Release the mouse button when you have restored the section you want.

Did You Know?

You can save a video project as a work in progress as a Photoshop file. If you are working on a video and you cannot finish it in one editing session, click File ⇨ Save As. The Save As dialog box appears. Type a name for your project in the File Name text entry box. Save the project as a PSD file.

You must decide how one video clip will *transition*, or change, to the next clip. You can decide to have one clip abruptly cut to the next, or have the first fade out to white, black, or a color and the second to fade in. Or you can have the first clip fade out while the second clip simultaneously fades in. This last transition is called a *cross fade*. You can add these transitions in Photoshop.

A cross fade ensures a smooth transition between clips. You can set the duration of a cross fade depending on the mood and effect you are trying to create. It is often easier to set the duration when you apply a cross fade and then adjust it later after you preview the effect.

The other type of fade effects can also be effective. You can use Fade with Black or Fade with White to indicate the passage of time, or a major transition from one place to another. Fade with Color opens the Color Picker, where you can choose a color for the transition.

1 With the video clips open in the Timeline, click the Transition button.

The Drag To Apply panel appears.

2 Click in the Duration box and type **3s**.

3 Click Cross Fade.

4 Click and drag Cross Fade between the video clips.

A black rectangle shows the relative duration of the transition.

5 Release the mouse button.

Ⓐ A Cross Fade transition icon appears below the thumbnail in the clip to the right of the transition.

6 Drag the Playhead close to the beginning of the transition.

7 Click the Play button.

8 To change the duration of the transition, position your cursor at the right end of the transition icon in the clip and click.

The cursor changes to the trim icon.

Ⓑ A window shows the current duration of the transition.

9 Drag the trim icon to the right to lengthen the transition, or to the left to shorten it.

Add FADE INS AND FADE OUTS

You can also begin your video with a transition, called a *fade in*, and end the video with a transition, called a *fade out.* Fade ins and fade outs are normally black, but you can also make them white or any color available in the Color Picker. Fade ins and fade outs are indicated by a blue rectangle with a white triangle that slopes up for a fade in and down for a fade out.

These transitions are effective for drawing the viewer into the completed video and allowing the

viewer to transition back to reality when the video finishes.

You can also control the time duration of fade ins and fade outs in the same way you controlled the time duration of transitions in task #96. The default Photoshop transition time for fade ins and fade outs is 1 second, which is too quick in nearly every case. A time of 2 seconds would seem to be a good minimum for a fade in and 3 seconds or longer for a fade out.

1 With the video clips open in the Timeline, click the Transition button.

The Drag To Apply panel appears.

2 Click the Duration box and type **2s**.

3 Click Fade With Black.

4 Click and drag Fade With Black to the beginning of the video.

A black rectangle shows the relative duration of the fade in.

5 Release the mouse button.

A A Fade In icon appears below the thumbnail at the beginning of the clip.

6 Drag the Playhead to the beginning of the video.

The preview goes black.

7 Press the spacebar to play the video.

8 Repeat steps 1 to 3, but set the duration to **3s**.

9 Click and drag Fade With Black to the end of the video.

10 Release the mouse button.

11 Click the Play button to play the clips with a fade in, transition, and fade out.

Convert a video clip to BLACK AND WHITE

The best thing about editing video in Photoshop is your ability to use the same tools to edit the video as you use to edit a still image. You can apply adjustment layers and filters just as you would with a still image to improve the video clip, including converting it to black and white and toning it.

When you add an adjustment layer with one video clip selected, Photoshop creates a special type of layer called a *clipping layer*. A clipping layer only adjusts the layer

immediately below it, so only one layer of the video, or one clip, is affected by the adjustment. You can convert the video to black and white and adjust it with sliders or the Targeted Adjustment tool. If the video is appropriate, you can tone it for even greater impact.

Just as with black-and-white still photos, black-and-white videos look better with added contrast. After creating a black-and-white adjustment layer and adjusting tonal values, increase the contrast using a curves adjustment.

① With video clips open in a video group, click the layer in the Layers panel of the video you want to convert to black and white.

② Click the Black & White adjustment in the Adjustments panel.

The Properties panel appears.

Ⓐ A Black & White adjustment layer with a layer mask appears in the Layers panel. A downward facing arrow indicates the layer is a clipping layer only affecting the layer immediately below it.

③ Adjust the sliders and use the Targeted Adjustment tool to adjust the tonal values.

④ Click and drag the Playhead to preview the adjustments on the entire clip.

⑤ Click the Adjustments tab and click the Curves adjustment button (▦).

The Properties panel opens.

Ⓑ A Curves adjustment clipping layer with a layer mask appears in the Layers panel.

⑥ Click and drag points on the tone curve to create an S-curve.

⑦ Click the Black and White layer thumbnail icon.

The Properties panel reopens.

⑧ Select Tint (■ changes to ☑).

⑨ Click the Tint color box.

Ⓒ The Tint Color Picker opens.

⑩ Type RGB values of **205**, **175**, and **150** into the number entry boxes.

The preview changes to sepia.

⑪ Click OK.

The video clip is sepia toned.

TIPS

Important!
If you click a video clip in the Timeline or the Layers panel and click the Play button (▶), you may not see that clip you expect playing. Unlike still imaging where you see what you click, video requires the Playhead (▣) to be positioned on the video clip you want to see, rather than just clicking a clip to select it.

Try This!
You can apply a black-and-white preset from the Preset drop-down menu. Try Green Filter for landscapes with trees, and Yellow Filter or Red Filter or even Infrared for desert and ocean scenes with interesting cloud formations.

Did You Know?
The first time you play a video and whenever you make a major change, it may not play smoothly, but subsequent plays are smooth. The first time through, Photoshop creates a preview, indicated by a thin green line that forms above the top video layer in the Timeline. Once the line is solid green, the preview is created and the video plays smoothly.

Digital cameras that capture video, particularly digital single-lens reflex (dSLR) cameras generally have excellent automatic white balance. But there are times when they are fooled, or you make an incorrect setting, and the white balance of your video is off. You can correct the white balance of a video clip in Photoshop.

In one way, you have an easier time correcting white balance in video. A video clip runs for a few seconds to a few minutes under the same

lighting conditions. You can scrub through the video until you find an object you know is neutral. You can click the neutral eyedropper on that object in the Curves Properties panel.

While you have curves open, you can also adjust the white and black points and the contrast. Then play through the video to ensure that the frame you chose to correct is truly representative of the entire clip.

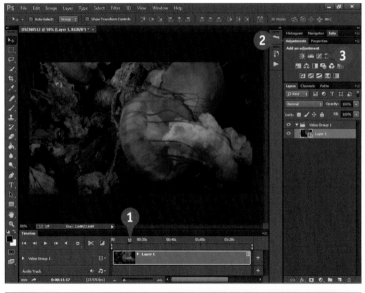

1 With a video clip open in the Timeline, click the Playhead and scrub through the clip to find an object you remember as neutral.

2 Click the Adjustments tab.

3 Click the Curves adjustment button.

The Properties panel appears.

4 Click the gray point eyedropper.

5 Click in the image on the neutral object.

6 Click the Set White Point eyedropper and click in the preview to set the white point.

7 Click the Set Black Point eyedropper and click in the image to set the black point.

8 Click the Playhead and scrub through the video to ensure the frame you applied white balance to is representative.

You need to sharpen video clips just as you need to sharpen still images. You can sharpen video in Photoshop, but the process is a little different from sharpening a still image.

With a still image, you can click an image or composite layer in the Layers panel and apply sharpening to it. However, for video, you must convert the video clip to a Smart Object in order to sharpen the entire clip. If you have a frame of a video clip open and apply the Unsharp Mask filter without converting the entire clip to a Smart Object, only that frame is sharpened. To apply

any Photoshop filter to the entire video clip, you must convert the clip to a Smart Object. All Photoshop filters other than Lens Blur are available for videos, including Oil Paint and the creative filters in the Filter Gallery.

You can apply adjustments, add audio, and add text prior to sharpening for final output, or for later compositing with other video clips. When you are ready to save or output the clip, convert the Video Group layer with the video clips to a Smart Object for sharpening.

① With the video open, right-click the video group in the Layers panel that contains the video clips.

② Click Convert to Smart Object from the menu that appears.

③ Click Filter ➪ Sharpen ➪ Unsharp Mask.

The Unsharp Mask dialog box opens.

④ Click and drag the sliders until the video in the preview is sharpened and there are no halos around high-contrast edges.

Note: If you oversharpen your video, light and dark outlines, called halos, appear around areas of high contrast. These are the same halos that appear with still images.

⑤ Click OK.

Note: Sharpening settings are less critical with video, because the images are not displayed for very long.

ADD BACKGROUND MUSIC *to a video*

No video is complete without a soundtrack. It could be the ambient sound recorded while you capture the video, or it could be a voice track that you add later as a voice-over narration. But what ties the video clips and the voice tracks together is the background music. Fortunately, you can add a background music track easily to a video.

Royalty-free background music is available from a number of sources, including stock photo houses such as iStockphoto. The selection is very large, with appropriate music for wedding videos to family holiday gathering

videos to photographer's portfolios. Commercially available popular or classical music purchased on CDs or downloaded is protected by copyright and should never be used.

Every video group created in Photoshop contains an empty audio track. You can fill the track with appropriate royalty-free music and it plays along with your video clips. You can have the music fade in when the video begins, and fade out as the video ends.

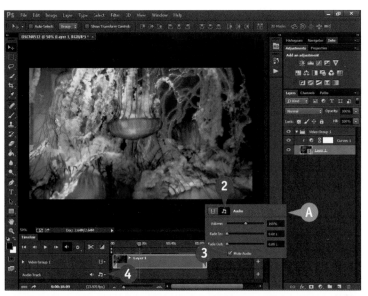

1 With a video open that has been trimmed and adjusted, click the layer options arrow (▶) in a video clip.

The video clip properties panel menu appears.

2 Click the music notes button.

A The audio properties panel menu appears.

3 Select Mute Audio (☐ changes to ☑).

Audio for that clip is muted.

4 Click the music notes button in the audio track in the Timeline.

The Audio Track menu appears.

5 Click Add Audio.

The Open dialog box appears.

6 Navigate to your music library and select the track to use for background music.

7 Click Open.

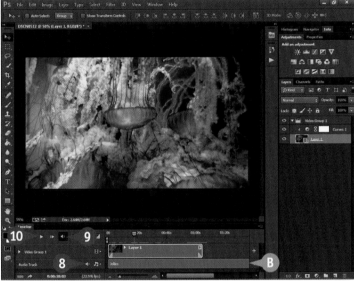

B The music track is added to the Audio Track layer in the Timeline.

Note: Audio tracks are displayed as green in the Timeline.

8 Click the Mute toggle button in the Audio Track to unmute the sound for the track (🔇 changes to 🔊).

9 Click the Mute toggle button for the video in the Timeline to unmute the sound for the video (🔇 changes to 🔊).

10 Click the Play button to hear the music.

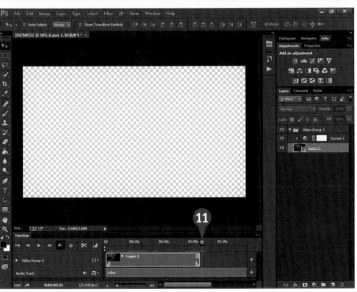

The music keeps playing after the video fades out.

11 Click and drag the Playhead just past the end of the video clip.

The background changes to a checkerboard.

12 Press the left arrow key repeatedly until the checkerboard disappears.

Note: If the left arrow key does not move the Playhead, you have not activated the video keyboard options. See the tips in task #94.

Adding a track of background music is an important start to finishing off a video and giving it a professional feel. But you can put some finishing touches on the music track to better fit it in with the visuals.

The music starts immediately as the video fades in and ends abruptly as the video fades out. You can have the audio fade in and fade out by adding a transition.

You can time the audio transitions to match the video transitions, or time them to occur independently of the transition times. You can begin the music without a fade in transition and end it with a longer fade out than the video fade out. Photoshop prepares the transitions smoothly and embeds them into the video project with no additional effort on your part.

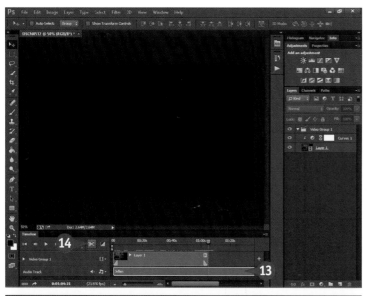

The screen is black.

13 Click the green audio track.

14 Click the Split at Playhead button.

The audio track splits into two sections at the Playhead position.

15 Click the section to the right of the Playhead.

16 Press Backspace (Delete) to delete the section of audio.

17 With the audio track still active, click the layer options arrow (▶) in the audio track.

A The audio properties panel menu appears.

18 Click and drag the Fade Out slider to match the fade out of the video clip.

19 Click and drag the Fade In slider to match the fade in of the video clip.

20 Press Enter (Return).

21 Click the Go to First Frame button.

22 Click the Play button to review the video with the audio track transitions.

TIPS

Did You Know?

You can quickly move to any time in a video clip without having to play the clip or even scrub through it. Place your cursor on the minutes and seconds timeline above the video clip and click. The Playhead (🔲) moves to the cursor position.

Try This!

You can play back the ambient sound you recorded while shooting the video at the same time the background music plays. Right-click the video clip. Click the music notes button (🎵) in the panel. Deselect Mute Audio (☑ changes to ☐). Right-click the audio track. Click and drag the Volume slider to lower the volume of the background music until you can hear the ambient recorded sound clearly.

ADD TEXT to a video

You can add text to a video to create a title. You can use the same sequence of steps to create text to appear anywhere in the video.

Adding text to a video is not quite as simple as adding text to a still image. If you select the Type tool, click a video frame, and type text, the text appears on every frame of the video as it plays. To control where the text appears and how long it plays, you need a new video group.

You add text to the new video group by selecting the Type tool and clicking in the preview. With the text added, you have all the controls over text in video you had when working with stills. You can resize it; move it; change its color, opacity and fill; and apply layer styles. You can add transitions to the type layer. By dragging the end points of the type layer you can set its duration, and by dragging the entire layer, you can set where it begins and ends.

1 With a video clip open, click the Filmstrip button.

2 Click New Video Group.

Ⓐ A new video group appears in the Timeline and the Layers panel.

3 Click and drag the Playhead until you can see a frame of the video.

4 Click the Type tool.

5 Set the type options in the Options bar or the Character panel.

6 Click in the preview.

7 Type your title text.

Ⓑ The text Video Group in the Timeline becomes purple to indicate a still image.

8 Size and move the type into position.

9 Click the Effects button in the Layers panel and select Stroke to add a stroke layer style to the text.

10 Click and drag the text Fill slider to zero.

11 Click and drag the trim icon in the text Video Group layer in the Timeline to the time marker when you want the title to end.

12 Click the Transition button.

The Drag To Apply panel appears.

13 Click Fade.

14 Click and drag the Duration slider to the amount of time you want for the title to fade out.

15 Drag Fade to the end of the text layer.

A rectangle shows on the layer to indicate the fade.

16 Click the Go to First Frame button.

17 Click the Play button to view the title.

TIPS

Important!

The stacking order in the Layers panel determines how video layers interact. Video groups are independent of one another. Any video group or layer outside of another video group functions independently of a video group below or layer above or below it.

Try This!

You can add another line of text with your credit. Repeat steps 4 to 8 to add a credit or copyright line below the title. Use the same font at a smaller size. Alt+click (Option+click) and drag the title layer style to the new text in the Layers panel. Repeat steps 12 to 15 to add the same transition to the new line of text. The credit line text looks and transitions just as the title text.

Did You Know?

You can add text in a video group and have it appear through the entire video. Add text using the steps in this task. Drag the end marker of the text layer in the Timeline to the end of the video. The title remains on-screen throughout the video to remind viewers they are seeing a particular event or person.

You can add motion to a still image by choosing a motion option and applying it to the still image in the Timeline. You can set the time duration that the still image is on-screen by increasing or decreasing the length of the image timeline in the video layer.

Unless you captured the image with an aspect ratio of 16 × 9, you must first crop and scale the image to fit the format and pixel dimensions of your high-definition video. With a single image, this is easiest to do in Photoshop. You can use the 16 × 9 crop preset for the Crop tool to crop the image and then set the pixel dimensions using the Image Size dialog box.

In the Timeline, you can apply motion to the image and transitions between images if you have multiple images. And because the still image is on its own layer in the Layers panel, you can apply adjustments to the image as you work.

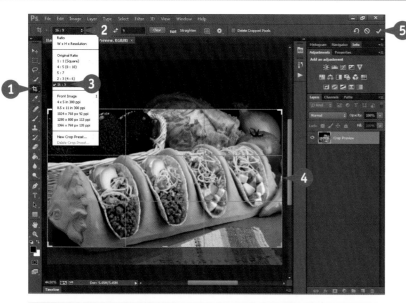

1 With a still image open in Photoshop, click the Crop tool.

2 Click the Preset Aspect Ratio drop-down menu.

The Preset Aspect Ratio menu opens.

3 Click 16 × 9 from the drop-down menu.

4 Position the crop on the image.

5 Click the Commit button.

The image crops.

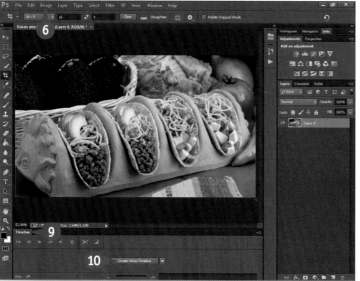

6 Click Image ➪ Image Size.

7 In the Image Size dialog box, type **1280** in the Width number entry box.

8 Click OK.

The image is in HD 720 format.

9 Click the Timeline tab.

Note: Click Window ➪ Timeline if the Timeline tab is not visible.

10 Click Create Video Timeline.

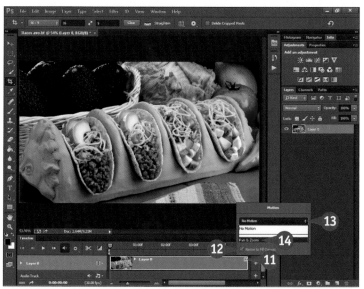

The image opens as a still image in the Timeline.

⑪ Click the layer options arrow for the layer.

The Motion panel opens.

⑫ Leave Resize to Fill Canvas checked.

⑬ Click the No Motion drop-down menu.

⑭ Click Pan & Zoom.

The Pan & Zoom options appear.

⑮ Type **180** in the Pan number entry box to pan the image from left to right.

⑯ Click Zoom In from the Zoom drop-down menu.

⑰ Click the Play button to view the pan and Zoom effect.

TIPS

Try This!

You can do more with multiple images in sequence in the Timeline than you can with a single image. With multiple images in sequence in the Timeline, you can apply different motion options to each one, or choose not to apply motion, and apply transitions between images. You can drag the duration of the images to different screen times. And you can add a soundtrack or voice-over, or intersperse the still images with video files.

Did You Know?

You can create a custom crop in Camera Raw to crop images to 1280 × 720 pixels in one step. Click the Crop button (🔲) in Camera Raw and right-click in the image. Click Custom from the menu. Select Pixels from the Crop drop-down menu and type **1280 × 720** in the number entry boxes. This HD video crop appears in the crop menu in Camera Raw. You can select and apply it with one click in the future.

After putting time and energy into creating a video, you want others to enjoy it. You can save the video file and show it on your own computer. But you can also save it in a video format that you can upload to YouTube or Vimeo to share with others.

The drop-down menu of video output formats is extensive. Options are available all the way from worldwide, professional broadcast-quality output to older Android mobile phones. YouTube and Vimeo each have one option for SD video and three options for HD video.

SD, or *standard definition*, Widescreen video is 16 × 9 format and 640 × 360 pixel dimensions.

The HD formats are 720p and 1080p with frame rates of 25 or 29.97. *720p* is 1280 × 720-pixel progressive video while *1080p* is 1920 × 1080-pixel progressive video. Choose a frame rate to match the frame rate of your camera. It is safe to ignore the other settings in the Render Video dialog box. Photoshop takes care of everything if you choose the correct preset.

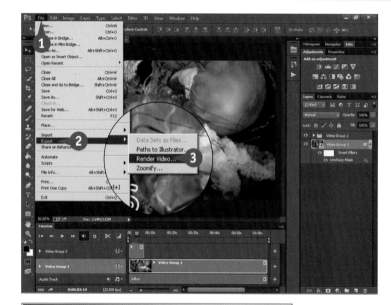

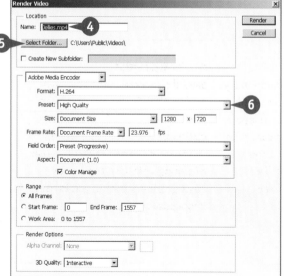

Save for YouTube

1 With a completed and saved video project open, click File.

2 Click Export.

3 Click Render Video.

The Render Video dialog box opens.

4 Type a name in the Name text entry box.

Note: Photoshop supplies the correct .mp4 extension if you do not.

5 Click Select Folder and choose a location to store the file.

6 Click the Preset drop-down menu.

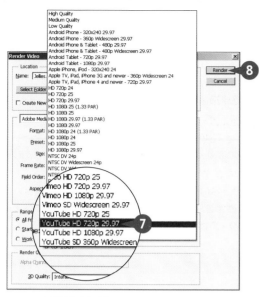

7 Click YouTube HD 720p at the frame rate of your camera.

Note: If your camera captures 1080p video and you edited the files at 1080p, choose YouTube HD 1080p 29.97.

8 Click Render.

A progress bar opens as the video renders.

#104

DIFFICULTY LEVEL

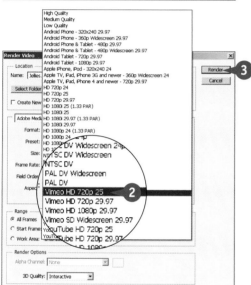

Save for Vimeo

1 Repeat steps 1 to 6.

2 In the Preset drop-down menu, click Vimeo HD 720p at the frame rate of your camera.

Note: If your camera captures 1080p video and you edited the files at 1080p and you are a Vimeo Plus or Pro subscriber, choose Vimeo HD 1080p 29.97.

3 Click Render.

A progress bar opens as the video renders.

TIPS

Important!

Before you render your video project to a common output format, save it as a layered PSD file with a unique name. Rendering a video project flattens the layers in the Timeline and makes them uneditable in the future. Rendering also compresses the files in the Timeline. Image and sound quality decrease, sometimes significantly.

Did You Know?

The render time depends on many factors. These include the length of the video, the number of layers, the complexity of the adjustments and filter you applied, and the speed of your computer. The progress bar can move very slowly. Be patient.

More Options!

Save the layered video as a high-quality MP4 file to show on your own computer. This is a better option than opening and closing the layered file and taking the risk of damaging it. Use the default High Quality preset in the Preset drop-down menu.

Chapter 11

Use Plug-ins to Extend Photoshop

Photoshop is designed to accept *plug-ins,* ancillary programs from third-party software designers. The Adobe Photoshop marketplace lists 452 at the present time. These plug-ins are designed to enhance the creative power of Photoshop by automating some of the tasks and extending some of the capabilities.

You can find plug-ins for creating special effects, manipulating type and illustrations, converting images to black and white, simulating film effects, reducing noise, retouching portraits, and more. There are plug-ins for 3-D projects and video, and they are available for every imaginable project. Prices vary from free to many hundreds of dollars for suites of plug-ins from a manufacturer. Most plug-ins that function properly in Photoshop CS5 and CS6 are compatible with CC, provided 32-bit plug-ins are used in the 32-bit versions of

Photoshop and 64-bit plug-ins are used in the 64-bit versions.

You can download trial versions of plug-ins from the manufacturers' websites to test and evaluate them. Trial versions are limited either to use for a short time period, or provide reduced functionality for saving images. The manufacturers' websites often have extensive tutorials to guide you in getting the most out of the plug-in and show examples of the effects possible when using them. But the best way to evaluate them is to download the trial version and test it on your own images.

The tasks in this chapter make use of plug-ins from Alien Skin, Anthropics, and Topaz Labs. These are but a few of the most popular plug-in companies. Others include onOne Software, Tiffen, Imagenomics, Auto FX, and many more.

DIFFICULTY LEVEL

You can use Alien Skin Eye Candy 7 to build effects that are difficult or nearly impossible to create in Photoshop alone. The effects are available for text and illustrations as well as images. You can create realistic metal, gel, and fur effects, and the results are far easier to create than using Photoshop alone.

Lightning is a new effect in version 7. You can create believable lightning flashes with no effort and a lot of creative options. The controls allow you to precisely position the lightning, adjust the brightness, spread the branching, and control the glow around the lightning. There is also a randomizing button that offers many more lightning effects for you to try.

By applying Eye Candy effects to a Smart Object layer, you can return to the effect later and fine-tune it for final output. Alien Skin offers other products such as Exposure, which simulates film effects, Blow Up for image enlargement, Bokeh for focus effects, and Snap Art to turn photos into art.

1 With an image open, right-click the Background layer.

2 Click Convert to Smart Object from the menu that appears.

3 Click Filter.

4 Click Alien Skin.

5 Click Eye Candy 7.

The Eye Candy interface appears.

6 Click the Effect button.

7 Click Lightning.

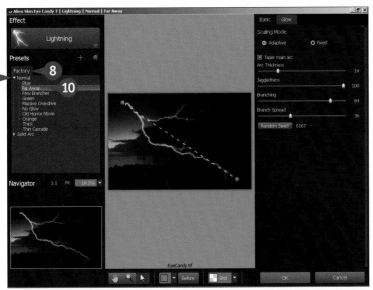

The default lightning appears on the image.

⑧ Click the Factory tab.

⑨ Click the Normal disclosure triangle.

⑩ Click Far Away.

⑪ Click and drag the position handles to position the main branch of lightning.

Note: You can drag the upper handle outside the image so that the lightning appears to come from outside the frame.

⑫ Click and drag the Arc Thickness slider to set the thickness and brightness of the main branch.

⑬ Click and drag the Branching slider to select different arrangements of the side branches.

⑭ Click and drag the Branch Spread slider to set the spread between the branches.

⑮ Click OK.

Eye Candy applies the changes to image as a Smart Object.

TIPS

Try This!

You can see hundreds of other lightning options. But before you do, click Random Seed in the Basic panel, and take note of the number next to the button. You must type this number in the Random Seed number text entry box to return to this lightning. Click the Random Seed button to view other prebuilt lightning in the group you chose in step 10.

More Options!

You can control the glow around the lightning. Click the Glow tab in the right panel. The Glow panel opens. Click and drag the Glow Width slider to adjust the size of the glow. Click and drag the Glow Opacity slider to adjust the opacity of the glow.

Did You Know?

You can preview the preset on your image for lightning and the other effects without selecting them. Drag your cursor over the list of presets without selecting them. The effect appears on your image in the thumbnail at the bottom of the left panel.

RETOUCH A PORTRAIT with
Anthropics Portrait Studio Plus 11

Portrait Studio is available in three editions from Anthropics Technology. The Standard edition only supports 24-bit TIFF and JPEG files and is a stand-alone application. The Studio edition supports RAW files and 16-bit TIFFs and installs as a stand-alone and a Photoshop plug-in. The Studio 64 edition is the Studio edition optimized for 64-bit Mac and Windows operating systems.

Portrait Studio does not support Smart Objects, nor does it place the retouching on a new layer, so it is important to

work on a copy of your image. The software not only automatically retouches your image, it also sculpts the skin area. The technology behind Portrait Professional is based on the analysis of thousands of photos of human faces to determine what makes them attractive. Unlike other automated portrait retouching software, the subject does not need to be facing the camera directly. You can use Portrait Studio to retouch multiple people in the photo and to retouch full-length portraits.

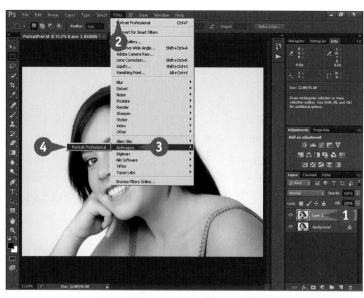

① With a portrait image open, press Ctrl+J (⌘+J) to duplicate the Background layer.

② Click Filter.

③ Click Anthropics.

④ Click Portrait Professional.

The Portrait Professional interface appears.

⑤ Click the gender button on the first screen.

The Adjust Outline screen appears.

⑥ Adjust any outline handles that the automatic face detection did not get quite right.

⑦ Press the spacebar to move to the next step.

The main screen opens with before and after views.

Ⓐ A default preset adjustment is selected.

⑧ Click and drag the Zoom slider to change the zoom level.

⑨ Click Show Skin Smoothing Controls.

⑩ Click the View After Only tab to view the corrections better.

#106

DIFFICULTY LEVEL

The Skin Smoothing Controls open.

The corrected image opens in the preview.

⑪ Click and drag the sliders to adjust the default skin smoothing.

⑫ Click Hide Skin Smoothing Controls.

⑬ Click the Touch Up brush to manually paint out blemishes.

⑭ Click the Restore brush to restore lost detail or a permanent skin marking.

⑮ Click other manual adjustments as needed.

⑯ Click Next.

⑰ Click Return From Plugin.

Portrait Professional makes the adjustments to the copy of the Background layer and returns you to Photoshop.

TIPS

More Options!

You can use Portrait Professional to adjust photos with multiple faces. Adjust the first face and click Other Faces (▣) in the Options bar. Portrait Professional returns you to the first screen to choose another face.

Try This!

Portrait Professional automatically thins and sculpts faces. You can turn this off completely or minimize the sculpting. Click the green button next to Face Sculpt Controls in the right column to disable the face sculpting entirely. Open the Face Sculpt Controls panel and click and drag sliders to the right to minimize the individual face sculpting controls.

More Options!

You can retouch the neck and shoulders of the subject as well as the face. Click View/Edit Skin Area in the Skin Smoothing panel. A purple overlay appears to show the skin area mask. Paint over other areas of skin to apply the same adjustments that you apply to the face.

ADD REALISTIC STAR BURSTS with Topaz Star Effects

Using Topaz Star Effects, you can add realistic star bursts to landscape, cityscape, portrait, and still-life photos. Cross-star filters were a mainstay of film photographers, but there is little control with a filter on your lens. Star Effects simulates these effects with far more variety and control.

Adding a starburst to a large light source such as a candle flame is difficult with traditional methods. Star Effects automatically discovers the highlights in the scene and

applies the effect you select to them. You can then control the brightness, color temperature, number of spikes and their orientation, glow, and flare. There is also a brush to add or remove the effect from selected light sources.

Topaz Star Effects is also effective for adding starbursts to jewelry even when there is no bright highlight and to a light reflected in a portrait subject's eye. Star Effects is only one of many photographic effects available from Topaz Labs.

1 With an image open, right-click the Background layer.

2 Click Convert to Smart Object from the menu that appears.

3 Click Filter.

4 Click Topaz Labs.

5 Click Topaz Star Effects.

The Topaz Star Effects interface opens.

6 Click Jewel Sparkle I.

7 Click Star Settings.

The Star Settings panel opens.

8 Select Vector Star from the Star Type drop-down menu.

9 Click Main Adjustments.

The Main Adjustments panel opens.

10 Click and drag the sliders until the stars look correct.

11 Click Apply.

12 Click OK.

Topaz Star Effects renders the filter and returns you to Photoshop.

TIPS

Try This!

Open an image taken in the evening with streetlights. Click one of the Lamp Post presets and adjust the sliders to set stars on each of the street lamps. Adjust the Temperature slider in the Color Adjustments panel to bring the color of the star closer to the color of the lights.

Remove It!

It is easy to get lost in the options of most plug-ins. Click Restore All at the bottom of the right panel in Topaz Star Effects to remove all of your adjustments and start over.

Did You Know?

Topaz and other plug-in companies have tutorials on their websites along with extensive help and examples to make it easier for you to get up to speed using the software.

Index

Index

Index

Index